Data and Text Mining

A Business Applications Approach

Thomas W. Miller

Upper Saddle River, New Jersey 07458

To the memory of my mother and father

Library of Congress Cataloging-in-Publication information is available.

Acquisitions Editor: Katie Stevens
Editor-in-Chief: Jeff Shelstad
Editorial Assistant: Rebecca Cummings
Executive Marketing Manager: Shannon Moore
Marketing Assistant: Patrick Danzuso
Managing Editor: John Roberts
Production Assistant: Joe DeProspero
Manufacturing Buyer: Michelle Klein
Design Manager: Maria Lange
Cover Design: Kiwi Design
Cover Illustration: Paul Klee, "Museale Industrie" (1879–1940, Swiss). Christies Images/Bridgeman Art Library, London/Superstock. © Artists Rights Society, New York, NY
Printer/Binder: Phoenix /Book Tech

Pearson Education LTD.
Pearson Education Singapore, Pte. Ltd
Pearson Education, Canada, Ltd
Pearson Education–Japan
Pearson Education Australia PTY, Limited
Pearson Education North Asia Ltd
Pearson Educación de Mexico, S.A. de C.V.
Pearson Education Malaysia, Pte. Ltd

10 9 8 7 6 5 4 3 2 1
ISBN 0-13-140085-1

Contents

PREFACE

Firms collect consumer responses from telephone, mail, and online surveys. They scan data from retail sales. They record business transactions and log text from focus groups, online bulletin boards, and user groups. Spurred on by lower costs of data acquisition, storage, retrieval, and analysis, business databases grow larger each day. Business managers work in a world in which data are plentiful and well-formulated theories rare. This is a world well suited to data and text mining.

Data and text mining represent flexible approaches to information management, research, and analysis. They are data-driven rather than theory-driven. They rely upon powerful computers and efficient algorithms. Relatively new and little understood by business and marketing managers, data and text mining are important enough to require an adequate introduction. That is the reason for this book.

This book advocates a disciplined approach to data and text analysis. It is through the development of meaningful models that data and text mining contribute to information management, research, and analysis. Models should fit the data, yielding small errors of prediction and classification. Models should be as simple as possible because simple, parsimonious models are easy to understand and use. Model selection in data and text mining is a matter of striking the proper balance between fit and parsimony. When analysts strike the proper balance, they develop models with explanatory power.

To serve as a business introduction to data and text mining, a book cannot rely upon statistics and computer algorithms alone. A business book must give students a feeling for the work of data and text mining and how it serves business needs. This book focuses upon business applications, including customer relationship management, database marketing, consumer choice modeling, market segmentation, market response modeling, sales forecasting, and the analysis of corporate databases. It reviews traditional and data-adaptive methods and shows how the results of data and text mining can be used to guide business decision making.

The book provides an introduction to data and text mining methods and applications. It shows how to use tools for data manipulation and integration, statistical graphics, traditional statistics, and data-adaptive methods. It shows output from data and text mining programs and reviews the literature, citing relevant books and articles in business, marketing research, statistics, computer science, and information management.

The book draws upon a rich set of business cases and data sets described at length in Appendix A. Cases promote experiential learning; students learn about data and text mining by doing data and text mining. Case documentation and data sets have been placed in the public domain, available on the Web site for the book. Additional cases and discussion are provided in Miller (2004).

Data and text mining offer great promise as technologies for learning about customers, competitors, and markets. But having the ability to organize and analyze large quantities of data does not excuse us from our obligation to conduct research in a responsible manner. Appendix B reviews the important topic of privacy in business research.

Recognizing that business and research professionals have strong feelings about computing software and systems, our coverage of data and text mining topics is sufficiently broad to accommodate users of many systems. The Web site for the book provides data, documentation, and examples for use with various software systems.

Examples in the book were prepared using S-PLUS, Insightful Miner, R, and Perl. Many leading researchers in statistics use S-PLUS and R, providing a substantial body of public-domain code for data mining applications. The Perl user community provides an extensive set of utilities for text processing. By relying upon public-domain systems and code, we can do more work for less cost, and we can write programs that run on many computer platforms. Both R and Perl, for example, have Apple Macintosh OS X, Microsoft Windows, Linux, and Unix implementations.

The book can serve as a textbook in business, marketing research, statistics, management information systems, computer science, information science, quantitative methods, decision science, and operations research. It may be used as a stand-alone introduction to data and text mining or as a technical reference for practitioners. Written in a non-technical, non-mathematical style, the book is accessible to many readers.

I have many people to thank for making this book possible. Wendy Craven of Prentice Hall was a key proponent of the book throughout its development, always willing to listen to ideas for making the book relevant to a wide range of business disciplines. Rebecca Cummings and John Roberts of Prentice Hall assisted in the final stages of production. Special recognition is due to Dana H. James for copyediting and indexing and to Amy Hendrickson, TEXnology, Inc., for her assistance in the development of LaTeX class and style files. Data entry, proofreading, graphics, and electronic typesetting services were provided by Teresa Cheng, Kristin Gill, and Krista Sorenson. Kim Kok, Giovanni Marchisio, Jeff Scott, and Michael Sannella of Insightful Corporation provided advice and technical assistance in the area of text mining. Hung T. Nguyen helped in writing the supplement for instructors. Reviewers and colleagues provided many helpful suggestions. For their feedback and encouragement in the reviewing process, I thank Lynd Bacon, Jerry L. Oglesby of SAS Institute Inc., David M. Smith of Insightful Corporation, and Michel Wedel. Most of all, my wife Chris and son Daniel stood by me in good times and bad, tolerating my unusual writer's lifestyle.

Thomas W. Miller
Madison, Wisconsin
February 23, 2004

Web site for book:
`http://www.prenhall.com/miller`

List of Figures

List of Exhibits

CHAPTER

1 WHAT IS DATA MINING?

> Aristotle (b 384BC) and Bacon (1561–1626) advocated an approach to scientific methodology that was used for close to two thousand years. They suggested amassing large quantities of data, searching for patterns, and then hypothesizing about such patterns. Galileo (1564–1642) advocated continuing in this vein but suggested that scientists should also do experimentation to check the hypotheses. The Galilean approach to scientific methodology (the Galilean scientific method) was widely accepted within the scientific community for about three hundred years; it was still in common use throughout the 19th century.... From a philosophy of science perspective, data mining follows the "scientific method" tradition of Galileo. (Press 2004, p. 2)

At midnight a new customer of Musicnotes.com, an online retailer, places an order for the sheet music of *Harry Potter and the Sorcerer's Stone.* It will be one of more than a hundred Harry Potter orders that day. Is this new customer likely to become a repeat buyer of digital sheet music? Or is this a "once-and-done" customer, acceding to the Harry Potter fad?

What is the probability that a new customer will be a repeat customer, and how does that probability vary from one type of customer to the next? Can we accurately classify customers using data gathered from a first order? And, if we classify correctly, will that classification be useful in targeted marketing? Firms like Musicnotes.com face questions like these every day. To answer the questions, firms need to identify relevant data and use flexible tools for data analysis.

Data mining is an approach to research and analysis. We find data, explore data, generate hypotheses, and learn from data. By being amenable to many ways of understanding and analyzing data, we learn more from data than we would with a single fixed approach to research and analysis. We are open to many things that data may reveal.

The focus of this book is business data, including information about firms and markets, products and prices, supplier actions and buyer responses. We mine the data of business to get information for managers. From data to information, from information to knowledge—we use methods and models to guide business decisions.

This chapter describes the process of data mining. It describes sources of business data and the ways of research. It reviews basic concepts from statistics and introduces data mining methods and applications, providing an overview of the field.

1.1 SOURCES OF BUSINESS DATA

Data mining falls at the intersection of various disciplines, including statistics, library and information science, and computer science. Using data mining tools, business analysts move from raw data to structured data, from structured data to analysis and models. They learn from data and apply that learning in business applications.

We think of two major types of organizations and information workers: information providers and information users (clients). Information providers generate, gather, and work with information as their primary activities. They supply information to other organizations. While also involved in generating, gathering, and grouping information, clients use information for their own purposes. The work that needs to be done may be summarized by referring to "The Four Gs" of research and information services, as shown in Exhibit 1.1.

Business data come in many forms, as summarized in Figure 1.1. Nonreactive measures and records of business and market transactions reveal actual marketplace behavior. When we think of data mining, we often think of its application to large corporate databases arising from the normal operations of business. But we can use these same tools for the analysis of smaller data sets, such as those arising from field experiments and sample surveys.

As shown in Figure 1.1, we can think of research as an interaction involving customers, business environments, measures, models, and methods. In surveys and designed experiments, respondents reveal their abilities, lifestyles, attitudes, and behavior. We can use data mining tools to explore data from respondent ratings, rankings, and choices. Data mining tools help us to evaluate consumer preferences for product and service features and to provide information for predicting consumer choice and product market share. Business and market response data follow from respondents interacting with the real business environment in the field, with hypothetical stimuli in laboratory experiments, or with survey instruments.

1.1.1 Types of Data

A critical step in data mining is understanding the nature of the data. Are the data categorical or continuous? Are they words (character strings), numbers, or dates? Do the data relate to research objectives? Can we identify response and explanatory variables in the data?

Categorical data represent named attributes. We have men and women. We note that they are employed, unemployed, or retired. We see that they live in distinct countries or regions. We watch as they choose among coffee, tea, water, juice, or soft drink. Continuous data have meaningful magnitude. We observe respondent rankings and ratings. We record counts, quantities, volumes, revenues, costs, and profits.

Exhibit 1.1 "The Four Gs" of Research and Information Services

Miller (2000) describes "The Four Gs" of research and information services. The job of research and information providers is to turn words and numbers into information—to unlock the meaning in data. The job is to gather, group, and generate information and then give information to others. These are "The Four Gs" as they relate to providers and clients of information services.

- **Gather Information.** Central to business and market research is the initial job of gathering information or data collection. Analysts gather primary information from business managers and consumers. They gather information from secondary sources. Traditional modes of gathering include face-to-face and telephone interviews, focus groups, mail surveys, observational studies, and online research. Successful research and information providers are efficient gatherers.

- **Group Information.** It is easy to be overwhelmed by the amount of information that comes our way each business day. To learn from data, firms organize, aggregate, and process data. They use model-based or data-adaptive statistical methods to transform, smooth, and reduce data, computing summary statistics, making parameter estimates and probability statements. Although analysts may not reduce data down to what Miller (1956) called "the magic number seven, plus or minus two" chunks of information, their grouping activities should yield a more manageable, more understandable organization of data. Successful research and information providers group data in meaningful ways, turning data into useful information.

- **Generate Information.** Research and information providers generate information when they develop new scales and coding schemes, specify models, make prior assumptions about parameters, or provide a theoretical organization for research. They generate information through insightful interpretation of research results. Some qualitative researchers speak of "grounded theory," in which a theory of consumer behavior, say, is generated from the recorded words of consumers. Interpreting textual data from in-depth interviews or focus groups and writing research reports are creative, generative processes. Researchers are distinguished from one another by their styles of interpretation and information generation. Successful researchers and information providers generate new information that is relevant to management.

- **Give Information to Others.** All organizations are involved in information gathering, grouping, and generating. But these activities would have little relevance to business if information were not communicated to management. Central to the information function is the process of giving information to others—to clients or information users. Successful research and information providers are good communicators, turning raw data into information and providing information that managers can understand.

Figure 1.1 Framework for Business and Market Research

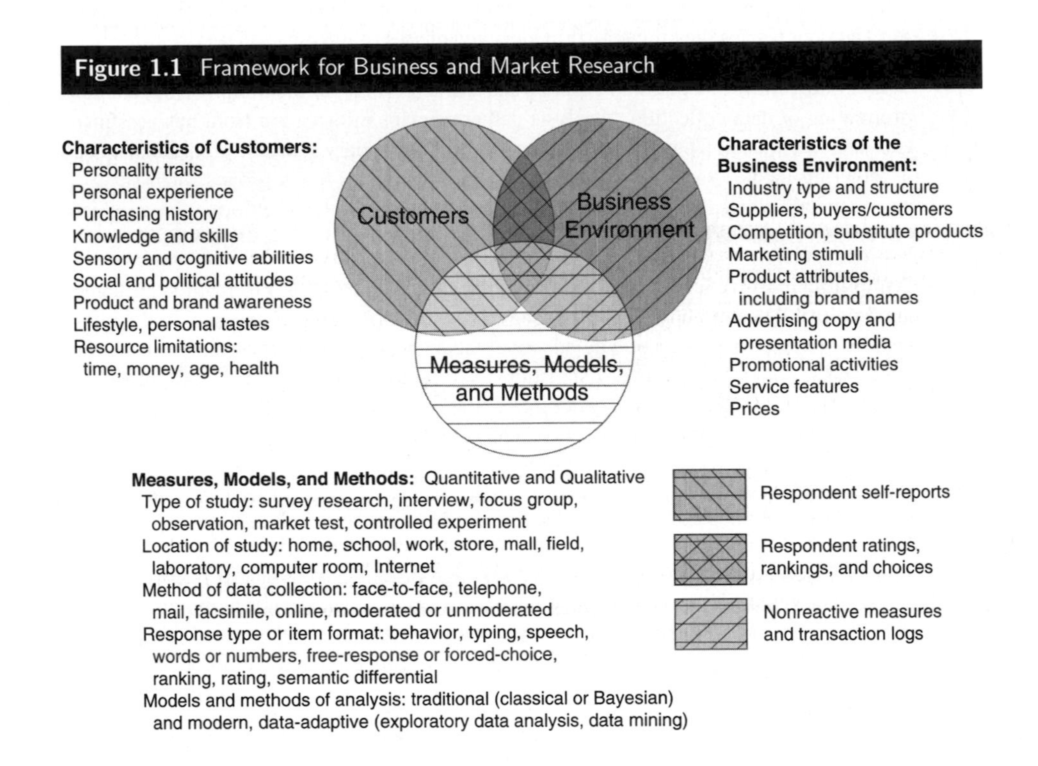

Source: Adapted from Miller (2002).

Much business research has a specific objective. We want to grow sales or reduce costs. We want to develop products that people buy. We want to use advertising that gets people's attention and to build the awareness of products and brands. We want to spend money on promotions that increase sales revenue. The goals of business are associated with response variables representing product choices, market shares, sales volume, and revenue. Response variables are the things we want to predict.

1.1.2 Information Supply Chain

Today's information supply chains can be complex, involving a host of providers of research and information services. The user or client can draw upon many sources of information, both internal and external. Information gathering, grouping, and generating activities are often automated, leading to an information supply chain as shown in Figure 1.2. Providers of information gathering software (survey or research tools) sell to intermediate providers of online research services. Providers of online research services, in turn, sell to custom research providers, and custom research providers sell to information users or clients. As we move from providers of general-purpose tools and data collection services to providers of more specialized research and consulting services, value is added through information integration and customization.

External providers of data, information, and research services include marketing and competitive intelligence professionals, database users and administrators, corporate librarians, competitive intelligence researchers, and anyone involved in recording and analyzing the transactions of business. Providers of information services include many small firms and independent agents, as well as large multinational research firms. There are firms at various points along the information supply chain. There are firms engaged in economic, business-to-business, business-to-consumer, database, and field research. Many providers of information services make use of data mining methods, and some providers specialize in data mining methods.

Figure 1.3 shows a classification of information provider organizations derived from hierarchical cluster analysis. Moving from the left-hand side of the figure to the right, groups of providers more similar to one another are merged to form larger groups or clusters. As a distinct group of information providers, data miners and modelers are seen as being most similar to librarians, fact finders, and competitive intelligence professionals. They focus upon facts, data, and details, and much of their work involves the analysis of secondary data sources.

What about the people who do data and text mining work? What kinds of skills are needed beyond an awareness of methods such as those discussed in this book? Quinn, Anderson, and Finkelstein (1998) pose an interesting model of professional intellect for business managers. Exhibit 1.2 shows how we might apply this model to data mining, research, and information services professionals.

Figure 1.2 An Information Supply Chain

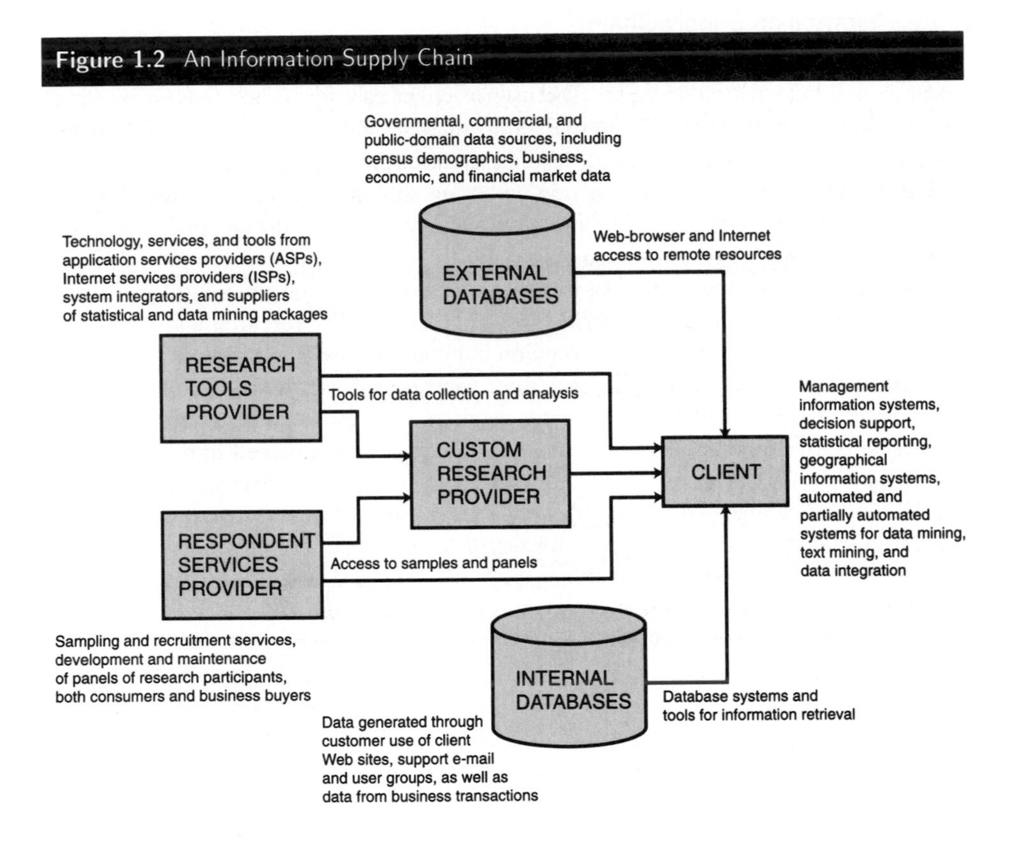

Source: Miller and James (2004).

Figure 1.3 Varieties of Research and Information Services

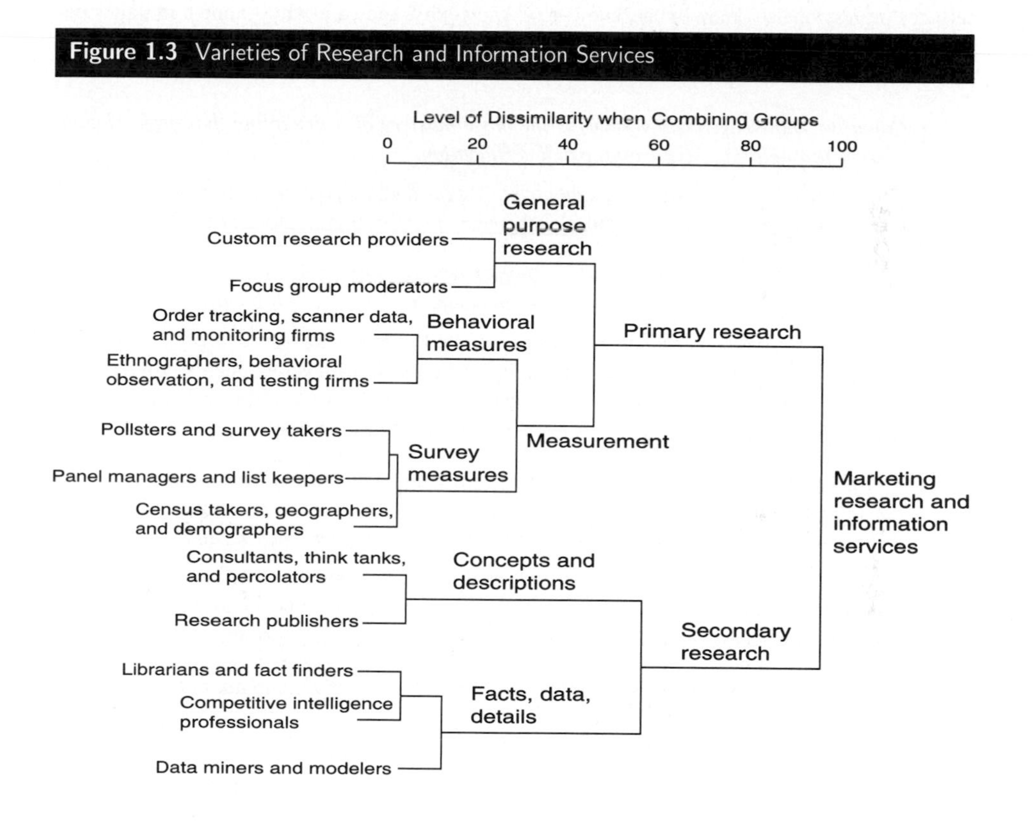

Source: Miller and James (2004).

Exhibit 1.2 Intellectual Characteristics of Information Services Professionals

Quinn, Anderson, and Finkelstein (1998) describe four intellectual characteristics of information services professionals—know-what, know-how, know-why, and care-why—shown in italics below. We consider how these characteristics might apply to the training of data mining, research, and information services professionals.

- *Cognitive knowledge (know-what) is the basic mastery of a discipline that professionals achieve through extensive training and certification.*

  This is what a certification test might cover. There should be balance: an understanding of both the language of business and the language of research and information.

- *Advanced skills (know-how) translate "book learning" into effective execution. This is the ability to apply the rules of the discipline to complex real-world problems.*

  One of the reasons business schools use the case study method is to simulate problem solving in real-world situations. Living case studies and projects with actual clients provide good training. From cases to projects, to internships, to jobs—experiential learning is essential to developing know-how. Students learn research by doing research.

- *Systems understanding (know-why) is deep knowledge of the web of cause-and-effect relationships underlying a discipline. It permits professionals to move beyond the execution of tasks to solve larger and more complex problems—and to create extraordinary value.*

  To know what projects to work on and what projects to avoid, to garner the resources needed to execute a project, to manage those resources, and to be a trusted consultant to management—these require the know-why that comes from experience.

- *Self-motivated creativity (care-why) consists of will, motivation, and adaptability for success.*

  We expect professionals in marketing research and information services to have a passion for their work and a willingness to help others. Think about the intangibles that we associate with a marketing research and information services professional: willingness to work, attention to detail, commitment to "getting it right," a healthy skepticism about the research claims of others, honesty in presenting information, high ethical standards, respect for data and the scientific method, and a willingness to be an independent thinker on the one hand and a leader on the other.

Source: Miller and James (2004). Reprinted with permission from Research Publishers LLC.

1.1.3 Making Sense out of Data

In an early book about data mining, Piatetsky-Shapiro and Frawley (1991) estimated that the amount of data doubles every twenty months. Given the vast amounts of data that are collected as part of the normal operations of business, many firms are forced to use data and text mining methods. There is what we might call a "data mining imperative."

Making sense out of data is essential to success in today's business environment. Methods of data and text mining help firms to find relevant data, identify patterns in data, and organize, group, and reduce data. What variables go together? What products are purchased together? Can we detect patterns and trends in sales response? Can we identify groups of customers or market segments? What is the competitive structure of the market? How do products within a category relate to one another?

Data mining tools can be used to find variables that explain or predict market response, as reflected in response variables. Explanatory variables may be found in data relating to consumers, products, and the business environment. For many data mining projects there are hundreds or thousands of potential explanatory variables. Data mining tools help us to sort through those variables to find the ones that work best in predicting market response.

Making sense out of data requires business understanding as well as data mining tools. An overview of the data mining process is provided in the Cross-Industry Standard Process for Data Mining (CRISP-DM), described by Chapman et al. (2000). Figure 1.4 shows the six major aspects of the CRISP-DM reference model, and Exhibit 1.3 provides a summary. The CRISP-DM model presents data mining as a cyclical, iterative process with data preparation and analysis informed by business understanding and with business understanding informed by data and models.

1.2 STATISTICS, MODELS, AND INFORMATION SYSTEMS

It would be hard to talk about data mining without also talking about statistics, models, and information systems. Some think of data mining as an approach to statistics or as a way of generating statistical models. To data mine effectively, we need to understand basic statistical principles and use efficient programs for data analysis.

1.2.1 Statistics: Variability and Bias

Fundamental to an understanding of statistics and data mining is the idea of variability. Behavior and attitudes vary from one person to the next. There are individual differences between and within cultures. Products vary from one manufacturer to the next, services from one provider to the next, and prices from one market to the next. Variability is both our friend and our nemesis.

When it comes to building models for individuals, firms, or markets, variability is our friend. Without variability in both explanatory and response variables, we could not identify meaningful relationships among variables. The values of some variables, such as promotion and sales, go up together. The values of other variables, such as competition

Figure 1.4 Phases of the Cross-Industry Standard Process for Data Mining (CRISP-DM)

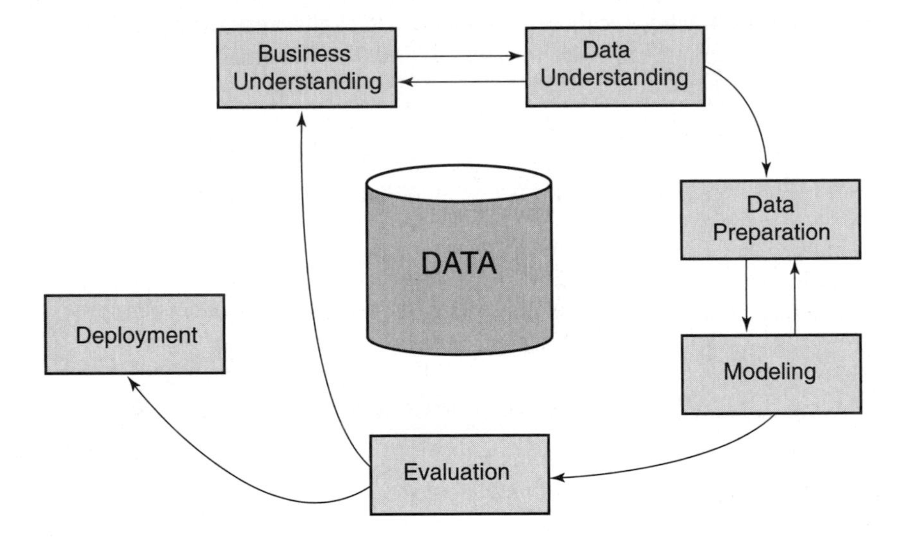

Source: Adapted from Chapman et al. (2000).

Exhibit 1.3 Cross-Industry Standard Process for Data Mining (CRISP-DM)

The Cross-Industry Standard Process for Data Mining (CRISP-DM) was the work of a consortium of data mining practitioners, headed by representatives from DaimlerChrysler, SPSS Inc., and NCR Corporation (Chapman et al. 2000). The CRISP-DM reference model describes six major aspects or phases of data mining. Here we provide a summary.

- **Business understanding.** Data mining begins with business understanding. The researcher focuses upon project objectives and requirements as they relate to business. It is important not to lose sight of the goals of research.
- **Data understanding.** To do the job of data mining, one must understand the data. What is the nature of the data? What is the quality of the data? Are there missing or miscoded data? Data understanding and business understanding go hand-in-hand. Do the data relate directly to business questions and research objectives?
- **Data preparation.** Data preparation is often the most time-consuming part of the data mining process. Decisions must be made regarding data to be used and data to be ignored. Data should be verified and edited where appropriate. The analyst needs to determine a method for dealing with missing data problems. And data must be organized in a way that permits subsequent analysis by computer.
- **Modeling.** This is the part of data mining that gets the most attention in textbooks. Researchers can choose from many methods, both traditional and data adaptive. The selected method should be appropriate to the data being analyzed. As described in this chapter, analysts seek models that fit the data well and are also simple or parsimonious.
- **Evaluation.** The analyst is encouraged to evaluate both the technical adequacy of the models and their suitability to the business problem at hand. With regard to technical adequacy, the analyst can evaluate goodness of fit to the data, suggesting possible model enhancements. She can select models using criteria that reflect model simplicity as well as goodness of fit. Graphical diagnostics may be used. A common evaluation procedure is to divide the sample into two or three subsamples, referred to as training, test, and verification subsamples. The analyst builds models on the training subsample and evaluates models on test and verification subsamples.
- **Deployment.** If data mining is to have value to management, research findings and models should guide business decision making. In some cases, models may be deployed in the daily operations of business. Models can be implemented in computer programs for product customization and personalization, customer acquisition and retention, credit scoring, and pricing, among other applications. Some models are agent-based, executing decisions based upon rules developed in earlier stages of data mining.

Figure 1.5 Effects of Bias and Variability

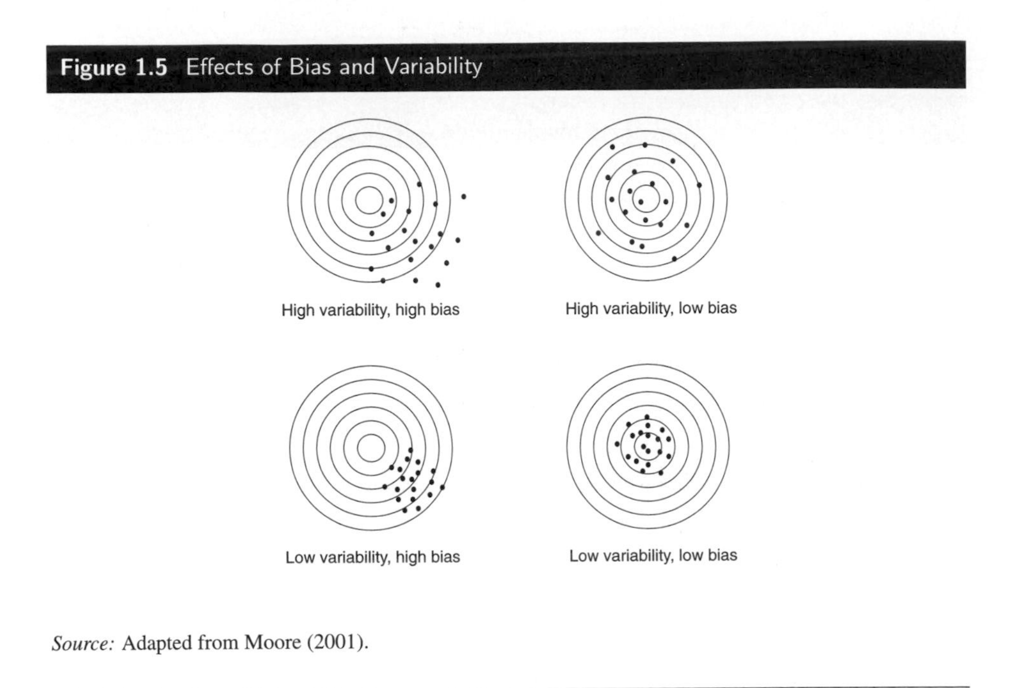

Source: Adapted from Moore (2001).

and sales, move in opposite directions. Whatever the direction of relationship between two variables, we must have variability in both variables in order to see the relationship.

Variability is also our nemesis because there is sampling variability—values of statistics vary from one sample to the next. The standard error of a statistic is a measure of the sampling variability of a statistic. In particular, it is the standard deviation of the sampling distribution for the statistic. Large variability across samples is associated with large variance in the population and small sample sizes.

Good research design attempts to reduce bias and sampling variability. Moore (2001) likens bias and variability to shooting arrows at a target. As shown in Figure 1.5, bias systematically moves statistics away from the true population value, shown as the center of the target. Variance randomly moves statistics away from the true population value. To reduce bias we use random sampling. To reduce sampling variability, also known as sampling error, we use large samples.

Much of traditional statistical practice has addressed the problem of sampling error. It has concerned itself with small sample problems. An engineer wants to find the optimal settings for temperature and air pressure for blowing glass or plastic against a mold. She asks, "How many experimental observations will be needed to be confident about estimates of product quality?" A medical researcher needs to determine whether a new drug is effective in treating asthma. She asks, "How many double-blind clinical trials must be run in testing drug against placebo?" A pollster wants to predict an election outcome. He wonders, "How many exit-poll interviews must be conducted to be confident of the prediction?" A marketing manager must decide whether or not to release a new product. She asks the marketing researcher, "How many consumers should be surveyed about their likelihood of purchasing the product? How many test markets should be used prior to a nationwide rollout?" These are small sample questions. Because the cost of data collection is high or the time frame short, researchers try to get answers they can trust from as little data as possible.

In data mining the problem is not small samples, but large samples. Rather than asking how small a sample is sufficient to be confident of statistical estimates, we ask how small a model is sufficient to summarize the large data set.

1.2.2 Probability Statements: Describing Uncertainty

We express uncertainty about events with probabilities. Events that are very likely have probability close to one; events very unlikely have probability close to zero. When we make inferences from samples to populations, we cast those inferences in terms of probabilities. There are two primary ways of making probability statements in statistics: classical and Bayesian.

Classical methods are implemented in standard statistical packages and are widely used in business and marketing research. With the introduction of computer-intensive estimation methods, Bayesian statistics has become a viable approach to business and marketing research. Even with effective estimation methods, Bayesian methods require customized programming in many applications.

The classical statistician takes what is called a frequentist approach to probability. He asks us to imagine that the observed sample is like one of many samples that could have been taken from a fixed but unknown population. In making inferences from the sample to the population, the classical statistician begins by imagining that something is true about the population (the null hypothesis), and, using the sample data, expresses an inference in terms of a conditional probability statement, a p-value, which has the general form:

$$Probability(Data|Null\ Hypothesis).$$

That is, he talks about the probability of observing the sample data given the assumption that the null hypothesis is true.

The null hypothesis is usually a statement that no one believes, a claim that two variables have no relationship in the population or that the means of two groups are exactly equal in the population. By collecting enough data, the classical statistician obtains a low p-value, indicating that either (1) a very low probability event has occurred with the null hypothesis being true or (2) the null hypothesis is false. When rejecting the null hypothesis because of the low p-value, the classical statistician claims to have obtained a statistically significant result. The classical statistician is uncertain about the true state of nature, the null hypothesis. The observed p-value is a way of expressing his degree of uncertainty.

Another approach to probability and inference is the Bayesian approach, which takes its name from Bayes Theorem. The Bayesian expresses uncertainty about the true state of nature by specifying prior probability distributions about characteristics of the population (priors about parameters). Then she uses sample data to update her priors, forming a posterior probability distribution. The Bayesian is able to make conditional probability statements of the form:

$$Probability(Hypothesis|Data).$$

That is, she talks about the probability of something being true about the population, given the data (and her priors). Bayes Theorem is used to move from priors to posteriors. Uncertainty about the true state of nature is reflected in the posterior probability distribution, which incorporates information from the prior and the sample data.

To understand the logic of classical inference, we must think about population, sample, and sampling distributions. To understand the logic of Bayesian inference, we must also understand prior and posterior distributions and how priors are updated to form posteriors. Conceptually, Bayes Theorem has the form:

$$Posterior = \frac{Likelihood \times Prior}{Evidence}.$$

The prior probability distribution is specified by the researcher. The likelihood is estimated from the sample data. And the denominator or evidence is merely a scaling factor that is used to make the posterior distribution a probability distribution with total area under the curve equal to one.

Data miners can be found in both the classical and Bayesian camps, and some may be found in a third camp, best described as exploratory data analysis. Not all research work needs to end in a probability statement. Exploration and description of sample data are worthy objectives in their own right, especially when samples are large. Hypothesis generation is just as important to research as hypothesis testing; discovery and pattern recognition are just as important as formal inference and theory validation.

1.2.3 Models

Few business people would think of describing themselves as "modelers," but models are basic to the things we do with data. When we measure, we use models. When we compute summary statistics and make histograms and scatterplots, we use models. When we design and run surveys and experiments, we use models. Because we need to work with data, we are modelers, whether we like to admit it or not.

Finding a good model for the data is the fundamental problem of data mining. We look for patterns in the data. We look for relationships. A good model helps us to summarize patterns and relationships. A model is at once a tool for representing data and a simplification of the data. We want models that fit the data well, and we want models that are easy to understand. The art and science of modeling involve striking the proper balance between goodness of fit and parsimony.

A quotation attributed to the statistician George Box, "All models are wrong, but some are useful," captures the spirit of modeling. Models can be wrong for many reasons. They can include the wrong explanatory variables, incorrect scales or transformations of variables, or incorrect mathematical specifications, such as a main-effects-only model when an interaction model is appropriate. Most models are incomplete in that they fail to include all relevant explanatory variables.

Some models are useful. They help us to represent large data sets with a few summary statistics, graphs, or formulas. We present many examples of models in this book, and we talk at length about statistical model selection and validation. But let's not forget that models should satisfy management needs as well as statistical criteria. According to Little (1970), to be most useful to managers, models should be:

- Simple (easy to understand)
- Robust (hard to get absurd answers)
- Easy to control (with inputs known, measurable, or obtained from subjective estimates)
- Adaptive (can be modified as new information becomes available)
- As complete as possible (with all critical variables included)
- Easy to work with (change the inputs and quickly get new output when playing "what-if" games)

1.2.4 Information Systems: Data Mining Software

The central thesis of this book is that data mining is not merely a collection of tools for data analysis. Rather, it is an approach to data analysis, a way of doing research. Nonetheless, we must have tools to do the work. Methods of analysis, whether model-based or data-adaptive, are often computer-intensive. Without powerful computers and efficient algorithms, there would be no data mining.

We organize and visualize data. We fit models to data. We examine thousands or millions of potential models to find the "right" model. The process of data mining can be exploratory. The process can be lengthy, involving many steps of data preparation and analysis. Specialized programs for data mining provide tools for managing the process.

Figure 1.6 provides a stylized user's view of a data mining application. A graphical user interface shows procedures, project workspaces, and processing logs in windows or distinct areas of the screen. The window for procedures, shown at the left-hand-side of the figure, provides icons for data preparation and analysis. The primary window, the area where analysts do their work, is the project workspace, shown as the largest area in the upper right-hand-side of the figure. Using analyst-selected icons for data preparation and analysis procedures, this window shows the steps involved in the data mining project. The window at the bottom right is the processing log, which provides a text-based report about executed procedures. Processing commands, execution times, and warning and error messages appear in the processing log.

A key advantage of data mining applications is their ability to provide documentation for complex research projects. The project workspace provides a map of the data mining process, showing the sequence of data preparation and analysis steps in the research

Figure 1.6 User's View of a Data Mining Application

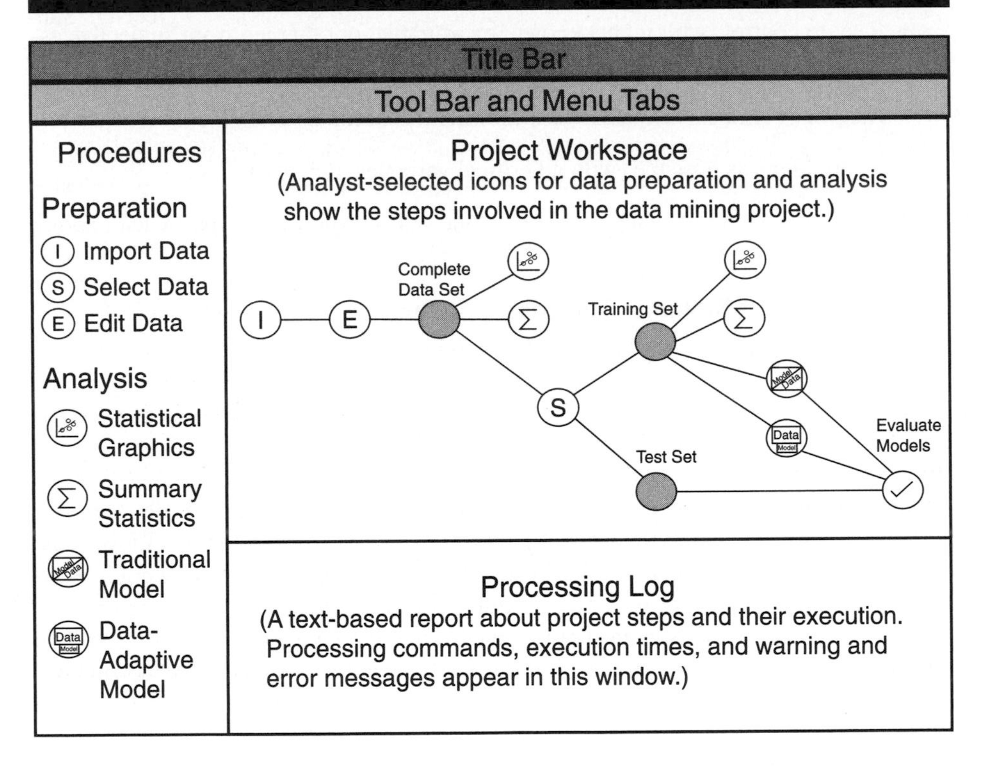

project. The processing log, which is generated automatically and can be maintained as a history file, provides a list of executed procedures and a report of processing results. Accordingly, work completed within a data mining application is self-documenting, simplifying the job of the individual statistician, modeler, or business analyst. With project data, programs, and documentation maintained in shared folders or directories, data mining applications make it easier for teams of researchers to work together.

There are many reputable suppliers of data and text mining software. SAS Institute, Inc. offers the Statistical Analysis System (SAS) and Enterprise Miner, as well as a Text Miner product that can be integrated with Enterprise Miner. SPSS Inc. has its Statistical Package for the Social Sciences (SPSS), Clementine (Helberg 2002), AnswerTree, and a variety of text analysis tools. Salford Systems provides CART (classification and regression trees), MARS (multivariate adaptive regression splines), and TreeNet. StatSoft products include Statistica Neural Networks and Data Miner. XLMiner from Cytel Systems provides data mining capabilities with Microsoft Excel as the user interface. Systems vendors have their own data mining offerings, including NCR's Teradata, IBM's Intelligent Miner, and online analytical processing (OLAP) tools for database systems from Oracle and Microsoft (de Ville 2001).

For examples in this book, we use products from Insightful Corporation, including S-PLUS and Insightful Miner, as well as public-domain software, such as the R system and the Perl language. The S-PLUS and R systems are implementations of the S language, originally developed at AT&T Bell Laboratories. These are flexible, object-oriented programming environments for implementing the specialized methods and models of data mining. The Insightful Miner system builds and documents data mining applications. It provides a user interface to the major tasks of data mining: selecting, preparing, and transforming data, model building, validation, and implementation. It extends the S-PLUS system by using efficient algorithms for working with very large databases. Insightful also offers the InFact text mining tool.

1.2.5 Information Systems: Databases and Data Interchange Standards

Business problems are often large data problems, involving massive data sets and document collections. Database systems are needed to manage the data and to provide efficient access to those data. Suppliers of database systems offer online analytical processing (OLAP) and data analysis tools for generating summary reports involving numerous variables or data fields. Many suppliers also provide data mining applications.

Many database systems are relational, with data organized into tables of rows and columns. Data can be numeric, dates, or alphanumeric character strings. A data dictionary provides a guide to the structure of the database. A database administrator defines this structure before data are entered into the database, imposing restrictions upon what data may be stored and how they may be stored. Because a relational database has a well-defined structure, information retrieval is easy. Rows and columns in one table can be linked with rows and columns in another table. A structured query language (SQL) helps the analyst form new tables by joining or intersecting portions of existing tables.

Business analysts and managers want to exchange information with one another; they want to share data and models across operating systems and applications. And when they share information, they want to do it seamlessly, without converting from one data format to another. An Excel user on an Apple Macintosh should be able to share her data and models with an R user on Linux. An analyst who has developed a credit scoring model in Insightful Miner should be able to deploy that model in a Java program for processing loan applications. Users don't want information about the data and models to be "lost in translation" when moving from one platform to another.

Proprietary data formats, long the bane of users needing to share data across systems, are being replaced by formats that comply with international standards for information interchange. Just as communication standards and formats like TCP/IP (transmission control protocol/Internet protocol), ftp (file transfer protocol), HTTP (hypertext transfer protocol), and HTML (hypertext markup language) made the Internet and the World Wide Web a reality, standards like XML (extensible markup language) will make program-to-program data interchange a reality.

Standards for data interchange promote communication and collaboration among research practitioners, just as they promote interprocess communication and coordination across computer systems. Many businesses have benefited from standards like EDI (electronic data interchange), which enable efficient business-to-business transactions between buyers and sellers. Acceptance of XML and other international standards is the first step in the direction of Web services linking networks of information providers and users. Data miners will be among the first to benefit from these technologies.

1.3 THE WAYS OF RESEARCH

How should we conduct research to learn about business, economic, and social phenomena? To know the ways of research, we must first understand the roles that models and data play in the research process. We distinguish among three basic ways of conducting research, as shown in Figure 1.7.

Data mining is data-driven, data-adaptive research. It begins with data and derives models from data. This type of research follows in the tradition of exploratory data analysis, popularized by Tukey twenty-five years ago (Mosteller and Tukey 1977; Tukey 1977). We begin with data and search for simple models to represent the data. Data mining often employs data-adaptive methods appropriate for large data sets and unstructured problems. It is well suited to applications in business and marketing.

Traditional research is central to the scientific process. This is empirical research as it has been conducted for many years—data and theory (models) are equally important. Formal hypotheses are stated and tested with empirical data. Traditional research is well suited for working with small to moderately sized data sets and well-specified problems.

A third way of research is model-dependent research, in which the model comes before the data. In fact, the model is often the source of the data. Simulation methods are examples of model-dependent research. These methods can be especially useful in applied research settings and in testing alternative statistical models and methods.

Figure 1.7 The Ways of Research

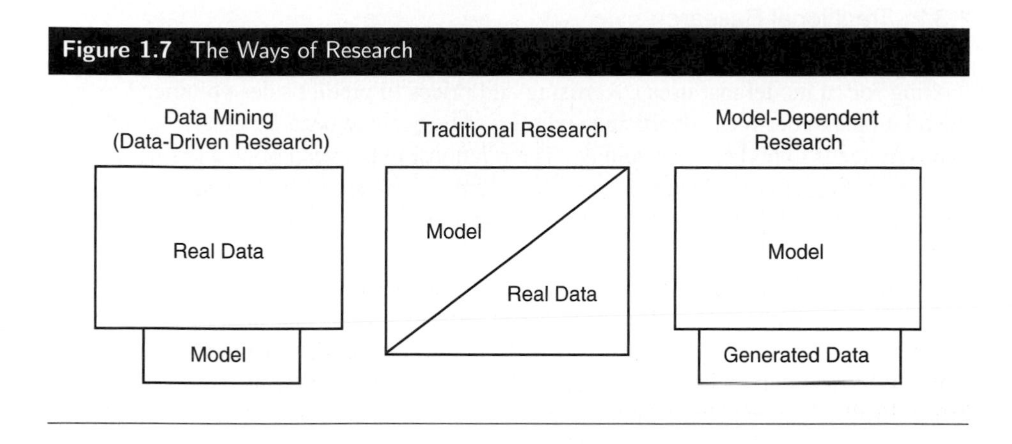

1.3.1 Data Mining

A business researcher might say, "I'm looking for a model that will predict sales, but I'm not sure what kind of model that should be. Advertising and prices could affect sales, but so could hundreds, perhaps thousands, of other variables." To simplify the process of finding a model to predict sales, the researcher lets the computer do the work. No need to restrict model selection to a set of models linear in their parameters. No need to limit the set of explanatory variables to advertising and price alone. With computer algorithms to do the work, the researcher allows the data to be the guide. An algorithm selects the form of the model, as well as the variables to be included in the model. The process of model selection is automated or partially automated. This is typical of data mining, a data-driven, data-adaptive approach to research.

Taking a data mining approach, the analyst begins by limiting the range of methods to be considered. Will these be tree-structured methods, neural networks with a single hidden layer, or a sum of smooth functions fit to the data? Will they be parametric or nonparametric? That is, the process begins by selecting a method or algorithm that makes sense for the data. After a method has been selected, the analyst lets the computer do the work. The process of model specification—finding the right model form—is automated or partially automated. Data mining is data-driven, data-adaptive research. It is a flexible approach to making sense out of data.

Traditional research is usually associated with traditional methods of statistical analysis. Data mining is usually associated with data-adaptive methods. As we will see in subsequent chapters, examples of traditional methods include regression and logistic regression, whereas examples of data-adaptive methods include tree-structured regression and classification, neural networks, and smoothing methods. Nothing prevents us from using either or both types of methods in the conduct of business research and in data mining.

1.3.2 Traditional Research

The traditional approach begins with theory. A researcher says, "I know what I'm looking for: a model that uses advertising and prices to predict sales volume. I expect the relationship between advertising and sales to be positive because greater advertising exposure leads to higher sales volume. The relationship between price and sales should be inverse; higher prices lead to lower sales volumes." To simplify the task of modeling, the researcher is likely to specify a linear model using variables in their original units or, perhaps, log units.

Traditional research is often parametric; it makes assumptions about the form of the population distribution. Having specified the model in advance, the analyst fits a specific model to the data; that is, the analyst estimates the parameters of the model from sample data. We use inferential methods, both classical and Bayesian, to make conditional probability statements about data and hypotheses. There are tests of goodness of fit to see how well the model fits the data. Diagnostics may be used to evaluate the specification and underlying statistical assumptions.

In taking a traditional approach to research, the analyst can begin with a management problem, specify a model, collect data relevant to the model, fit the model, and test the fit. This sequence of steps describes what many researchers do. Care is taken to ensure that the selected model fits the data. The process is often repetitive, with alternative specifications and subset models being tested and retested. If there is lack of fit or if model assumptions appear to be violated, ample opportunities exist to step back to specify new models for testing. Analysts intervene in the process. Analysts use their judgment in specifying the form of models and in restricting the domain of subset models to be tested.

Specify, fit, test; specify, fit, test. How does the analyst know when to stop? Analysts, searching across a set of subset models, begin the process anew with each full model specification. In practical terms, the process stops when the analyst runs out of time or patience. A report is due to management. A decision has to be made.

1.3.3 Model-Dependent Research

Taking a model-dependent approach to research, the analyst identifies the business problem to be addressed, defines and implements a model, and develops a computer program for the model. The program is designed to generate data under hypothetical business conditions or scenarios. Researchers who practice model-dependent research often refer to themselves as modelers. This approach to research is popular among management and decision scientists.

What makes model-dependent research a meaningful research enterprise and not just a computer modeling game is its goal of mimicking real business-world phenomena. Data generated from the computer model are supposed to resemble real business data, relationships, and events. To judge the utility of model-dependent research, we compare generated data with real business data. The modeler says, "Here is a model for the behavior of a system. Let's put the model in a computer program and see what happens as it runs."

Model-dependent research is often used in conjunction with other research methods. In statistical simulations, for example, analysts generate data to test the performance of alternative computer algorithms, statistical methods, and model selection criteria. They can test models derived from traditional and data-adaptive methods using data generated to conform to specific business conditions. Furthermore, models can be used for "what-if" analyses, evaluating business strategies under alternative market scenarios.

We expect growth in model-dependent research in the coming years. Of particular interest are agent-based models of business and market phenomena. Software agents representing individual consumers and firms, imbued with artificial life, values, and behavioral propensities, interact with one another. Modelers set initial conditions and let the agent-based simulation run. They watch what happens as software agents interact with one another.

Like data mining, model-dependent research is often computer-intensive. Nonetheless, we can think of data mining and model-dependent research as being at opposite ends of a research continuum. Data mining begins with real data; its product is a model representing real data. Model-dependent research, on the other hand, begins with a model; its product is generated data, showing the behavior of the model or of virtual agents in a virtual world. Data mining involves data-based model generation, whereas model-dependent research involves model-based data generation.

Theory first or data first—what is the right way to do research? Put data miners, traditional researchers, and modelers in the same room, and they may end up fighting with each other. Curiously enough, they are rarely in the same room. Traditional research is the domain of most social science and business academics. Modeling is the choice of many management scientists and operations researchers. Applied statisticians, although receptive to the idea of exploratory data analysis, have been slow to adopt data mining as a viable approach to model selection and inference. It has been the computer scientists who have been the strongest proponents of data mining, and their success has prompted others to reevaluate their views about this exciting approach to research.

1.4 DATA MINING HYPE AND REALITY

Controversy surrounds data mining. In some circles the term "data mining" has a negative connotation. Economists have been particularly harsh in their criticism of research that eschews theory, describing data mining as "data dredging" or a "fishing expedition." Arthur Conan Doyle in *A Study in Scarlet* had Sherlock Holmes saying, "No data yet.... It is a capital mistake to theorize before you have all the evidence. It biases the judgments." In a parody of these words, Leamer (1990) quotes an economist as saying, "No theory yet. It is a capital mistake to look at the data before you have identified all the theories."

There is the hype of data mining, much of it coming from vendors of software products and services. They describe data mining as automated or partially automated data analysis, often ignoring the fact that data mining involves considerable time. To attract business customers, software vendors often describe data mining practitioners as business analysts, rather than statisticians. Vendors of database software tout data mining as a database application, a collection of software tools for information retrieval and analysis. To hear many vendors talk, we might think that learning about data mining was merely a matter of learning how to use software, ignoring the fact that good data mining practice relies upon an understanding of business problems and statistical concepts.

The hype about data mining suggests that insight into business problems is automatic or easily obtained by using software. Consider this quotation, which refers to neural networks, a data mining method:

> Artificial intelligence systems, based upon the emerging technology of neural networks, can sift through mountains of data and identify shopping trends and product opportunities, weigh promotional possibilities, segment groups of customers, and present marketers with clear conclusions and suggestions. (Bessen 1993, p. 153)

The reality of data mining practice is different from the hype. Data mining tools offer no panaceas, no ultimate solutions to perennial questions about research. Are measurements reliable and valid? Are there errors in measurement? Should we be concerned about missing or miscoded data items? Are samples representative of the population of interest? Is there bias in the selection of individual cases? What should we do about missing or miscoded data? Business analysts need to address these questions, regardless of their approach to research.

Large samples, often associated with data mining problems, can be both a benefit and a curse—we have the smaller standard errors associated with large samples, but we also have more work to do in preparing the data for analysis. Large databases have many measured variables and more opportunities for missing and miscoded data items. Data rarely come to us in a form that is directly usable for analysis and modeling. Much time is spent preparing data for analysis.

Consider the hypothetical time lines in Figure 1.8. In developing a research plan or proposal, an analyst might consider data collection, analysis, and modeling phases to be of comparable length. The reality of research, however, often diverges from the plan or proposal. Data collection takes longer than planned, and much time is spent cleaning and preparing data for analysis.

The reality of data mining is that this approach to research, like other approaches, requires time to prepare input data, to analyze data, and to interpret and evaluate results. Following Pyle (1999), we see data preparation as a critical component of data mining:

> After finding the right problem to solve, data preparation is often *the* key to solving the problem. It can easily be the difference between success and failure, between usable insights and incomprehensible murk, between worthwhile predictions and useless guesses. (Pyle 1999, p. xvii)

Figure 1.8 Research Time Lines: Plan versus Reality

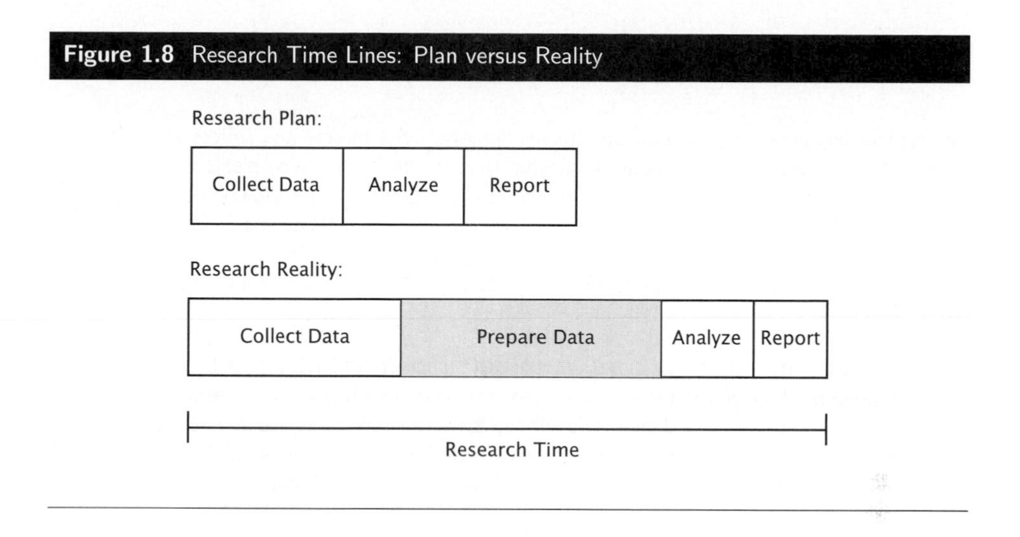

Data preparation is often a collaborative exercise involving business analysts and information systems professionals. Much of the work of data preparation falls on the shoulders of information systems professionals who have programming and database expertise. Cross (2001) identifies various data preparation processes, including data recognition, parsing, filtering, and transformation. To these we add data cleaning, including the handling of missing data items. Exhibit 1.4 describes data preparation processes.

Some think of data mining as exploratory data analysis for large data sets. Others see it as a collection of traditional and data-adaptive tools. We describe data mining as a way of doing research or learning about data. Flexible, data-driven, and data-adaptive it is. Automatic it is not. To do a good job of data mining in business, we must do a good job of analysis, drawing upon a knowledge of the business context, measurement methods, statistics, computer programs, and modeling.

Traditional versus data-adaptive methods, specification of form, model fitting and selection, parametric and nonparametric models—many discussions of modeling methods and processes seem abstract. To show how traditional and data-adaptive processes differ, we can draw upon business cases. Market research and the transactions of business provide rich sources of data. The fundamental task is to make sense out of data, to learn from data. Seeing data mining applications helps us to understand data mining methods.

Exhibit 1.4 Data Preparation Processes

The typical business database contains transactions between buyers and sellers and acts as a source of information about customers. Rather than serving a specific research objective, the typical business database is intended to serve diverse and, as yet, unspecified objectives of future research. Rarely do data often come to us in a form suitable for analysis and modeling. Data are often unstructured, and we must impose structure. Data may be improperly structured, and we must restructure them prior to any data analysis. Data preparation, as described below, involves processes important to ensuring data integrity as well as proper structure.

- **Recognition.** A first step in data preparation is to identify relevant data sources and to recognize which data items are relevant to the research problem at hand. Some use the term "data mart" to refer to a database developed to serve a specific research objective. To build a data mart, which is a collection of data extracted from other databases (both internal and external to the firm), we must recognize relevant data for inclusion in the data mart.

- **Parsing.** The verb "to parse" has a grammatical meaning: to resolve a sentence into its component parts of speech. Statements in a computer language must also be parsed. Statements follow grammatical rules and must be broken down into their component parts in order to be executed. Likewise, data parsing involves structuring and restructuring data for further analysis. We take data in their original form and reformat them, so they may serve as input to data analysis programs. A common parsed structure has individual cases (units of analysis) as rows and attributes (explanatory and response variables) as columns.

- **Filtering.** Having recognized data relevant to research and having reformatted them for analysis, we move on to the next step, filtering. Data filtering involves selecting specific rows and columns of data for further processing. When working with massive data sets, it is often convenient to work with samples or subsets of the data. Sampling of cases is a filtering process. Selecting specific attributes or columns is also a filtering process. Business judgment as well as statistical criteria may be used to identify those data attributes most relevant to research objectives.

- **Cleaning.** Data filtering and data cleaning often go hand in hand. Cleaning refers to processes that ensure data integrity. We check to see that each data item has a valid code and that codings are consistent across data attributes. Data outliers or unusual data values often result from incorrect data entry; these should be corrected prior to further analysis. Researchers must decide what to do about missing data items. Cases or attributes for which most data values are missing might be eliminated from the data set. For many missing data items, the analyst decides whether to replace missing data items with statistically generated values. There are many methods for doing this, including sophisticated methods of data imputation.

- **Transformation.** Often we must recode or transform data prior to data analysis. We change values or formats of selected fields. Mathematical formulas may be used to transform data from one measurement scale to another. We often combine categories or values within an attribute to create a new coding for the attribute. We can look at the values of two or more attributes to create values for a new attribute. And using summary statistics for entire columns of data, we can standardize or normalize the values of selected attributes.

1.5 BUSINESS APPLICATIONS

If data mining is to be described as a "fishing expedition," let's get the story straight. The data miner, like the fisherman, is sometimes successful, sometimes not. But, as any good angler knows, success in fishing is more than a matter of chance. Just as it makes sense to use the right tackle and bait in fishing, it makes sense to use the right tools in data mining. And just as the fisherman needs to know where to fish, the business researcher needs to know which problems are amenable to analysis.

We can use data mining methods to explore data or search for structure. We can use them to complement or supplement traditional methods of analysis. Data mining methods may be used for explanation and prediction. Let's review common application areas in business.

- **Brand Loyalty and Buyer Behavior.** Some customers are product- and brand-loyal; they purchase the same products and brands repeatedly. Other customers switch from one product or brand to the next, influenced by lower prices, promotions, or a desire for variety. Switching costs can be high in product categories that require consumer learning, such as computer software. In other categories, such as cellular phones, products and services may be viewed as interchangeable, and switching costs are low. Models of buyer behavior help us to understand buying processes, including trial purchase, repeat purchase, brand loyalty, and switching. Methods of analysis draw upon applied probability (stochastic) models, recurrent events data (reliability) analysis, and survival data analysis.

- **Competitive Intelligence.** Learning about the competition is critical to business success. The Internet and World Wide Web provide access to a vast information store for research about the competition and competitive products. We can use data mining tools to organize and reduce data and to search for relevant information. The methods of text mining are especially useful in this area.

- **Consumer choice modeling.** Choice is fundamental to business, and models that predict consumer choice are of great value to management. Some people buy a firm's products; others do not. Some buy only on discount. Some buy but don't pay their bills. Some shop online; others shop in person. Adding up the choices of individual consumers across products within a category, we get estimates of market shares. Finding out what makes people choose one product over another is a key to successful marketing. Logistic regression is a traditional method of choice modeling. Classification trees and neural networks are examples of modern data-adaptive methods for choice modeling.

- **Credit scoring and fraud detection.** Businesses want customers who buy in volume or at high margin, and businesses want customers who pay their bills. Credit scoring helps firms to find and keep customers who pay their bills and to drop customers who don't. Past financial behavior and current financial circumstance can be good predictors of future financial behavior. Data mining models may be used for credit scoring, identifying those individuals who are credit risks.

- **Customer relationship management.** Customer relationship management is a natural extension of direct or database marketing. This is the one-to-one marketing approach, as described by Peppers and Rogers (1993). Firms build relationships with customers over time. A record of business transactions serves as a guide for fostering further transactions. Systems for customer relationship management can integrate business transactions data with marketing research data (Miller and James 2004). Firms can use what they know about customers to develop individualized or customized marketing plans.

- **Direct and database marketing.** Direct and database marketing are common applications for data mining. Direct marketing firms contact prospects and customers directly, sending promotional brochures. These firms can increase profits by mailing only to those prospects and customers most likely to buy. Data mining models may be used to identify these customers. Anand and Büchner (2002), for example, discuss applications of data mining techniques in cross-selling, finding prospects for additional products from an existing customer list.

- **Market basket analysis.** Data relating to the things we buy and the prices we pay are important to retail management. These are the empirical ramifications of demand. Walking through the aisles of supermarkets, we see hundreds of thousands of items from which to choose. The market basket of products we take to the checkout counter reveals our product preferences in a way that no survey could fully capture. Individual items, identified by stock keeping units (SKUs) and universal product codes (UPCs), might be grouped by product or category type. Sometimes called affinity or association analysis, market basket analysis asks, "What goes with what?" There are obvious things, like hot dogs and hot dog buns, and party favors and ice. There are reports, sometimes surprising, sometimes bogus, of less obvious things going together, like diapers and beer. We can use market basket analysis to guide product placement in stores and to develop co-marketing and product bundling plans. More generally, we can apply market basket analysis in the study of consumer lifestyles and behavior.

- **Market response modeling and sales forecasting.** Explanatory variables associated with the marketing mix (product characteristics, price, promotions, and advertising) affect market response, consumer demand, or sales. Traditional regression and modern data-adaptive regression are appropriate tools for many response modeling and sales forecasting problems.

- **Market segmentation** Mass marketing involves using a common method to sell to everyone. One-to-one marketing involves customizing a firm's marketing plan to fit the needs of each individual consumer. Targeted marketing falls between mass marketing and one-to-one marketing, and market segmentation is a tool for targeted marketing. We identify groups or segments of customers who are more similar to one another than to customers outside their respective groups or segments. Segments are often based upon geo-demographic data. "Location,

location, location," long the mantra of business, has relevance today despite our migration toward a networked nation. Many products and services are location-dependent. Grocery and convenience stores, restaurants, laundromats, and health and fitness clubs know that there are advantages in being close to where people live and work.

- **Pricing.** Pricing decisions can be informed by models for market response. They can also be built upon information about competitor pricing policies and consumer response to product features and product availability, as we learn from consumer choice studies. Data mining models can guide decisions about pricing.

- **Product positioning.** How do products within a category compare with one another? What is the nature of the product space? Which products serve as close substitutes for one another? How important is brand name as a differentiator of products? These product positioning questions may be addressed by multivariate methods, as we shall see in the next chapter.

- **Information management.** Last but not least in our list is the most general of data and text mining applications: information management. Managers complain of information overload. There are too many documents to read, too many statistics to understand. Some define the field of statistics as the science of "data reduction." Data and text mining can be of great assistance to the modern manager in reducing the amount of information that she must review.

Business managers have the dual responsibility of serving customers and investors. To serve customers, managers need to understand demand, as observed in the marketplace and as reflected by measured customer needs, behavior, and attitudes. To serve investors, managers must provide a positive return through interest payments, dividends, and capital appreciation. They need to offer the right products at the right times, at the right prices. Retailers, manufacturers, and service organizations need to understand their customers and the business environment. All can benefit by learning from customer and market data. There is much data, much to learn about data, and much to learn about data mining.

An extensive study at the University of California–Berkeley (Lyman et al. 2000) estimated that the world's yearly production of information (across print, film, optical, and magnetic media) is 1.5 billion gigabytes, the equivalent of 250 megabytes per person. Plain text accounts for 24 terabytes of data per year. The Berkeley study estimated that Web content increases by 0.1 terabytes each day, or 35.6 terabytes per year. Estimates of surface Web content (static publicly available Web pages) for the year 2000 stood at 2.5 billion documents, between 25 and 50 terabytes of directly accessible data. Only two years earlier, Lawrence and Giles (1998) had estimated the surface Web to contain at least 320 million pages. Beyond the surface Web, there is the deep Web, which consists of databases and dynamic Web content accessible through the Web. The Berkeley study estimated the deep Web to be 400 to 500 times the size of the surface Web. To keep up with information, we need data and text mining.

1.6 FURTHER READING

Reviews of data mining technologies and applications have been provided by Bacon (2002) and Benôit (2002). Breiman (2001) presents a review of traditional versus data-adaptive methods, which he refers to as the "data modeling" versus "algorithmic" cultures, respectively. Some use the term "statistical learning" to refer to the wide range of data-adaptive methods. Detailed discussion of statistical learning and data mining methods may be found in Hastie, Tibshirani, and Friedman (2001), Cherkassky and Mulier (1998), and Hand, Mannila, and Smyth (2001). Comprehensive reviews of methods and applications are provided in volumes edited by Klösgen and Żytkow (2002), Ye (2003), and Bozdogan (2004). A number of authors have focused upon applications in the area of customer relationship management (Berson, Smith, and Thearling 2000; Dyché 2002; Greenbert 2002). Miller and James (2004) discuss the integration of marketing research and customer relationship management.

Discussion of various aspects of data preparation may be found in Pyle (1999) and Cross (2001). Witten and Frank (2000) suggest methods for automatic data cleaning. Rubin (1987), Little and Rubin (1987), and Schafer (2000) review missing data issues and statistical methods for data imputation. Additional sources provide introductions to databases, XML, and data interchange standards (Ray 2001; Chaudhri, Rashid, and Zicari 2003; Date 2003).

Moore (2001) provides an elementary introduction to statistical concepts. Snedecor and Cochran (1989) offer an overview of classical statistical methods. Churchill and Iacobucci (2002), Malhotra (2004), and Miller and James (2004) review the application of classical methods in marketing research. Gelman et al. (1995), Carlin and Louis (1996), Berry (1996), Congdon (2001, 2003), and Rossi and Allenby (2003) review the logic and methods of Bayesian statistics. Tanner (1996) provides an advanced treatment of algorithms for the computer implementation of Bayesian methods. Selected references compare classical and Bayesian approaches as they apply to working with large quantities of data (Ridgeway and Madigan 2003; Press 2004) and text (Mosteller and Wallace 1984).

Detailed reviews of software systems for data mining have been provided by Klösgen and Żytkow (2002) and Haughton et al. (2003). Gentle (2002, 2003) provides overviews of computational methods for data analysis. For S-PLUS and R programming, Chambers (1998) and Venables and Ripley (2000) are the standard sources. For models and methods in S-PLUS, we suggest Chambers and Hastie (1992), Pinheiro and Bates (2000), Harrell (2002), Venables and Ripley (2002), Crawley (2002), and Krause and Olson (2002). Lam (2001) reviews techniques for working with S-PLUS for Windows. Zivot and Wang (2003) discuss applications in finance and econometrics. Insightful Corporation offers user documentation for the S-PLUS and Insightful Miner systems (`http://www.insightful.com`). To learn about R, the reader can refer to Venables, Smith, and R Development Core Team (2001), Fox (2002), Dalgaard (2002), Maindonald and Braun (2003), and the Web site for the Comprehensive R Archive (`http://cran.r-project.org`).

CHAPTER 2 TRADITIONAL METHODS

> We recognize that we don't live in a world of ones and zeroes, of truth and falsehood. Real life, including real-life engineering and computer science applications, must deal successfully with vagueness and imprecision, with linguistic variables and noisy data. We must increasingly learn to live with near-optimum answers. We must realize that global optimization is a myth. We don't do it as humans; neither should we, in most cases, expect our machines to do it. (Kennedy and Eberhart 2001, p. 423)

What is it like to do data mining? We prepare data for analysis. We explore data with statistical graphics. We convert many numbers to a few numbers using methods and models as our guides. We solve business problems as well as we can given the limitations of business data and the methods and models at our disposal. Predicting market response, prices, sales, or consumer choice is by no means an automatic process. There are many hurdles on the way to finding models that work.

Computer scientists specializing in data mining distinguish between supervised and unsupervised learning. When learning from data is guided by a response variable, they call it supervised. When there is no identifiable response variable, they call it unsupervised. Figure 2.1 provides an overview of traditional methods organized by type of response variable or research objective (continuous or categorical) and by type of learning (supervised or unsupervised). The four listed methods are those we review in detail in this chapter. We use regression to predict response magnitude. We use logistic regression and cluster analysis for classification. And the method of principal components is one of many ways of searching for communalities among many measures and producing product positioning maps. Additional traditional methods and applications may be placed within the context of this fourfold overview.

In this chapter we introduce traditional methods. We review regression, logistic regression, and multivariate methods. We discuss the application of traditional methods in predicting market response and consumer choice and in product positioning, market basket analysis, and market segmentation. References to the literature are provided at the end of the chapter.

Figure 2.1 Classification and Application of Traditional Methods

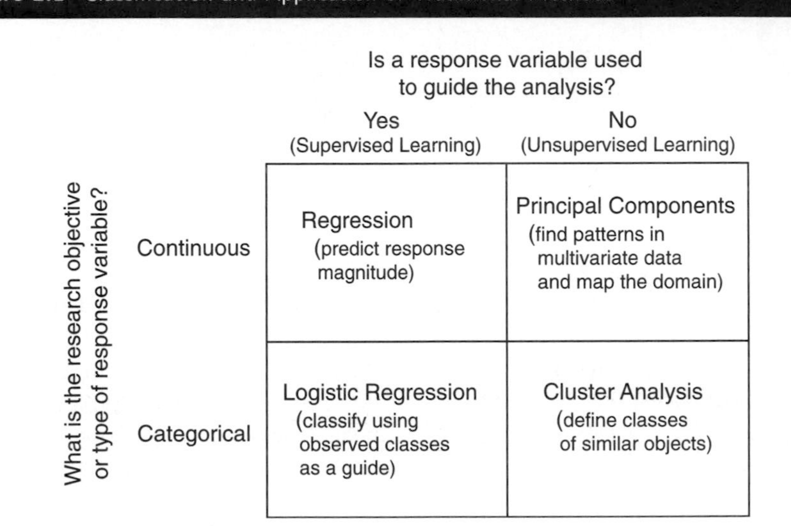

2.1 DATA PREPARATION AND VALIDATION

We have noted that much of the work of data mining is data preparation. Raw data come to us unstructured, and we must impose structure. Raw data come with miscodings, errors of omission, inconsistent or invalid responses, unusual responses or outliers, and missing data items. We need to fix data problems when we can.

Let's learn by doing. Let's see what data preparation means by working with real data from a real business case. To provide a detailed example, we turn to the DriveTime case from Appendix A. DriveTime is an automobile dealership that sells used vehicles to people with less than perfect credit. The firm keeps detailed records about its vehicle inventory and wants to use data mining to guide its inventory decisions. Which cars and trucks are the best sellers? Which are the worst?

2.1.1 Data Recognition, Filtering, and Cleaning

The DriveTime data set includes rows (records or cases) for 35,875 vehicles, including sixteen columns of continuous variables and seventeen columns of categorical variables. These data have been extracted from a much larger corporate database. Initial filtering of attributes was done by DriveTime analysts, with selected attributes (columns) being those thought relevant to the task of predicting time to sale, as described in the case. We note that there are 1,397 rows with missing data items, and we eliminate these rows for this example, leaving 34,478 vehicles with complete data.

Knowing that there are great differences between cars and trucks, it may make sense to build separate models for cars and trucks. Focusing upon cars, we note that there are 27,417 cars, and the great majority of these (18,365) are coded as `SEDAN`. The next most frequent category is `COUPE` (4,704). Station wagons could be coded either as `STATION WAGON` (1,291) or `WAGON` (745), and there are 18 car records coded as `JEEP`. Curiously, 613 cars are coded as `PICKUP`; these could be trucks miscoded as cars, cars miscoded as pickups, or small pickups that are thought of as cars.

Building a single model for all car types could be problematic, given the low frequencies of many types and possible misclassification of some vehicles. Given the predominance of sedans, most of which we can hope have been correctly classified as cars, let's start by building models for sedans. Accordingly, we build a reduced data set for sedans, deleting sedan records also classified as minivans, pickups, sport utility vehicles, and other non-car, non-sedan categories. This gives us a sedan data set with 17,506 vehicles.

To continue with our data cleaning and filtering efforts, we select a subset of columns to begin our research. Imagine that there are two types of problems to be addressed: vehicle pricing or cost models associated with the response variable `TOTAL.COST` and time-to-sale models associated with `LOT.SALE.DAYS`. To keep the analysis manageable for the purposes of demonstration, we can use our judgment to select the potential explanatory variables. Some explanatory variables may be of little use in predictive models because they have low variability or low frequencies across categories. For example, the variable `DOORS.NADA` has codes `2DR`, `3DR`, and `4DR`, but almost all sedans have four doors. Suppose we believe that the important variables include `MILEAGE`, `VEHICLE.AGE`, `REGION`, `VEHICLE.CATEGORY`, `MAKE`, `MODEL`, `COLOR`, and `DOMESTIC.IMPORT`, and we transform some of these variables before we begin our modeling work.

2.1.2 Data Transformation

Looking at sedans, we see that the variable `VEHICLE.CATEGORY` has codes for economy car (`ECO`), large family car (`FAM/L`), mid-sized family car (`FAM/M`), and small family car (`FAM/S`). There are two codes for luxury cars, highline domestic (`HL/D`) and highline foreign (`HD/F`), that we should recode simply as luxury cars because, in building predictive models, we have the binary categorical variable `DOMESTIC.IMPORT` to represent the attribute domestic-versus-import. Furthermore, the make of the vehicle reflects this information. Let's define a new variable `VEHICLE.TYPE` to accommodate the revised coding for `VEHICLE.CATEGORY`.

Another easy transformation concerns the variable `REGION`, which has numeric codes in the original data file. For ease of interpretation, we define a new variable called `STATE` with abbreviated state names corresponding to the numeric codes for regions; twelve regions are converted to eight state names.

Some DriveTime categorical variables have low-frequency categories and require transformation prior to their use in predictive models. The variable `COLOR`, for example, has twenty-seven distinct categories or values. Colors like pink, yellow, and chrome have very low frequencies, so including all twenty-seven color categories in our models would present problems. A better approach, assuming that we want to use color in our models at all, would be to define a new categorical variable for color.

How many categories to use and how to map the original twenty-seven colors into the new colors are matters of judgment. Suppose we call our new color variable `COLOR.SET` and give it eight categories, as shown in Exhibit 2.1. In defining this new color variable, we specify categories that cover the entire range of colors, and we make sure that each new category has a sufficiently large frequency to warrant its use in modeling work. Sometimes catch-all or "other" categories must be used. In the DriveTime case, the `COLOR.SET` category `GOLD`, for example, covered a wide range of colors, including gold, tan, cream, yellow, and brown tones.

The variable `MAKE` has codes for twenty-seven manufacturing firms or divisions, but many codes have low frequencies. Our transformation strategy for this variable is to ignore manufacturing firms or divisions with fewer than 150 vehicles in the sedan data set. We define a new variable `MAKEX` with the code `OTHER` representing the makes of vehicles with low frequencies; `MAKEX` has twenty distinct codes.

The variable `MODEL` is more problematical than `MAKE`. With its 107 distinct codes, we are less inclined to include it in predictive models. Feeling that complete make and model information may be useful when we examine fitted models, however, we combine the character strings of `MAKE` and `MODEL` into a single labeling or identifying variable called `MAKE.MODEL`.

Exhibit 2.2 provides statistical summaries for the four continuous and seven categorical variables that we retain in the sedan data set. These are the variables we use in subsequent modeling work for the DriveTime case. One of the categorical variables, `OVERAGE`, which refers to vehicles that remain on the lot more than 90 days, will be used when we discuss logistic regression later in the chapter.

Details, details, details—good research is a matter of attending to details. Care must be taken in preparing data for analysis. The work takes time; it can be tedious. But the work must be done if we are to trust the results of data mining. The old adage of computer programmers holds true: "Garbage in, garbage out." We must make sure that we are not throwing garbage into our data mining programs. The most important, most salient of variables in business models are often derived variables involving scale transformations or ratios of original variables. Many of the decisions made in preparing data for data mining are arbitrary decisions based upon judgment, but they are decisions that must be made if research is to proceed. Good research depends upon good judgment. Good research also requires a plan for validation.

2.1.3 Partitioning for Validation

Before we begin modeling work, we should know how we are going to judge the adequacy of models. For predictive models we adopt a partitioning strategy using the computer to divide the full sedan data set into two or three disjoint sets for analysis. That is, we can use part of our data to develop models and another part to evaluate or validate models.

Figure 2.2 shows a strategy for partitioning into two data sets, identified as training and test sets, or into three data sets, identified as training, validation, and test sets.

Exhibit 2.1 DriveTime Sedan Color Map with Frequency Counts

Values of Original Variable (COLOR)	*Values of New Variable* (COLOR.SET)								*Count*
	BLACK	WHITE	BLUE	GREEN	RED	PURPLE	SILVER	GOLD	
Aluminum/Silver	0	0	0	0	0	0	1234	0	1234
Beige	0	0	0	0	0	0	0	123	123
Black	1216	0	0	0	0	0	0	0	1216
Blue	0	0	2149	0	0	0	0	0	2149
Blue - Dark	0	0	16	0	0	0	0	0	16
Blue - Light	0	0	53	0	0	0	0	0	53
Bronze	0	0	0	0	0	0	0	15	15
Brown	0	0	0	0	0	0	0	64	64
Burgundy/Maroon	0	0	0	0	0	1410	0	0	1410
Cream	0	0	0	0	0	0	0	76	76
Chrome/Stainless Stl	0	0	0	0	0	0	1	0	1
Copper	0	0	0	0	0	0	0	9	9
Gray	0	0	0	0	0	0	618	0	618
Gold	0	0	0	0	0	0	0	1003	1003
Green	0	0	0	3309	0	0	0	0	3309
Green - Dark	0	0	0	59	0	0	0	0	59
Green - Light	0	0	0	20	0	0	0	0	20
Lavender	0	0	0	0	0	8	0	0	8
Mauve	0	0	0	0	12	0	0	0	12
Orange	0	0	0	0	9	0	0	0	9
Pink	0	0	0	0	7	0	0	0	7
Purple	0	0	0	0	0	366	0	0	366
Red	0	0	0	0	1406	0	0	0	1406
Tan	0	0	0	0	0	0	0	414	414
Taupe	0	0	0	0	0	0	0	11	11
Teal	0	0	289	0	0	0	0	0	289
Turquoise	0	0	2	0	0	0	0	0	2
White	0	3603	0	0	0	0	0	0	3603
Yellow	0	0	0	0	0	0	0	4	4
Count	1216	3603	2509	3388	1434	1784	1853	1719	17506

Exhibit 2.2 Summary Statistics for the Full Sedan Data Set

	TOTAL.COST	LOT.SALE.DAYS	MILEAGE	VEHICLE.AGE
Min:	1375	0	82	1.0
1st Qu.:	4300	7	67242	4.0
Mean:	4895	47	76950	5.4
Median:	4852	24	77961	5.0
3rd Qu.:	5444	74	89090	7.0
Max:	9813	300	119250	12.0
Total N:	17506	17506	17506	17506.0
Std Dev.:	935	53	16979	1.8

VEHICLE.TYPE		DOMESTIC.IMPORT		VEHICLE.AGE.GROUP	
ECONOMY:	2142	Domestic:	12035	ONE-THREE:	2127
FAMILY.SMALL:	3069	Import:	5471	FOUR:	3393
FAMILY.MEDIUM:	6897			FIVE:	4012
FAMILY.LARGE:	2940			SIX:	3437
LUXURY:	2458			SEVEN+:	4537

MAKEX		STATE		COLOR.SET		OVERAGE	
BUICK:	1674	AZ:	2335	BLACK:	1216	NO:	14011
CADILLAC:	174	CA:	3621	BLUE:	2509	YES:	3495
CHEVROLET:	2142	FL:	3147	GOLD:	1719		
CHRYSLER:	396	GA:	1725	GREEN:	3388		
DAEWOO:	160	NM:	522	PURPLE:	1784		
DODGE:	1015	NV:	514	RED:	1434		
FORD:	2287	TX:	4348	SILVER:	1853		
GEO:	403	VA:	1294	WHITE:	3603		
HONDA:	389						
HYUNDAI:	286						
KIA:	389						
MAZDA:	731						
MERCURY:	705						
MITSUBISHI:	330						
NISSAN:	1610						
OLDSMOBILE:	1512						
PLYMOUTH:	461						
PONTIAC:	1547						
TOYOTA:	971						
OTHER:	324						

Figure 2.2 Data Partitioning for Model Evaluation:"" Training, Validation, and Test Sets

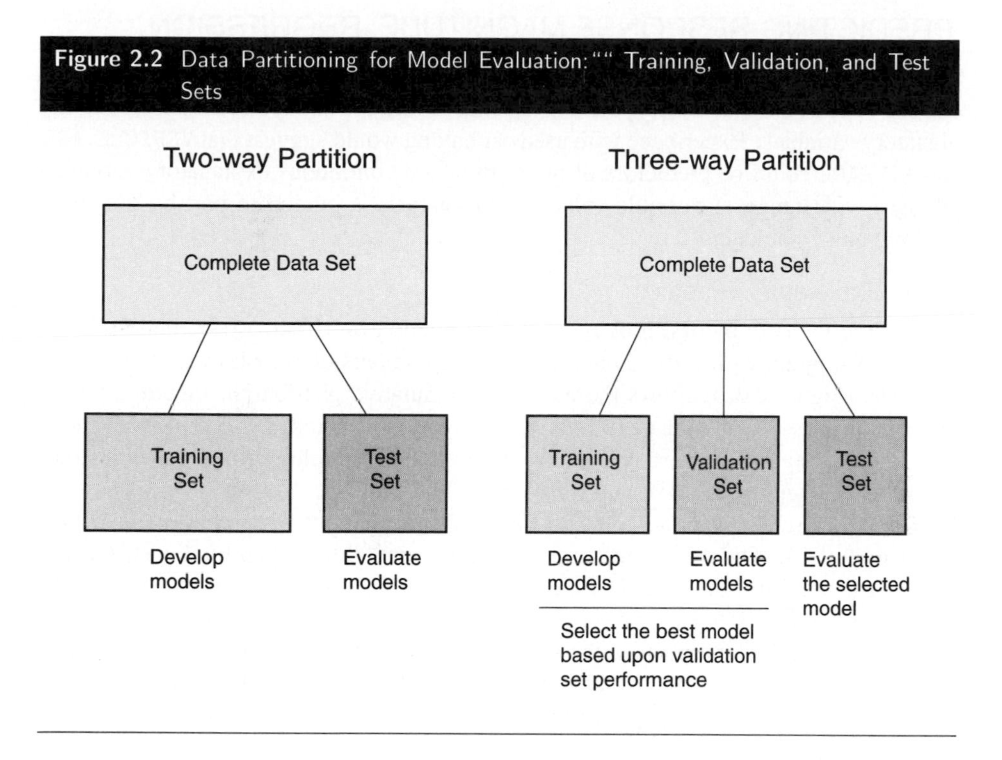

Training sets are used to develop models; we fit models to training data using optimization criteria. Validation and test sets are used to evaluate models, to see how well models work on new or hold-out data. For example, for the DriveTime case we can use a three-way partition. Instead of developing models for the full sedan sample of 17,506 vehicles, we can develop using 50 percent of the data (8,753 vehicles) in a training set. Then we select models based upon 25 percent of the data (4,377 vehicles) in a validation set. Finally, having chosen the model that works best in the validation set, we evaluate its performance in a test set consisting of the other 25 percent of the data (4,376 vehicles).

How shall we evaluate models? Statistical criteria for model selection depict goodness of fit and parsimony. Goodness of fit statistics show how well models fit the data. Parsimony relates to the complexity of models; simpler, more parsimonious models are easier to understand. We also evaluate models based upon their value in serving management objectives. We want models that work. When deploying models, we look for positive business results. Both statistical criteria and management criteria are quantifiable and may be computed for training, validation, and test sets.

2.2 PREDICTING RESPONSE MAGNITUDE: REGRESSION

Let's use the sedan training data to build a model for predicting the cost of sedans. We can use `TOTAL.COST` as our response or dependent variable and look for appropriate explanatory variables. Experience with used car buying would suggest that `VEHICLE.AGE` and `MILEAGE` could be predictors of price; these are continuous explanatory variables taking a wide range of possible values. Our analysis is guided in part by graphical explorations of the data.

2.2.1 Exploratory Graphics

We explore the data by first looking at the distribution of `TOTAL.COST`. Figure 2.3(a) shows a histogram with vertical bars representing numbers of vehicles within total cost intervals. Figure 2.3(b) shows the empirical cumulative distribution function, which indicates that the distribution of `TOTAL.COST` is symmetric across a wide range of values. Each point along the curve represents the proportion of vehicles falling below the total cost value shown on the horizontal axis of the plot.

Figure 2.3(c) shows a box plot for these same data. Box plots were the invention of Tukey (1977). The center line in the box represents the median total cost; outside lines of the box show the hinges of the distribution. Hinges are values close to the first and third quartiles, or twenty-fifth and seventy-fifth percentiles, respectively. Whiskers extending to the left and right of the box are drawn to observations that fall closest to within one and a half times the width of the box from the hinges. Observations outside the endpoints of the whiskers are called outliers; these are shown as solid vertical lines to the left and right of the whiskers. Given the large number of observations in the sedan training set, groups of vertical outlier lines appear as solid black boxes on this plot.

Box plots are quite useful for comparing distributions across groups of observations. In exploring the DriveTime sedan data, for example, we can see that total cost varies with the make of vehicle, as shown in Figure 2.4, but total cost varies little with the color of vehicle, as shown in Figure 2.5.

Figures 2.6 and 2.7 show scatterplots for `TOTAL.COST` with `VEHICLE.AGE` and `TOTAL.COST` with `MILEAGE`, respectively. Smooth lines fit through these plots show the general direction of relationships; as expected, higher mileage and higher aged vehicles have lower cost. But there is substantial variability around the smooth curves in these figures, showing that sedan cost is not fully explained by either age or mileage of a vehicle. In the plot of `TOTAL.COST` on `VEHICLE.AGE`, individual vehicles are shown by open circles positioned at their value on the variable `TOTAL.COST`. When there are many vehicles close together in cost, the open circles overlap to form a solid line. In the plot of `TOTAL.COST` on `MILEAGE`, we use small dots rather than open circles to represent data points in order to visualize individual vehicles. Graphics like this can be quite useful in data mining, given the large number of points that must be plotted on the same graph.

Figure 2.3 Exploring the Distribution of Total Cost

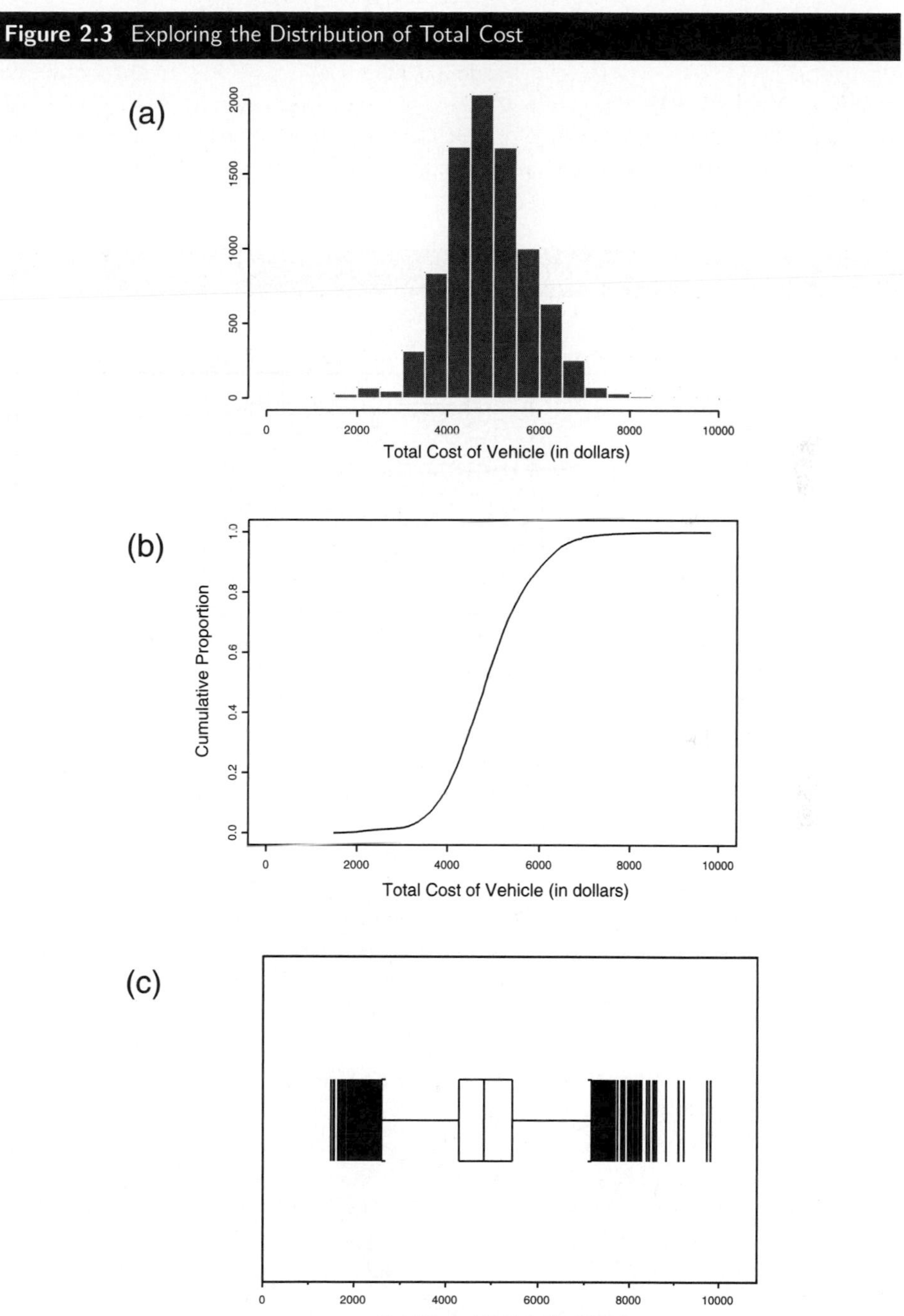

Figure 2.4 Vehicle Make and Total Cost

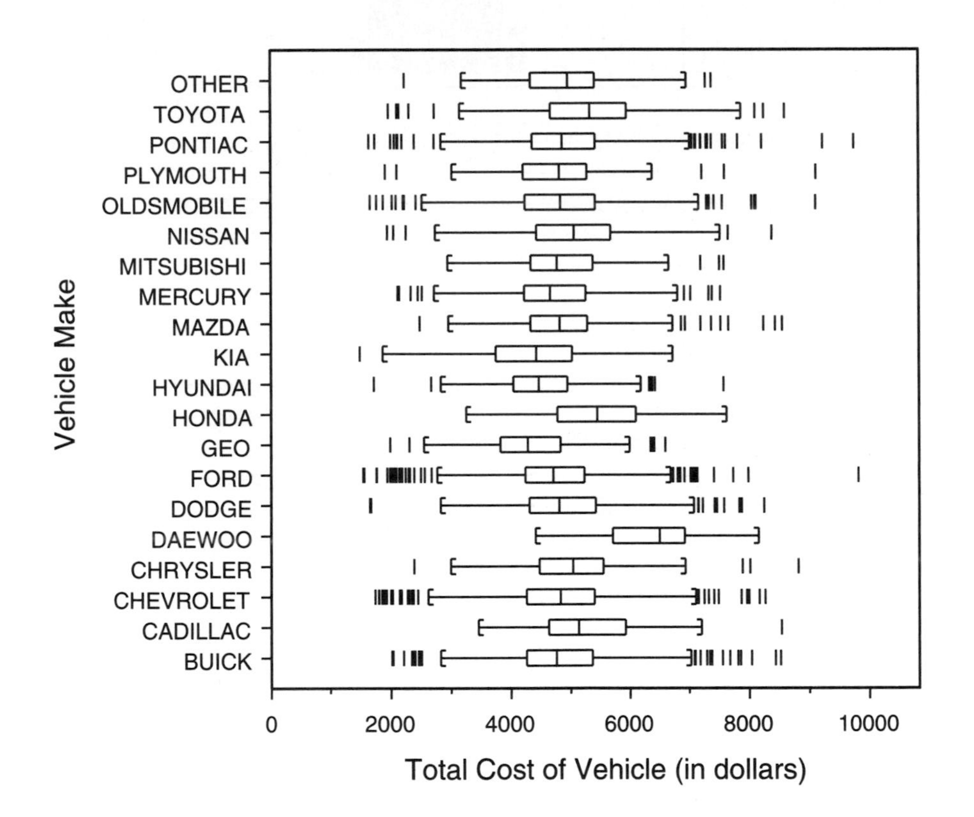

Figure 2.5 Vehicle Color and Total Cost

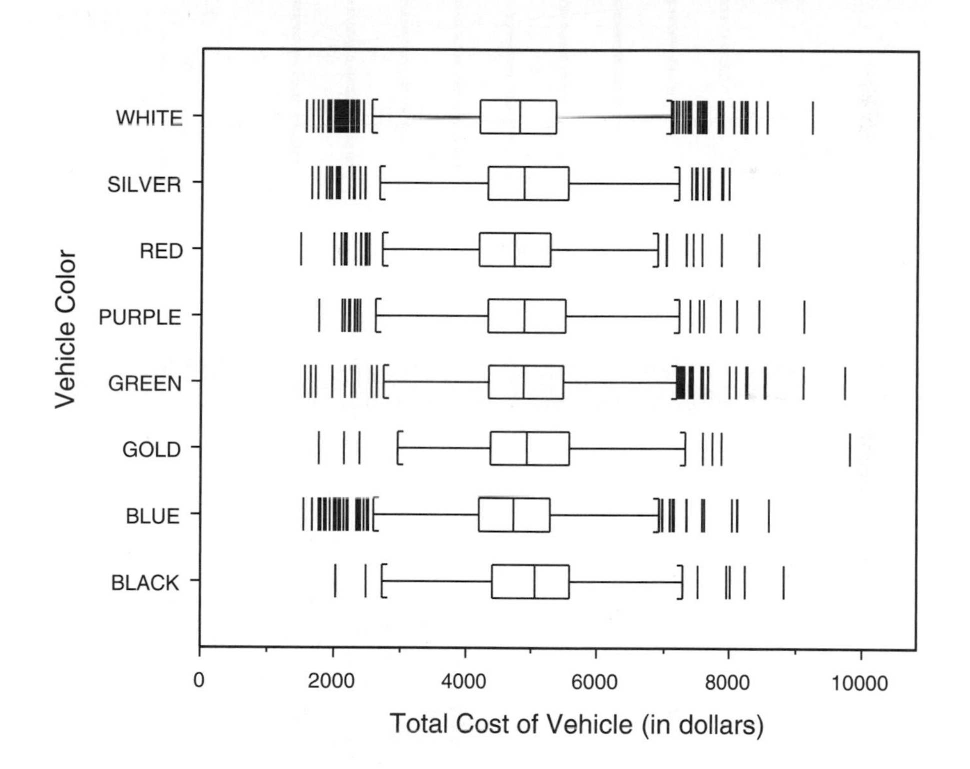

Figure 2.6 Vehicle Age and Total Cost

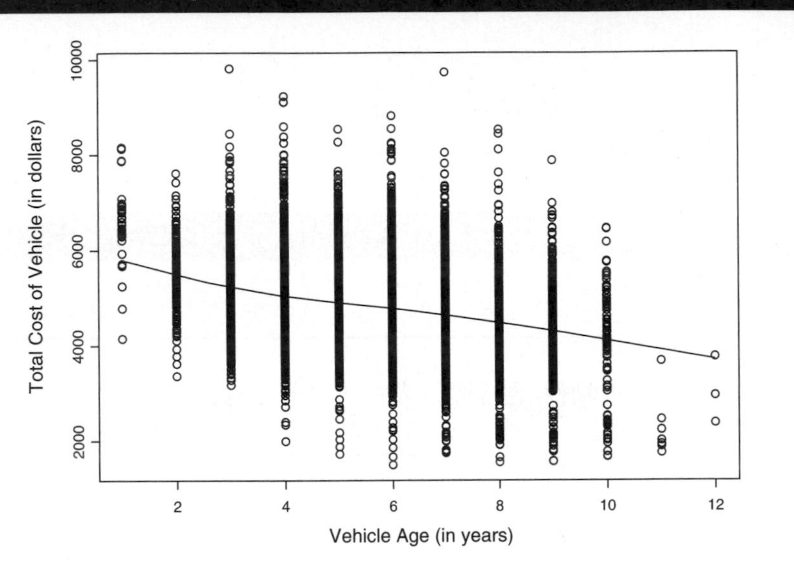

Figure 2.7 Vehicle Mileage and Total Cost

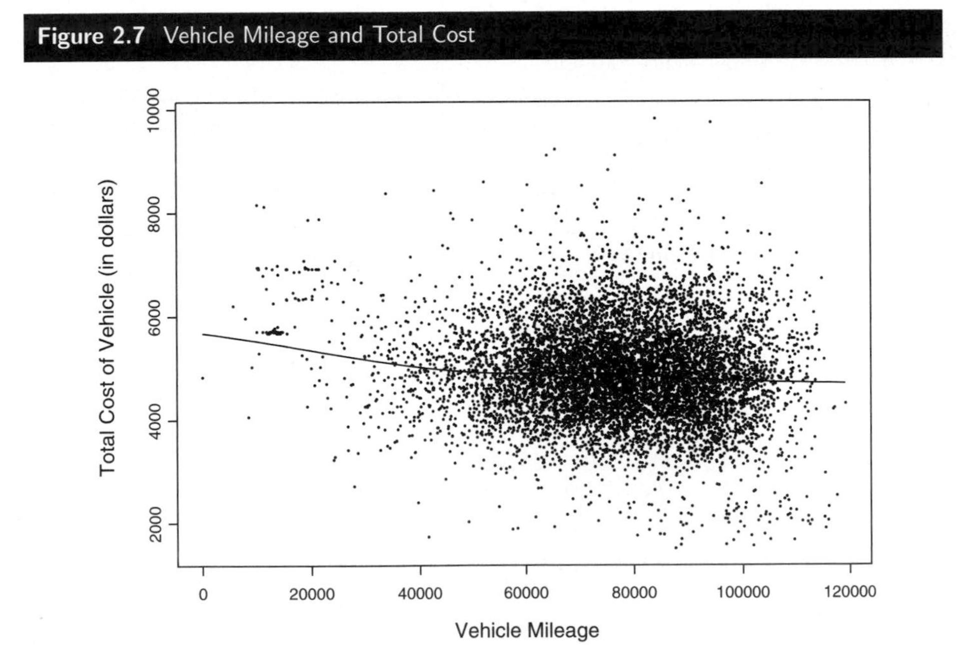

Exhibit 2.3 Simple Linear Regression

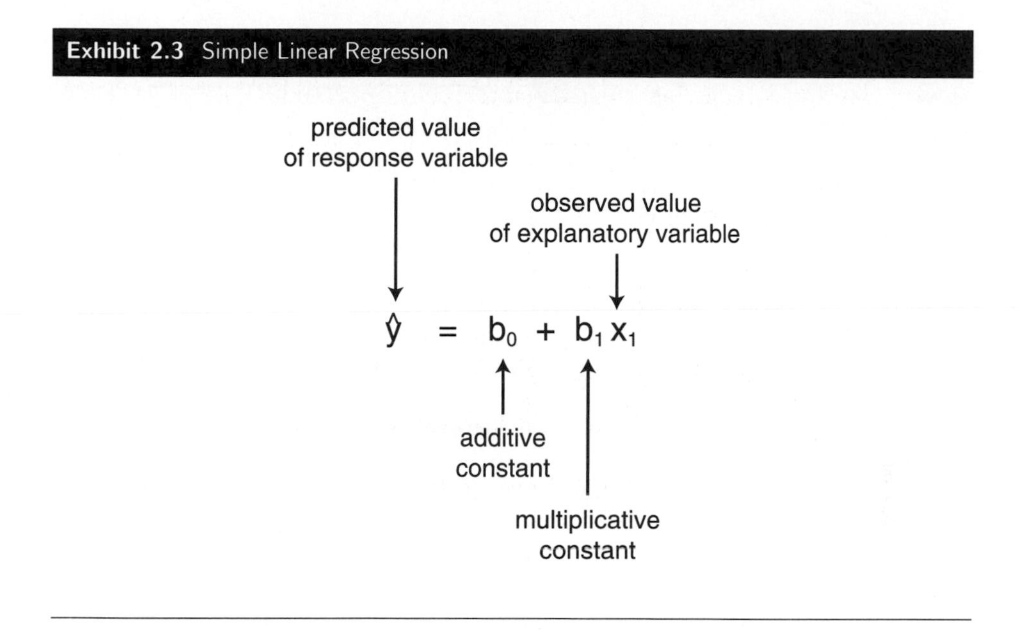

2.2.2 Regression Modeling Methods

We can use regression models to examine large sets of explanatory variables. Regression is a popular method of data analysis in business. The research objective is to predict a continuous response, a variable with meaningful magnitude. Explanatory variables are the variables we use to do the prediction; these may be continuous variables or appropriately coded categorical variables. Potential explanatory variables and the form or structure of the model are identified in advance.

To show the mathematics behind a traditional regression model, we note that a regression model is linear in the parameters, adding or multiplying by regression coefficients acting as constants in the equation. In symbols, a fitted regression equation looks like this:

$$\hat{y} = b_0 + b_1 x_1.$$

Exhibit 2.3 describes the symbols in a simple linear regression model—there is one response variable, one explanatory variable, and a linear function relating the two variables.

Adding a second explanatory variable yields a more complex model, a linear predictor with two explanatory variables, x_1 and x_2:

$$\hat{y} = b_0 + b_1 x_1 + b_2 x_2.$$

When there is more than one explanatory variable in the linear predictor, we are using multiple regression. It is common to have many explanatory variables in applied business problems. Explanatory variables in regression are either continuous variables with

Exhibit 2.4 Simple Linear Regression for Predicting the Total Cost of Sedans

```
Residuals:
   Min    1Q Median  3Q  Max
 -3304 -590   -57.7 530 5103

Coefficients:
              Value  Std. Error  t value  Pr(>|t|)
(Intercept)  5778.6        31.0    186.6       0.0
VEHICLE.AGE  -163.7         5.4    -30.3       0.0

Residual standard error: 889 on 8751 degrees of freedom
Multiple R-Squared: 0.095
F-statistic: 916 on 1 and 8751 degrees of freedom, the p-value is 0
```

meaningful magnitude or indicator variables (contrasts representing categorical variables or factors). To represent a multiple regression model with p explanatory variables, we write:

$$\hat{y} = b_0 + b_1 x_1 + b_2 x_2 + \ldots + b_p x_p.$$

2.2.3 Regression Modeling Example: DriveTime

Let's work through the DriveTime example using traditional linear regression to build predictive pricing models for sedans. We begin with a simple linear regression, using `TOTAL.COST` as the response and `VEHICLE.AGE` as the lone explanatory variable. The regression equation estimated from the sedan training data provides the following formula:

$$\text{Predicted} \;\; \texttt{TOTAL.COST} = 5778.6 - 163.7(\texttt{VEHICLE.AGE}).$$

Exhibit 2.4 shows the results of the fit, with estimated coefficients and standard errors for the intercept term and the slope (weight applied to `VEHICLE.AGE`). The R^2 statistic, 0.09475, indicates that just under 10 percent of the variability in `TOTAL.COST` may be accounted for by `VEHICLE.AGE`. Simple linear regression involves fitting a straight line through the set of points. Regression determines the intercept and slope of the line so that the sum of the squared errors in prediction is minimized; this is known as the least squares criterion.

Exhibit 2.5 reveals a multiple linear regression with a set of explanatory variables, including `VEHICLE.AGE`, `MILEAGE`, `VEHICLE.TYPE`, and `MAKEX`. Notice how multi-level categorical variables (multinomials) are represented by contrasts associated with all but one of the categories or levels. This more complex model has the form:

$$\text{Predicted }\ \texttt{TOTAL.COST} = 6482.496 - 268.029(\texttt{VEHICLE.AGE})$$
$$-0.006(\texttt{MILEAGE}) + \ldots. + 222.615(\texttt{MAKEX} = \texttt{OTHER})$$

Writing the entire equation would involve listing the coefficients for the intercept and all twenty-five weights applied to explanatory variables and contrasts. Using this more complex model results in a better fit to the sedan training data, yielding an R^2 value of 0.2808. That is, more than 28 percent of the variance in TOTAL.COST may be accounted for by the linear combination of explanatory variables we have selected. The p-values for each of the four explanatory variables are less than 0.05, showing that each of the four explanatory variables (VEHICLE.AGE, MILEAGE, VEHICLE.TYPE, and MAKEX) has a statistically significant relationship with the response, TOTAL.COST. But there could be other important variables we have not included in our model. There is much unexplained variability in sedan cost. Some of this unexplained variability could be associated with the condition of vehicle, for example.

Conceptually, multiple regression involves fitting a plane (or hyperplane) through the set of points in space. This is impossible to visualize in more than three dimensions, so we think in terms of generalizing from simple linear regression and focus upon the algebraic representation of the model. Multiple regression sets the coefficients of the regression equation in a way that minimizes the sum of the squared errors in prediction. In other words, like simple linear regression, multiple regression satisfies a least squares criterion.

It is tempting to interpret estimated coefficients in multiple regression as though they were not part of a set of estimated coefficients. Researchers might look at the signs of individual coefficients to see if they make sense, reflecting assumed relationships between individual explanatory variables and the response. But multiple regression is not just a series of simple regressions stacked on top of one another. The multiple regression coefficients should be interpreted as a set, and signs of individual coefficients are sometimes counterintuitive. We also note that multi-category (multinomial) explanatory variables are represented by multiple binary indicator variables in the table of coefficients. To determine whether a multi-category explanatory variable contributes significantly to the regression model, we look to the classical p-values in the analysis of variance table.

2.2.4 Evaluating Linear Regression Models

Returning to the multiple regression for predicting sedan total cost, we see that each of the four explanatory variables used in the model has a statistically significant relationship to the response. Relationships are weak, but, given the large size of the sedan training set, it is easy to reject null hypotheses that population parameters are equal to zero. This is a common observation in data mining work. Many relationships are judged to be statistically significant even though they are weak relationships.

The term "statistical significance" sounds impressive, but statistical significance is not the best criterion upon which to judge the adequacy of models or the importance of

Exhibit 2.5 Multiple Linear Regression for Predicting the Total Cost of Sedans

Coefficients:	Value	Std. Error	t value	Pr(>|t|)
(Intercept)	6482.496	63.666	101.820	0.000
VEHICLE.AGE	-268.029	6.019	-44.529	0.000
MILEAGE	-0.006	0.001	-9.463	0.000
VEHICLE.TYPE=FAMILY.SMALL	283.170	32.769	8.641	0.000
VEHICLE.TYPE=FAMILY.MEDIUM	470.390	30.377	15.485	0.000
VEHICLE.TYPE=FAMILY.LARGE	726.573	35.875	20.253	0.000
VEHICLE.TYPE=LUXURY	730.016	39.038	18.700	0.000
MAKEX=CADILLAC	856.097	88.480	9.676	0.000
MAKEX=CHEVROLET	-404.185	37.959	-10.648	0.000
MAKEX=CHRYSLER	136.610	63.472	2.152	0.031
MAKEX=DAEWOO	-64.534	107.311	-0.601	0.548
MAKEX=DODGE	-280.572	46.907	-5.981	0.000
MAKEX=FORD	-473.945	37.780	-12.545	0.000
MAKEX=GEO	-418.138	63.688	-6.565	0.000
MAKEX=HONDA	776.067	69.287	11.201	0.000
MAKEX=HYUNDAI	-956.534	73.312	-13.047	0.000
MAKEX=KIA	-1077.735	69.020	-15.615	0.000
MAKEX=MAZDA	-22.219	51.496	-0.431	0.666
MAKEX=MERCURY	-293.593	51.703	-5.678	0.000
MAKEX=MITSUBISHI	-226.370	68.486	-3.305	0.001
MAKEX=NISSAN	96.944	45.457	2.133	0.033
MAKEX=OLDSMOBILE	-60.509	40.341	-1.500	0.134
MAKEX=PLYMOUTH	-334.661	62.573	-5.348	0.000
MAKEX=PONTIAC	-48.943	40.688	-1.203	0.229
MAKEX=TOYOTA	532.826	49.959	10.665	0.000
MAKEX=OTHER	222.615	72.618	3.066	0.002

```
Residual standard error: 793 on 8727 degrees of freedom
Multiple R-Squared: 0.28
F-statistic: 136 on 25 and 8727 degrees of freedom, the p-value is 0

Analysis of Variance Table,  Response: TOTAL.COST
```

	Df	Sum of Sq	Mean Sq	F Value	Pr(F)
VEHICLE.AGE	1	7.2e+008	7.2e+008	1150	0.000
MILEAGE	1	3.5e+006	3.5e+006	6	0.019
VEHICLE.TYPE	4	6.8e+008	1.7e+008	271	0.000
MAKEX	19	7.4e+008	3.9e+007	62	0.000
Residuals	8727	5.5e+009	6.3e+005		

individual explanatory variables within models. Statistical significance has a specific meaning: we say that statistics are statistically significant when they lead to the rejection of a null hypothesis. A typical null hypothesis states that there is no relationship between variables in the population or that the population regression coefficient is exactly equal to zero. It is not hard to reject such a hypothesis when samples are large. Furthermore, tests of significance as we have seen in the regression models above are based entirely upon the training data set. To use them as our evaluation of the adequacy of models would be to use the same data to evaluate our models as we have used to build our models.

To evaluate regression models, we must go beyond the data to which they have been fit. We noted that our simple linear regression accounted for less than 10 percent of the response variability and that our multiple regression accounted for about 28 percent of the response variability. But these figures were based upon the training data. When we evaluate models on the same data to which we have fit those models, our evaluations are likely to be favorable. To get an honest evaluation of the models, we should see how well they perform on other data. This is the reason we partition the data set into training, validation, and test sets before we begin modeling work.

How well do our simple and multiple regression methods perform on validation and test sets? To assess performance in predicting a continuous response variable, we examine differences between observed and predicted scores. In terms of mathematics, let y be an observed response value and $\hat{y}$ be a predicted response value. The difference between values $(y - \hat{y})$ is called a residual, which is an error in prediction. When the observed response is higher than the predicted response, we have a positive residual; when the observed is lower than the predicted, we have a negative residual. When observed and predicted values are close, we have good predictions. To get an index of goodness of fit to a data set, however, we cannot merely average the residuals. This is because the sum (and, hence, the average) of the residuals across the training data set is zero in traditional linear regression. Accordingly, in calculations of goodness of fit (or badness of fit) in predicting a continuous response, we use squared residuals or absolute values of residuals. The mean squared error is the average of the squared residuals for a data set, and the mean absolute error is the average of the absolute values of residuals.

In reviewing printed results from the regression analyses, we cited another goodness of fit statistic, R^2. Sometimes referred to as the coefficient of determination, R^2 is the square of the correlation between observed and predicted responses and may be computed for training, test, and validation sets. R^2 varies between zero and one and may be interpreted as a proportion. It represents the proportion of response variability explained by a linear regression model. Another goodness (or badness) of fit statistic is the relative squared error, which, like an R^2 statistic, provides an indication of how well a regression model performs relative to the naive model that predicts that the response value of each observation is equal to the mean of the response variable across all observations in the data set.

In reviewing goodness of fit statistics, we note that adding terms to a regression model, as we did in moving from the simple linear regression model to the multiple regression model for sedan total cost, will always yield better goodness of fit values.

That is, more complex models do better in the training set. Before we deploy models in business applications, we need to find models that we can trust. We use test and validation sets in model evaluation and model selection because they provide an honest appraisal of model performance and, hence, model utility in business applications. It is not sufficient to show that a model works with the data on which it was developed (the training set). We must also show that it works with other data (validation and test sets).

Diagnostic plots may be used to evaluate regression models. Figure 2.8(a) shows a plot of regression residuals against predicted values. Nonlinear patterns in such plots can indicate problems with the specified model. We detect no such patterns in this plot. Figure 2.8(b) shows a normal probability plot of regression residuals. Departures from the straight line representing normal ordinates can indicate departures from normality, calling into question the assumption that errors are normally distributed. We see some evidence of this at the high end of the distribution.

Further evaluation of regression models should consider the business implications of their use. Models for total cost, such as developed above, can be used to make decisions about vehicles at auction. That is, DriveTime can use regression models in its bidding process, purchasing only vehicles that appear to be underpriced at auction. Lowering the cost of vehicles, while maintaining the quality of vehicles (as reflected by how long it takes to sell them), will lead to increased profits.

2.2.5 Applications of Regression

Developing a model to predict vehicle cost or price is one example of regression. There are many other applications of regression in business. A broad class of regression models, for example, is market response models. Suppose we want to predict sales or market share—continuous variables with meaningful magnitude. What explanatory variables could we use? Higher prices are usually associated with lower sales volume (the law of demand from economics). Heavy advertising and increased visibility through improved product placement in stores could result in higher sales. Sales promotions, price discounts, and volume purchase deals are likely to result in higher sales. Competitor advertising and promotional activities could also affect sales. Models built within this context are market response models. We study how sales volume varies with changes in the marketing mix (price, product attributes, promotion, advertising, and distribution).

In addition to the DriveTime case, numerous cases from Appendix A illustrate well the applications of regression in business, marketing, and economics. The Boston Housing Study is a market response study of sorts, with price varying with geographic, environmental, and housing characteristics. Movie-Going Surveys give us an opportunity to examine price expectations across consumers from various socio-economic groups and regions of the United States. Musicnotes.com data give us an opportunity to study sales across time with time-series regression. Veterans Organization Direct Marketing data may be used to search for variables associated with the level of donor contributions, variables that could be useful in targeted marketing efforts.

Figure 2.8 Diagnostic Plots for Linear Regression

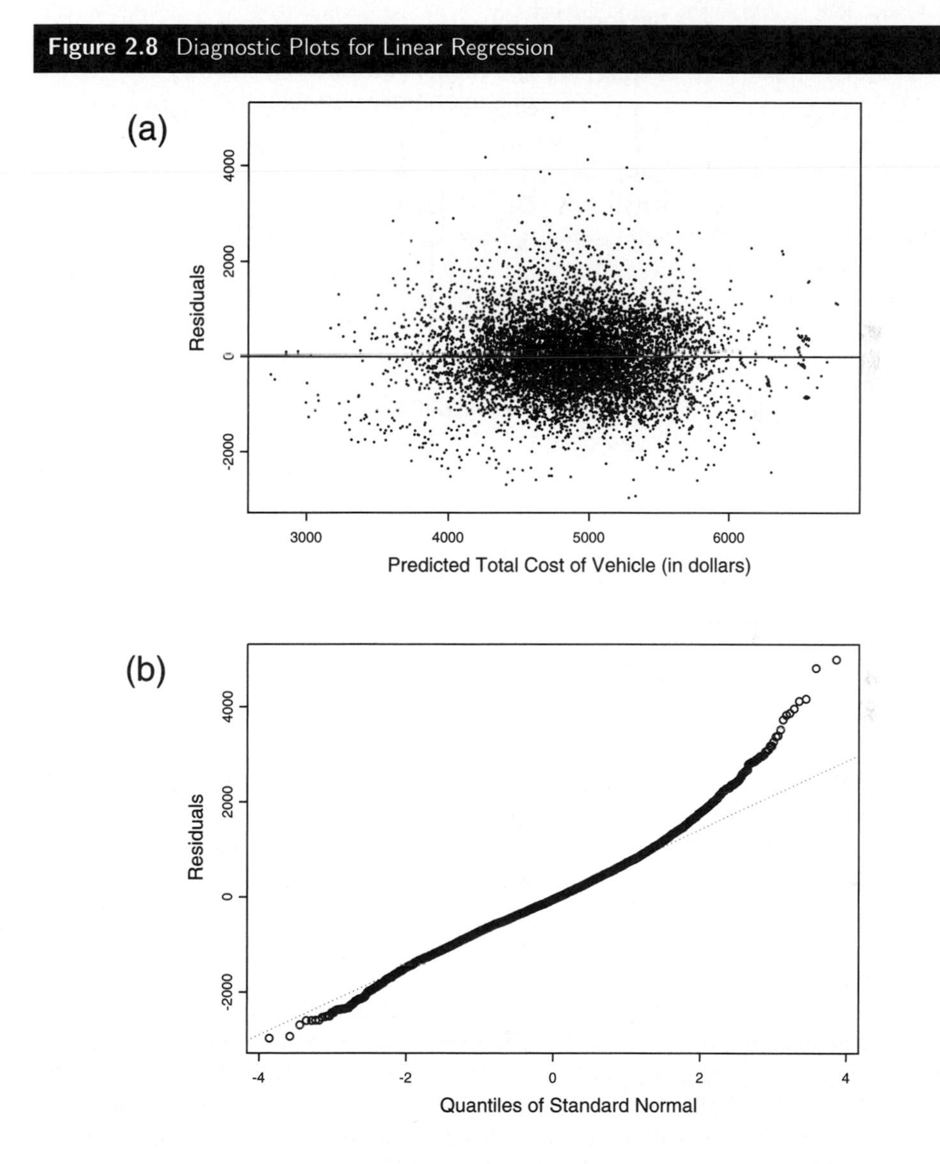

Exhibit 2.6 Simple Logistic Regression

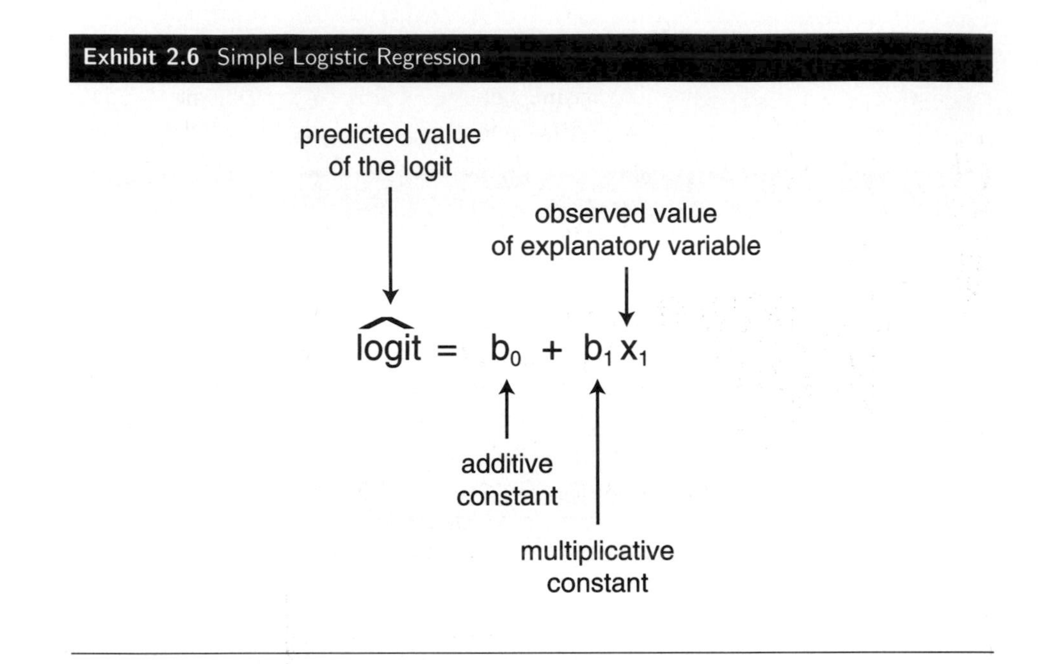

2.3 PREDICTING CHOICE: LOGISTIC REGRESSION

Regression is an appropriate method for predicting a continuous response. But what do we do when response variables are discrete or categorical? When the categorical variable takes two possible values, such as "yes" or "no" and "buy" or "don't buy," we use logistic regression.

For logistic regression, as with regression, there is a linear predictor composed of explanatory variables. The values of explanatory variables are multiplied by logistic regression coefficients that act as constants in the equation for the linear predictor. What makes logistic regression different from regression is that we are predicting a binary rather than a continuous response. This binary response, which could represent a buyer's choice or a type of consumer or firm, must be transformed prior to its use in logistic regression. For logistic regression we use the logit (pronounced "low jit") as the response transformation.

Exhibit 2.6 shows a simple logistic regression equation with one explanatory variable in the linear predictor. As with regression, it is easy to develop linear predictors with two or more explanatory variables, and explanatory variables are either numeric variables with meaningful magnitude or indicator variables (contrasts representing categorical variables or factors). To understand the logic behind logistic regression, we begin with the mathematical logic behind the logit, as described in the next section.

2.3.1 The Logic of the Logit

How shall we understand the logit? Let's see how it applies within the context of a real business problem. A DriveTime business objective is to reduce the number of days vehicles are on the lot. One way to further this objective is to stock vehicles that sell faster. Which vehicles sell faster? That is an empirical question, one that data mining methods can help to answer.

Let's continue the sedan modeling work by thinking in terms of predicting overage vehicles, those vehicles that remain on the lot more than ninety days. We define the variable `OVERAGE` as taking the value `YES` when `LOT.SALE.DAYS` is greater than ninety and the value `NO` when `LOT.SALE.DAYS` is ninety days or less.

The logit is a mathematical transformation that takes us from probabilities to numbers that take all possible values on the real number line. To understand the logic of the logit, we return to what we know about ratios and logarithms from high school algebra.

A probability is a number that varies between zero and one. For practical purposes we will assume that we are working with probabilities on the open interval between zero and one $(0, 1)$; that is, each event has some nonzero probability. A ratio of nonzero probabilities may take any positive real value. We call this ratio of probabilities the odds ratio. The odds of `OVERAGE` being `YES` is the ratio of probabilities: $\frac{p(\texttt{YES})}{p(\texttt{NO})}$, where $P(\texttt{NO}) = 1 - P(\texttt{YES})$. For example, if $p(\texttt{YES})$ were 0.25, then $p(\texttt{NO})$ would be 0.75, and the odds of `OVERAGE` being `YES` would be $0.25/0.75$ or 1 to 3. The odds ratio is always positive because it is computed as a ratio of two positive numbers—probabilities.

The logit is the log of the odds ratio. Like any log function, the logit takes a quantity that varies along the domain of all positive real numbers and maps it into the range of all real numbers. If the probability of `OVERAGE` being `YES` is greater than the probability of `OVERAGE` being `NO`, then the logit will be positive. If the probability of `OVERAGE` being `YES` is less than the probability of `OVERAGE` being `NO`, then the logit will be a negative number. And if the two probabilities are equal, then the logit will be zero (the log of 1). In symbols, we would write:

If $p(\texttt{YES}) > p(\texttt{NO})$, then $log(\frac{p(\texttt{YES})}{p(\texttt{NO})}) > 0$.

If $p(\texttt{YES}) = p(\texttt{NO})$, then $log(\frac{p(\texttt{YES})}{p(\texttt{NO})}) = 0$.

If $p(\texttt{YES}) < p(\texttt{NO})$, then $log(\frac{p(\texttt{YES})}{p(\texttt{NO})}) < 0$.

Logistic regression (named after the logit) and regression fall within a class of models called "generalized linear models." Many ideas from linear regression carry over into work with generalized linear models. Both regression and logistic regression have a response that we are trying to predict; the response is continuous for regression and binary for logistic regression. Most importantly, across the set of generalized linear models, linear predictors have a common mathematical form; they are linear equations. For linear predictors, explanatory variables may be either continuous variables with meaningful magnitude or indicator variables (contrasts representing categorical variables or factors).

2.3.2 Logistic Regression Example: DriveTime

Exhibit 2.7 shows logistic regression results for the DriveTime case. Using the sedan training set, we predict `OVERAGE` from `VEHICLE.AGE`, `MILEAGE`, `VEHICLE.TYPE`, and `MAKEX`. Multi-category (multinomial) explanatory variables are represented by multiple binary indicator variables in the table of coefficients. To determine whether multi-category explanatory variables contribute significantly to the logistic regression model, we look to classical p-values in the analysis of deviance table. In this example, three of the four explanatory variables (`VEHICLE.AGE`, `VEHICLE.TYPE`, and `MAKEX`) contribute significantly to the logistic regression model.

Figure 2.9 provides a graphical representation of logistic regression. For each vehicle, we compute the linear predictor using the fitted model from Exhibit 2.7. Higher values of the linear predictor are associated with higher estimated probabilities of being an overage vehicle. Tick marks at the top of the plot show actual overage vehicles (those not sold within ninety days); tick marks at the bottom show vehicles that are sold within ninety days.

Figure 2.10 provides another graphic representation of logistic regression, a density trellis plot. The top panel of the plot shows estimated probabilities of being overage for vehicles that are actually overage. The bottom panel shows estimated probabilities of being overage for vehicles that sell within ninety days. Looking from the bottom to the top panels, we should see a shift to the right—vehicles that are actually overage have higher estimated probabilities of being overage. This provides a graphical demonstration of the predictive power of logistic regression.

When we need to predict whether a vehicle is overage, we use a cutoff rule for the estimated probability that the vehicle is overage. A 0.50 rule, for example, would have us predicting that a vehicle is overage if the estimated probability of being overage is higher than 0.50, whereas a 0.25 rule would have us predicting that a vehicle is overage if the estimated probability of being overage is higher than 0.25. Different rules yield different predictions for many vehicles. Figure 2.11(a) shows how the 0.50 cutoff plays out with the sedan training set, and Figure 2.11(b) shows results for the 0.25 cutoff.

To evaluate fully the value of logistic regression models, we turn to their use in making business decisions. The DriveTime case provides a telling example. With the sedan training data as our guide, consider the current purchasing situation. Sedan purchases, like other vehicle purchases, are made without the aid of statistical models. Using no model or the "null model," as it is sometimes called, is like predicting that all vehicles will be sold within ninety days when, in fact, 20 percent are overage vehicles. Using the null model, management is 80 percent accurate in its predictions, but DriveTime has lower profits due to the 20 percent overage.

Suppose, instead, management uses logistic regression and a 0.50 cutoff to guide its vehicle purchasing. In this case management refuses to purchase vehicles with a 0.50 or more estimated probability of being overage. Exhibit 2.8(a) shows that this method of purchasing vehicles continues to yield a 20 percent overage. Accordingly, logistic regression with a 0.50 cutoff provides no advantage over the null model.

Exhibit 2.7 Logistic Regression for Classifying Vehicles as Overage or Normal Sales

```
Coefficients:                          Value  Std. Error  t value
(Intercept)                    -1.8888e+000 2.0276e-001  -9.3154
VEHICLE.AGE                     2.2259e-001 1.9188e-002  11.6008
MILEAGE                         7.9013e-006 2.0322e-006   3.8880

VEHICLE.TYPE=FAMILY.SMALL      -4.9673e-001 1.0426e-001  -4.7645
VEHICLE.TYPE=FAMILY.MEDIUM     -7.2312e-001 9.7449e-002  -7.4204
VEHICLE.TYPE=FAMILY.LARGE      -1.0601e+000 1.1673e-001  -9.0814
VEHICLE.TYPE=LUXURY            -1.24719     0.12973      -9.6140

MAKEX=CADILLAC                 -1.87075     0.36405      -5.1387
MAKEX=CHEVROLET                -0.61203     0.11279      -5.4263
MAKEX=CHRYSLER                 -1.38505     0.24429      -5.6697
MAKEX=DAEWOO                    2.47491     0.29136       8.4943
MAKEX=DODGE                    -1.32451     0.17112      -7.7402
MAKEX=FORD                     -1.04477     0.11981      -8.7199
MAKEX=GEO                      -0.44474     0.18046      -2.4645
MAKEX=HONDA                    -1.87151     0.28538      -6.5579
MAKEX=HYUNDAI                  -0.90878     0.27250      -3.3350
MAKEX=KIA                      -0.90510     0.24543      -3.6878
MAKEX=MAZDA                    -1.26053     0.17375      -7.2549
MAKEX=MERCURY                  -0.78019     0.16196      -4.8171
MAKEX=MITSUBISHI               -1.50367     0.27669      -5.4346
MAKEX=NISSAN                   -0.51676     0.13598      -3.8004
MAKEX=OLDSMOBILE                0.23164     0.10756       2.1537
MAKEX=PLYMOUTH                 -0.78189     0.20084      -3.8931
MAKEX=PONTIAC                  -0.77575     0.12296      -6.3088
MAKEX=TOYOTA                   -0.82748     0.15281      -5.4149
MAKEX=OTHER                    -1.34561     0.26471      -5.0834


Analysis of Deviance Table,  Response: OVERAGE

             Df  Deviance  Resid. Df  Resid. Dev  Pr(Chi)
        NULL                    8752      8857.3
VEHICLE.AGE   1    146.21       8751      8711.1  0.00000
MILEAGE       1      0.44       8750      8710.7  0.50585
VEHICLE.TYPE  4    112.53       8746      8598.1  0.00000
MAKEX        19    437.19       8727      8160.9  0.00000
```

Figure 2.9 Graphical Representation of Logistic Regression

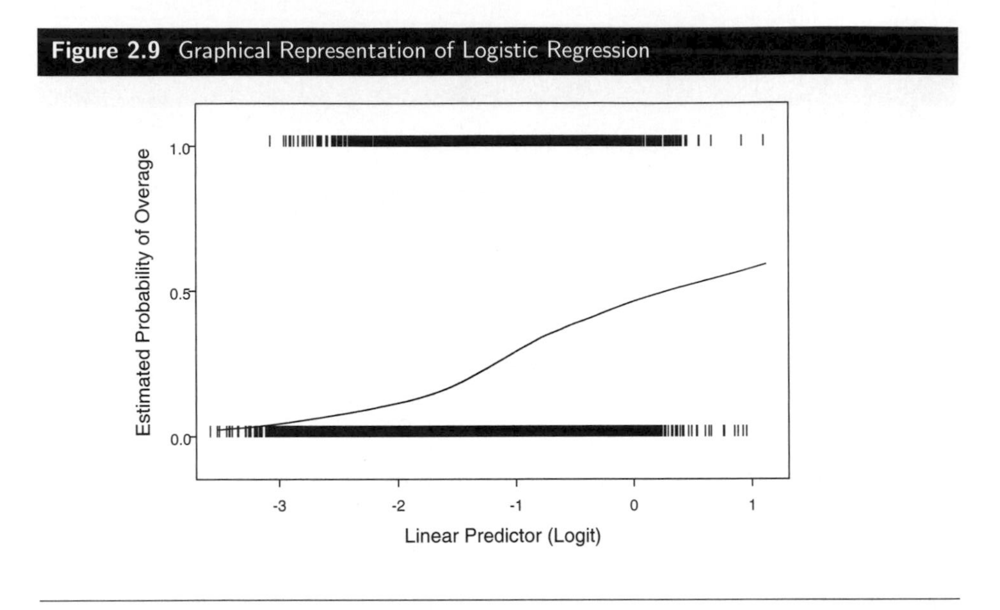

Suppose management adopts a 0.25 cutoff, refusing to purchase vehicles with a 0.25 or more estimated probability of being overage vehicles. Exhibit 2.8(b) shows that this method of purchasing vehicles yields a 14 percent overage, a 6 percent reduction.

The 0.25 cutoff looks good in the training set. Before we deploy a logistic regression model or a particular cutoff rule, however, we should obtain an honest assessment of its utility in test and validation data sets. Note that overage percentages in the DriveTime case can be converted into dollars of profit for the firm. A worked example from the case write-up in Appendix A suggests that a 5 percent reduction in overage would increase annual profits by more than $3 million.

Statistical performance and business results—both are important to the evaluation of data mining methods. Logistic regression is a traditional method for predicting a binary response, and, with the application of an appropriate cutoff rule, logistic regression works well in the DriveTime case, demonstrating the business value of models.

2.3.3 Logistic Regression Applications

Like many firms, DriveTime can benefit from higher inventory turnover. DriveTime managers know that improved profits will follow from faster vehicle sales. If DriveTime managers can stock the kinds of vehicles that sell faster and avoid stocking those likely to become overage vehicles, then profits will improve. This is a good example of how logistic regression can be applied to a real business problem. There are many such examples.

When predicting customer choice or categorizing consumers by type, we could be working with a logistic regression problem. The response variable is a discrete, identifi-

Figure 2.10 Using a Two-Panel Density Trellis to Evaluate a Logistic Regression Model

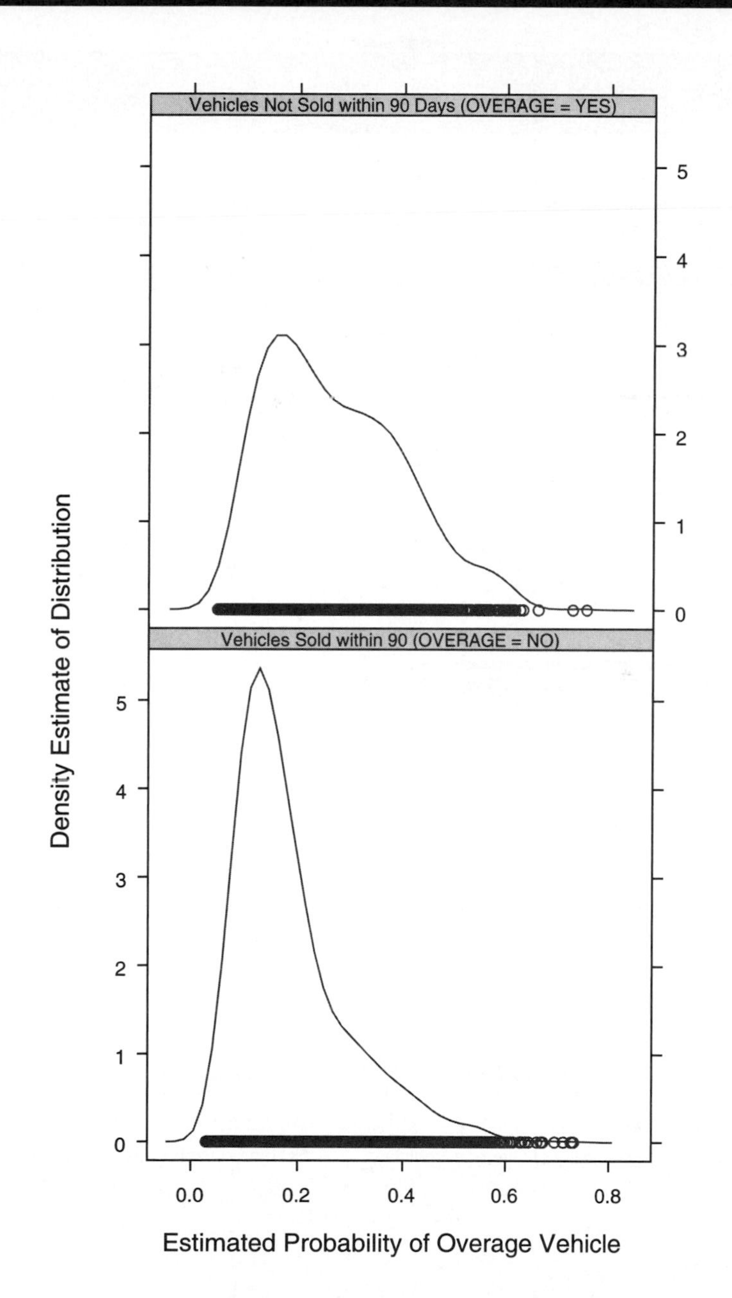

Figure 2.11 Alternative Classification Rules for Logistic Regression (Cutoff = 0.50 versus Cutoff = 0.25)

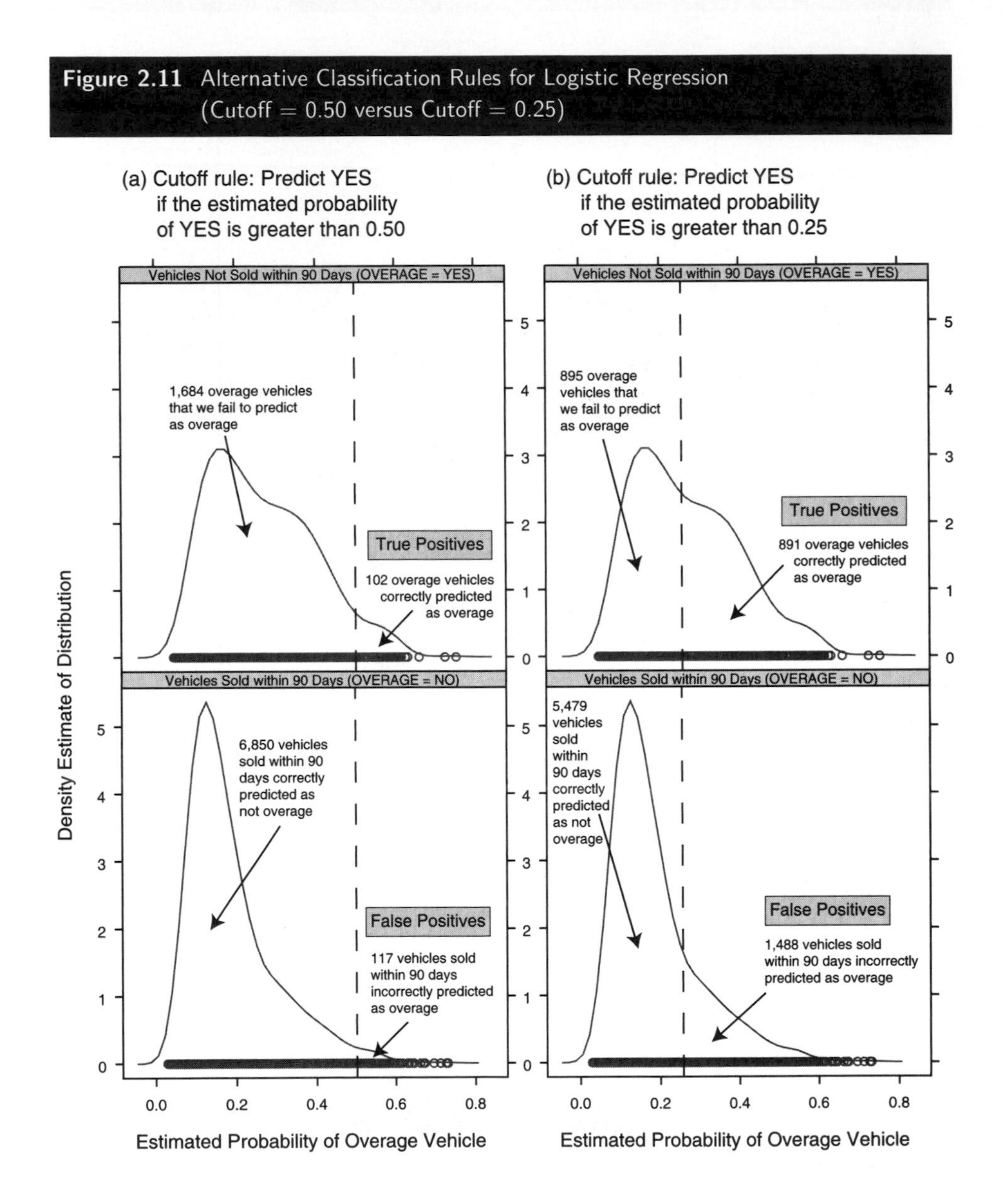

Exhibit 2.8 Demonstrating the Business Value of Models: Classification with Logistic Regression in the DriveTime Case

(a) Cutoff rule: Predict YES if the estimated probability of YES is greater than 0.50

Predicted Overage	Actual Overage (Training Set) YES	NO	
YES	102	117	219
NO	1,684	6,850	8,534
	1,786	6,967	8,753

True positive rate
= 102 / 1,786 = 0.06

False positive rate
= 117 / 6,967 = 0.02

Logistic regression predictive accuracy using a 0.50 cutoff
– (102 + 6,850) / 8,753
= 0.79

Resulting overage using 0.50 cutoff:
1,684 / 8,534 = 0.20

(b) Cutoff rule: Predict YES if the estimated probability of YES is greater than 0.25

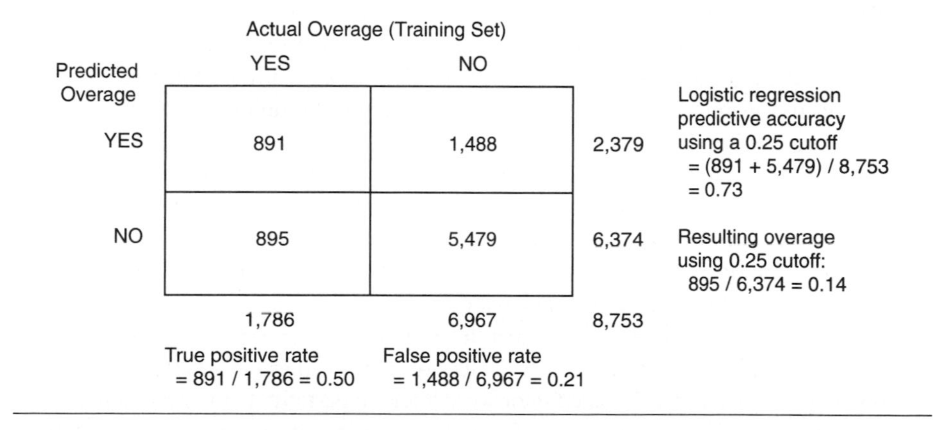

Predicted Overage	Actual Overage (Training Set) YES	NO	
YES	891	1,488	2,379
NO	895	5,479	6,374
	1,786	6,967	8,753

True positive rate
= 891 / 1,786 = 0.50

False positive rate
= 1,488 / 6,967 = 0.21

Logistic regression predictive accuracy using a 0.25 cutoff
= (891 + 5,479) / 8,753
= 0.73

Resulting overage using 0.25 cutoff:
895 / 6,374 = 0.14

able category or class—buyer or non-buyer, brand loyal or brand switcher, credit worthy versus credit risk. Relevant explanatory variables arise from the normal operations of business. We record customer characteristics as we execute business transactions, noting mailing addresses, birthdays, and credit card usage. Alternatively, we could conduct experimental research, studies that record consumer-stated choices in response to alternative product characteristics, prices, and brand name. Logistic regression has many uses.

Numerous cases from Appendix A involve applications of logistic regression. The AT&T Choice Study draws upon corporate data relating to consumer telephone habits and financials, providing an opportunity for choice modeling. Movie-Going Surveys, another case, includes numerous binary measures from the movie-going public, permitting the study of relationships with consumer demographics. Veterans Organization Direct Marketing looks at donors versus non-donors. Logistic regression has relevance to data that arise in text mining applications as well; the E-Mail Text Categorization case is an example. In the discussion below, we show how data from the Wisconsin Dells case may be used in market basket and product positioning studies, using methods such as principal components and cluster analysis. These same data provide rich opportunities for applying logistic regression to the solution of real business problems.

2.4 FINDING SIMILARITIES AND PATTERNS: PRINCIPAL COMPONENTS

Although regression and logistic regression, as reviewed above, can involve many explanatory variables, they are not "multivariate methods" as the term is used by statisticians. Linear and logistic regression are univariate when they are applied to studies with one response variable. Moving on to principal components and cluster analysis, we deal with methods that are properly described as multivariate methods.

In many business research settings we have observations on many variables, but no clearly identifiable response and explanatory variables. A common objective would be to identify underlying dimensions in the data, reducing the number of variables with which we have to work; the method of principal components is useful in this setting. To gain a better understanding of product positioning or the competitive structure of markets, we may want to draw maps of the product space or of consumers within the product space. Another objective would be to identify customer segments or groups. Multivariate methods address these business objectives. To illustrate the methods, we turn to the Wisconsin Dells case from Appendix A.

The Wisconsin Dells case draws data from more than a thousand face-to-face interviews conducted with visitors to the Dells. As part of the interviews, visitors were asked whether they had participated in or were likely to participate in any of thirty-three distinct activities. The resulting data for these activities constitute a binary response matrix, much like we would obtain in a typical market basket study.

There are 1,393 individuals with complete data on all variables. We divide the data into a training set of 1,000 individuals and a test set of 393 individuals. Focusing upon

Figure 2.12 Principal Component Eigenvalues for Wisconsin Dells Activities

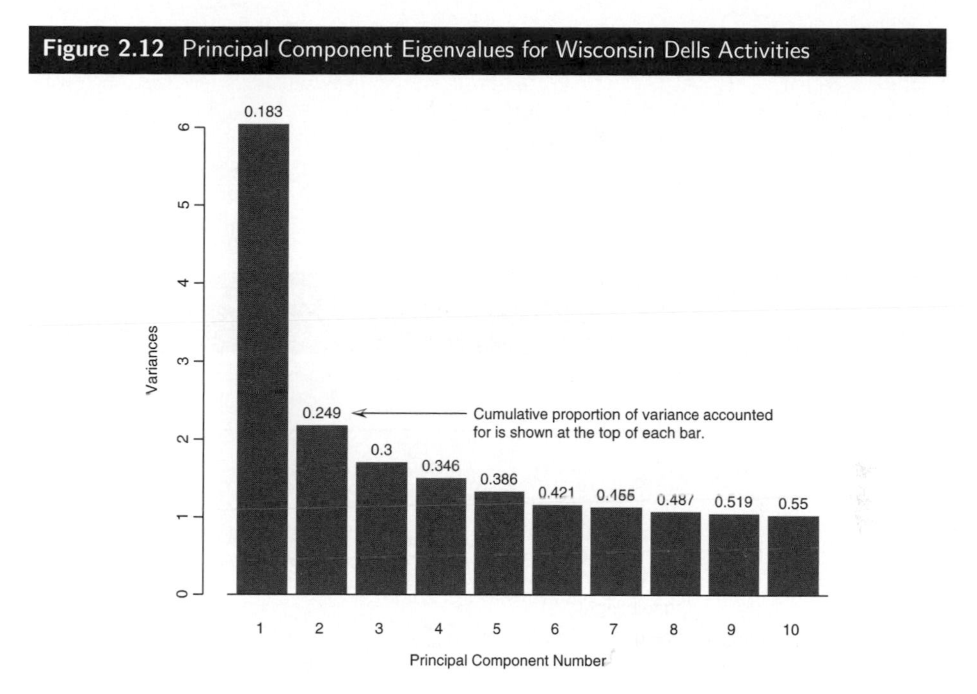

the training set for now, we have a binary data matrix consisting of one thousand rows for interviewees and thirty-three columns for activities. Entries in the matrix are one if an individual participated in or planned to participate in the activity and zero if not.

We can develop a product (activities) map for the Wisconsin Dells directly with principal components analysis. Similarities between activities may be represented as correlations between pairs of activities. The method of principal components is based upon the linear algebra of eigenvectors and eigenvalues. It yields uncorrelated underlying dimensions or components that help to summarize the pattern of correlations among many variables.

To map Dells activities in two dimensions, we can extract principal components from the binary data matrix. Principal components may be fit to the covariance matrix of the activities or the correlation matrix of the activities. The usual method, which we employ in this example, is to extract principal components from the correlation matrix. Principal components look for common variability across the set of activities, with the first principal component extracting the maximum variability. Results for the first ten principal components are shown in Figure 2.12.

We note that the first two principal components extract just under 25 percent of the variance in the data. This may seem like a small percentage, but, given our objective of obtaining a simple plot or product map of the activities, it may be sufficient. An activities map across the first two principal components or dimensions is shown in Figure 2.13.

Figure 2.13 Map of Wisconsin Dells Activities Produced by Plotting Loadings on the First Two Principal Components

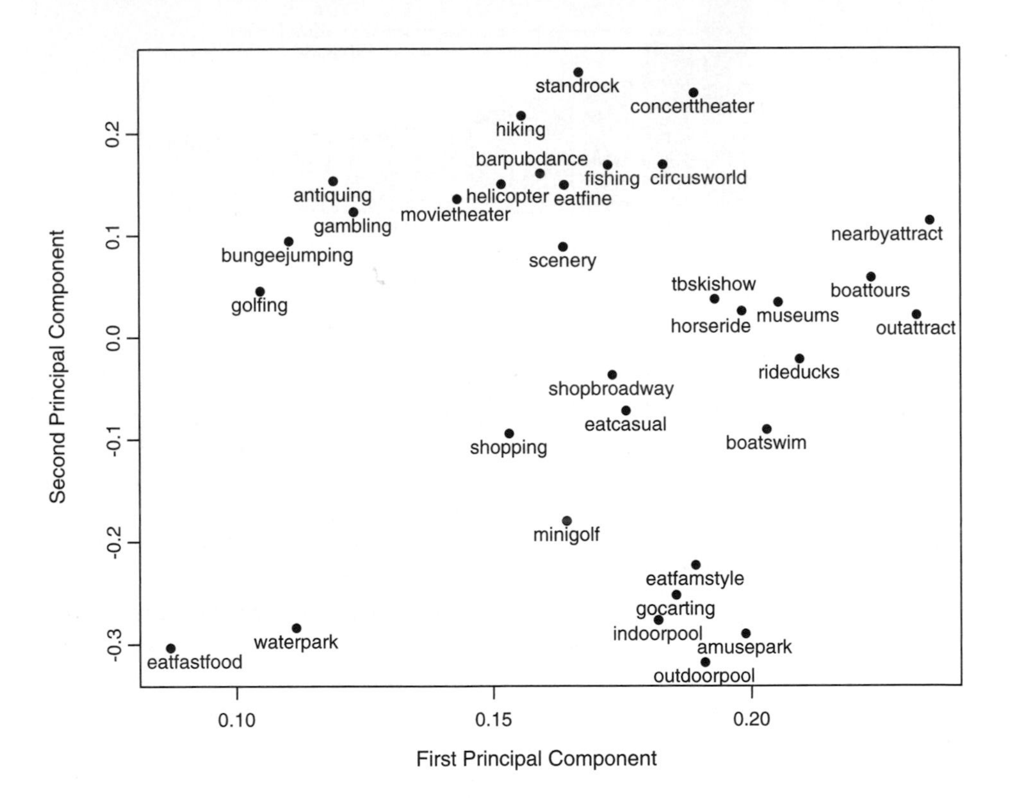

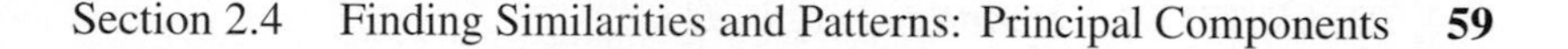

Figure 2.14 Map of Wisconsin Dells Activities Produced by Multidimensional Scaling

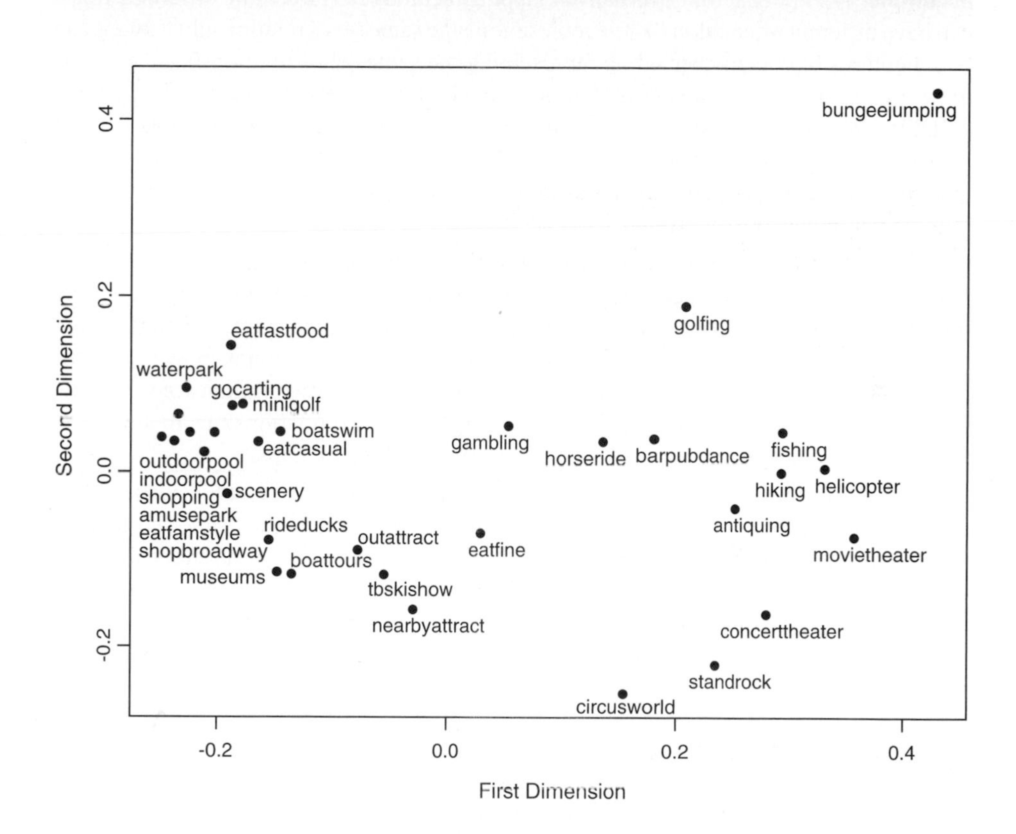

The method of principal components is often the starting point for other analyses, such as those employing factor analysis or multidimensional scaling. For actual product maps, especially those drawn from binary data, such as those in the Dells study or in market basket models in general, nonmetric multidimensional scaling would seem a more appropriate technique. A multidimensional scaling solution for the Dells training data is given in Figure 2.14. Input data for this example consisted of Jaccard dissimilarities, as discussed in the next section.

The multidimensional scaling solution in Figure 2.14 shows a group of activities in close proximity: `outdoorpool`, `indoorpool`, `shopping`, `scenery`, `amusepark`, `eatfamstyle`, among others. These are activities in which most Dells visitors participate. They have low Jaccard dissimilarities, so they appear close to one another on the map. In many research contexts, activities close together on maps are similar to one another and, hence, potential substitutes for one another.

Notice, as well, that the activities map from multidimensional scaling looks different from the map obtained from principal components analysis. This is a common occurrence—solutions from alternative mapping methods can look quite different. Maps can have different orientations while representing the same set of relationships. Maps can be reflections of one another while representing the same set of relationships. Furthermore, in this example we are using alternative methods to represent data from thirty-three variables in a two-dimensional plane. Principal components analysis attempts to form linear combinations of variables using correlations as input. Multidimensional scaling is nonmetric and uses dissimilarities as inputs. We should not be surprised or concerned that the mappings look different.

We use multivariate methods to study relationships among many variables. The language of principal components, factor analysis, multidimensional scaling, and other multivariate methods suggests that we are trying to identify underlying or latent dimensions in the data. In practical terms, we want to reduce the amount of data and the number of dimensions being considered. A plot of points in two dimensions is easier to understand than a large table of numbers. It is hard to see relationships in a 33×33 matrix of correlations, but it is not hard to see relationships in maps.

When different multivariate methods yield decidedly different results, as they often do, the analyst uses her best judgment to choose the method that makes the most sense. She should ask which method of analysis is most appropriate for the input data and which method of representing those data is most relevant to the business problem at hand. Some maps could make more sense to management than others. Or, perhaps, as we may see below, a clustering or grouping of the objects makes more sense than a map.

2.5 IDENTIFYING GROUPS OR SEGMENTS: CLUSTER ANALYSIS

Cluster analysis may be used to identify groups of objects, whether those objects be products, markets, or individual consumers. To show how it works, let's continue with our efforts to understand the Dells case. What activities go together in this market basket of activities? This is a cluster analysis question that we will approach in two ways: hierarchical clustering and non-hierarchical clustering (partitioning).

To prepare the Dells training data for input to hierarchical cluster analysis, we begin by converting the 1000×33 data matrix X to a distance matrix D that shows the distance or dissimilarity between each pair of activities. There are many ways to compute distances or dissimilarities between pairs of binary variables. We use the Jaccard dissimilarity index, which seems to work well in market basket problems. (See Exhibit 2.9.) The resulting matrix D is a symmetric 33×33 matrix, with each item in the matrix being a number between zero and one representing the degree of dissimilarity between a pair of activities.

Cluster analysis is appropriate for classification problems in which classes are not known in advance. We use interrelationships among objects to define the classes. Objects that are similar to one another in terms of their values on measured attributes in the data

Exhibit 2.9 Indices of Similarity and Dissimilarity between Pairs of Binary Variables

The Jaccard index of dissimilarity is obtained from the 2×2 table for two binary variables. The table below shows how to compute the Jaccard indices of similarity and dissimilarity from the frequencies a, b, c, and d in the 2×2 table. In many research problems the Jaccard index of dissimilarity makes more sense as an index of dissimilarity than the proportion of dissimilar observations. For pairs of low-incidence binary variables, the proportion of dissimilar observations is low because most observations are in the `NO/NO` cell of the 2×2 table. These `NO/NO` observations are more a reflection of low-incidence than similarity between the binary variables. In computing the Jaccard dissimilarity index, we drop the `NO/NO` cell frequency, thus avoiding problems with low-incidence binary variables. Similarity and dissimilarity indices play an important role in methods like multidimensional scaling, cluster analysis, and nearest neighbor analysis. Market basket analysis often begins with consumers or individual market baskets defining the rows of a binary data matrix and products or services defining the columns. Indices of similarity show how likely it is that two products will be included in a shopper's market basket. Further discussion of indices of similarity and dissimilarity may be found in Kaufman and Rousseeuw (1990).

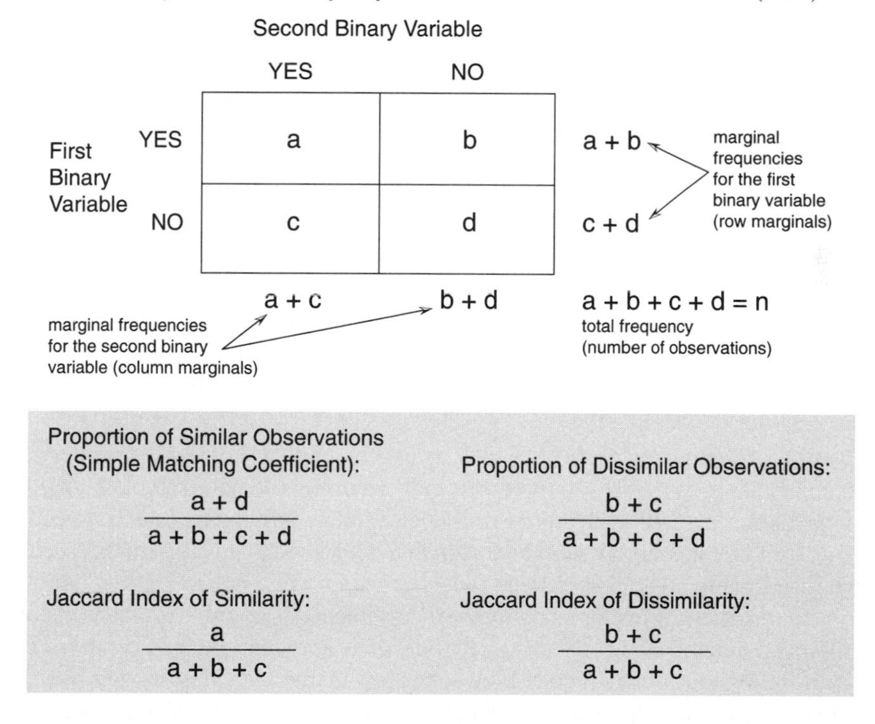

set get placed in the same cluster. Objects within a cluster should be more similar to one another than they are to objects in other clusters.

Our analysis for the Dells training data involves a clustering of products or activities. Along with the product positioning maps we drew earlier, the hierarchical cluster analysis output, shown in Figure 2.15, helps us to understand the product space of Dells activities, as well as the competitive environment among Dells businesses. This particular analysis was carried out using a hierarchical agglomerative clustering algorithm in S-PLUS, derived from the work of Kaufman and Rousseeuw (1990). Quite often, products or activities within the same cluster are potential substitutes for one another.

Cluster analysis can also be used to examine similarities and differences among customers. Market segmentation involves identifying groups or segments of customers. Customers within a segment are more like one another than they are like customers in other segments. Results from market segmentation studies are often used in targeted marketing efforts. Hierarchical or non-hierarchical methods may be used. Wedel and Kamakura (1999) provide a detailed review of these methods.

2.6 OTHER TRADITIONAL METHODS

A full discussion of traditional methods would require many additional pages, but we can at least mention major varieties of traditional methods. There are many types of regression, including specialized methods used by marketing researchers and econometricians. Traditional logistic regression may be extended to the prediction of multi-category responses, as well as multivariate responses. As we indicated earlier, regression and logisitic regression fall within the class of methods known as generalized linear models. This class of parametric models includes Poisson regression for the analysis of counts, log-linear models for higher-order contingency table analysis, and survival models.

Marketing researchers use conjoint analysis and choice studies to address product design and pricing questions. Consumer rankings and ratings of product profiles yield the raw data of conjoint analysis; these data are often analyzed with regression. Consumer choices among product profiles yield data that are analyzed with logistic regression or multinomial logit models.

Business research problems often have a time component. For most examples in this book, our focus is on traditional methods for the analysis of cross-sectional data. That is, we have think of data as having been collected at one point in time, and we concern ourselves with explaining variability across individuals. When we use cross-sectional models, we imagine that observations (whether they be observations about individual consumers, products, firms, or markets) are independent of one another. Although many data mining applications involve cross-sectional data, as evidenced by most of the cases in Appendix A, many others require time-series and hierarchical data models.

Time series observations are rarely independent; observations close in time tend to be more alike than observations distant in time. To address time series problems and their accompanying data, organized as they are across time, as well as across individuals, firms, products, or markets, requires models that reflect the structure of the data. We can

Figure 2.15 Hierarchical Clustering of Wisconsin Dells Activities

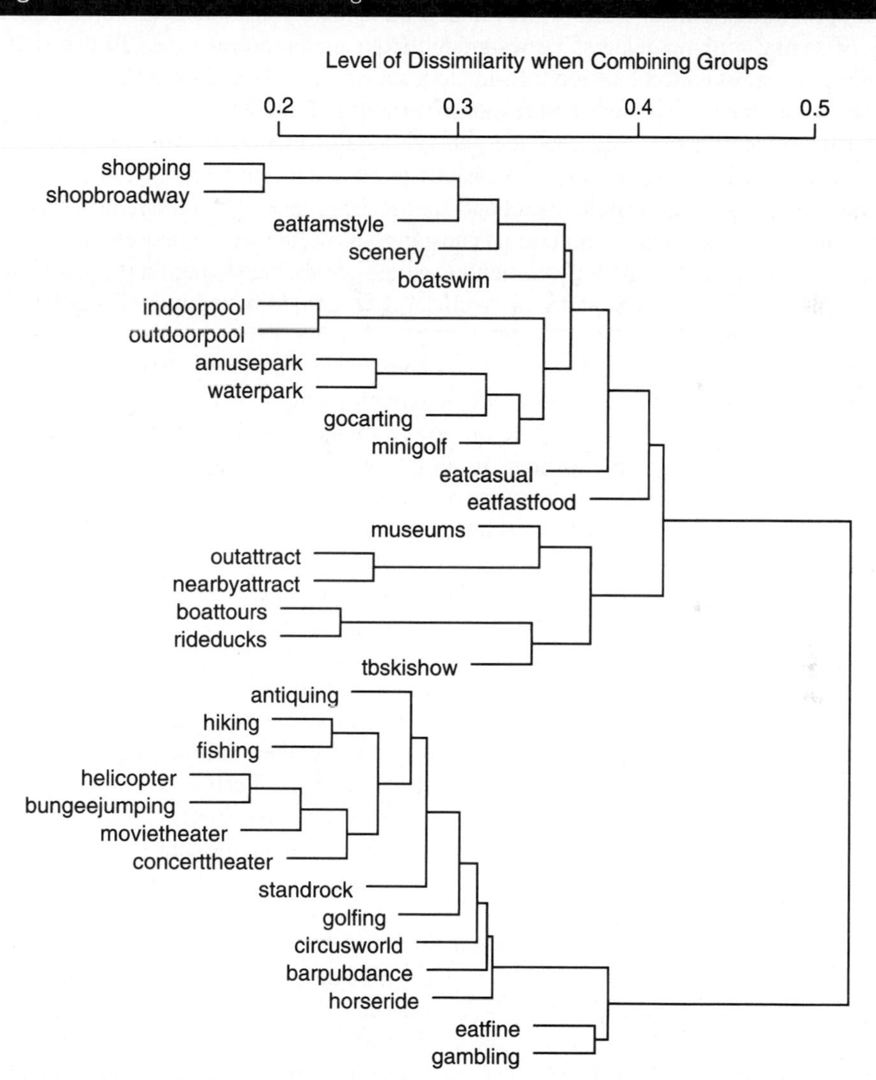

use time series regression models, including many from the domain of econometrics. We can use panel (longitudinal) data models when working with observations organized in time as well as cross sectionally. These models are especially useful in demand estimation and sales forecasting.

Many business research problems have a spatial component. Geographically proximal observations tend to be more alike than geographically distant observations. Methods of spatial statistics address issues arising from spatial correlation. To use spatial statistics we must collect location information, such as latitude and longitude, as well as information about explanatory and response variables of interest.

Hierarchical models represent the general class of models in which observations are organized across two or more dimensions. Data organized hierarchically are commonplace in business research. Panel and spatial data models are hierarchical models. Furthermore, we can think of individual consumers as falling within households, households within communities, and communities within cities, states, regions, or countries. Traditional methods for analyzing hierarchical data include mixed models of classical statistics and hierarchical Bayes models.

To estimate the likelihood of losing a customer from one time period to the next, or to estimate customer lifetime duration, we need methods that can accommodate censored data. This is because a firm is able to observe complete lifetime data (from winning a new customer to losing that customer) for only a subset of the customer base. Data for many customers, the active customers, is censored or incomplete. Survival models and recurrent events data analysis are especially designed to address problems with censored data. These models are useful in studies of customer retention.

There are many multivariate methods to consider. Correspondence analysis and higher-order (multi-mode) multidimensional scaling methods provide methods for the mapping of individuals, as well as products, in space. Discriminant analysis (linear discriminant functions) may be used as an alternative to logistic regression and multinomial logit models in classification problems. We introduced regression of a univariate response upon a set of explanatory variables—this is called multiple regression. But there is also multivariate regression, in which the response itself is a set of variables. We have seen univariate analysis of variance for evaluating the contribution of explanatory variables in multiple regression. There is also multivariate analysis of variance for evaluating the contribution of explanatory variables in predicting a set or vector of responses.

Much of our discussion up to this point has focused upon parametric methods, which make assumptions about the nature of the population distributions. There are also many traditional nonparametric methods to be considered. Most notably are those employing computer-intensive technologies for the estimation of standard errors and confidence intervals. Randomization tests, Monte Carlo methods, jackknife, and bootstrap methods are sometimes called resampling methods. These are nonparametric, computer-intensive methods that may be used by traditional researchers as well as data miners. In the context of traditional research, these methods involve using sample data over and over again in order to obtain estimates of standard errors, confidence intervals, and p-values.

2.7 FURTHER READING

Traditional methods are an important class of tools for data mining. There are many excellent sources for linear regression models, including Weisberg (1985), Neter et al. (1996), Draper and Smith (1998), Cook and Weisberg (1999), and Harrell (2002). For reviews of logistic regression, see Christensen (1997) and Le (1998). Andersen et al. (1993), Le (1997), and Therneau and Grambsch (2000) review survival data analysis; Nelson (2003) reviews recurrent events modeling. Regression, logistic regression, and survival data analysis methods fall under the general class of generalized linear models, as discussed by McCullagh and Nelder (1989). See Bishop, Fienberg, and Holland (1975), Fienberg (1980), and Christensen (1997) for a discussion of log-linear models, and see Cameron and Trivedi (1998) for Poisson regression and the analysis of counts.

The edited volume by Hinkley, Reid, and Snell (1991) provides excellent discussion of traditional methods, models, and statistical theory. Specialized articles and books review model selection methods and the application of Akaike and Bayes information criteria (Akaike 1973; Schwarz 1978; Burnham and Anderson 2002). Model selection methods for classification problems are reviewed by Hand (1997). An introduction to resampling statistics may be found in Hesterberg et al. (2003). For a more detailed review of these methods, refer to Efron and Tibshirani (1993) and Davison and Hinkley (1997).

Recommended readings in the general area of multivariate methods include Seber (1984), Manly (1994), Sharma (1996), Gnanadesikan (1997), and Johnson and Wichern (1998). In addition to principal components, a method that is discussed in most multivariate texts, related techniques include multidimensional scaling (Cox and Cox 1994; Borg and Groenen 1997) and correspondence analysis (Greenacre 1984; Weller and Romney 1990; Greenacre 1993). Biplots, the multivariate analog of scatterplots, provide graphical summaries of relationships among products, brands, or consumers (Gower and Hand 1996). Kaufman and Rousseeuw (1990), Corter (1996), and Everitt and Rabe-Hesketh (1997) discuss distance and dissimilarity measures and their analysis. Many multivariate texts review discriminant analysis; McLachlan (1992) provides a detailed review of this methodology.

Methods of clustering and classification, both traditional and data-adaptive, have received special attention from Hand (1997) and Duda, Hart, and Stork (2001). For cluster analysis, in particular, see Kaufman and Rousseeuw (1990) and Everitt, Landau, and Leese (2001). Alternative segmentation methods include model-based clustering methods, sometimes referred to as latent-class methods and finite mixture methods, as reviewed by Wedel and Kamakura (1999).

Applications of traditional methods and models in economics, business, and marketing research are discussed by Leeflang et al. (2000), Franses and Paap (2001), Hanssens, Parsons, and Schultz (2001), and Frees and Miller (2004). Lilien, Kotler, and Moorthy (1992) and Lilien and Rangaswamy (2003) focus upon marketing models. For a review of applications from the marketing research practitioner's point of view, see Chakrapani (2000). Louviere, Hensher, and Swait (2000) and the edited volume by Gustafsson, Herrmann, and Huber (2000) discuss conjoint and choice-based methods.

CHAPTER 3
DATA-ADAPTIVE METHODS

> One might have thought—as at first I certainly did—that if the rules for a program were simple then this would mean that its behavior must also be correspondingly simple. For our everyday experience in building things tends to give us the intuition that creating complexity is somehow difficult, and requires rules or plans that are themselves complex. But... in the world of programs such intuition is not even close to correct. (Wolfram 2002, p. 2)

Traditional research is big on theory. Hypotheses, both scientific and statistical, play as important a role as the data used to test them. Traditional research is well suited to the academic world. Not so with data mining. Data come first with data mining. Data mining is well suited for the applied world of business research, in which data are plentiful and well developed theories are rare.

Traditional methods can fail us when working with very large data sets. Traditional methods require prior specification of models. They make assumptions about data that are rarely true in practice. When the number of explanatory variables is large, it is difficult to specify and evaluate all candidate models. When the number of observations is large, weak or unimportant relationships among variables may be identified as statistically significant. Model specification and selection are difficult when working with large data problems. Analysts spend an inordinate amount of time specifying and respecifying models in an attempt to find the "right" model.

Suppose we use computers to fit models. Computers are especially good at repeating things. Iteration, recursion, resampling, searching across a domain of explanatory variables to find an optimal combination of variables and values for predicting a response—these are the things computers do well. We use computers to execute procedures we would never do by hand. And when analytics or mathematical deduction fail us, we turn to solution by computer brute force. Most data-adaptive methods would not exist were it not for raw computing power.

To conduct research in today's business environment, analysts turn to data-adaptive, automated or partially automated tools for data reduction and analysis. These are important tools for data mining. In this chapter we review tree-structured classification and regression, smoothing methods, neural networks, and other methods. Our challenge is to provide a conceptual, nonmathematical overview of modern data mining methods, making them accessible to business managers. We start with a few words about graphics.

3.1 EXPLORING AND VISUALIZING DATA

A good way to begin learning from data is to look at them, as we have been doing since our discussion of traditional models. Trellis plots show relationships between two variables while conditioning on one or more additional variables. Plotting smooth curves through scatterplots helps us to see patterns we might otherwise miss. Univariate density plots, bivariate scatterplots, and scatterplot matrices can be quite useful in data explorations. Models with complicated analytical forms, such as a logistic regression model with many explanatory variables, can be rendered understandable to management by using statistical graphics.

Returning to the DriveTime case, we can use graphics to explore further relationships among explanatory variables and responses. In the previous chapter, we saw the distribution of `TOTAL.COST` represented by a histogram, box plot, and empirical cumulative distribution function. Another way to represent univariate distributions is to use density plots; these work quite well when there are large numbers of observations, as in most data mining applications. Figure 3.1(a) shows a density plot for `TOTAL.COST` and Figure 3.1(b) a density plot for `LOT.SALE.DAYS`. These are simple plots that tell a story. Here we see that the univariate density for `TOTAL.COST` is symmetric, whereas the density for `LOT.SALE.DAYS` is asymmetric with a preponderance of observations associated with short sales cycles. Both distributions extend over a wide range of values.

Short vertical lines along the horizontal axes of the density plots are affectionately called "rugs." These represent individual observations. Tick marks, like plotted points on some graphs, are often jittered. When we jitter, we add a small amount of uniform random noise to each data value before plotting. Jittering is a useful visualization technique because it permits cases with identical data values to be seen as distinct observations on the graph.

Figure 3.1(c) presents a scatterplot showing the relationship between `TOTAL.COST` and `LOT.SALE.DAYS`. We use very small points to represent observations in the scatterplot because there are more than eight thousand DriveTime sedans in the training set. The smooth curve fit through the scatterplot reveals a weak positive relationship between the variables; there is wide variability around the curve.

Another way to represent relationships between variables in large data sets is to use hexbin plots, following methods described by Carr et al. (1987) and Carr (1991). Hexbinning involves bivariate binning into hexagonal cells. We organize continuous bivariate data into hexagonal bins and use shading, coloring, or amount of hexagon filling to indicate the number of observations in each bin. Figure 3.2 shows a hexbin plot for `TOTAL.COST` and `LOT.SALE.DAYS` with amount of hexagon filling representing the number of observations falling within each hexagonal region.

Figure 3.1 Data Explorations with Statistical Graphics

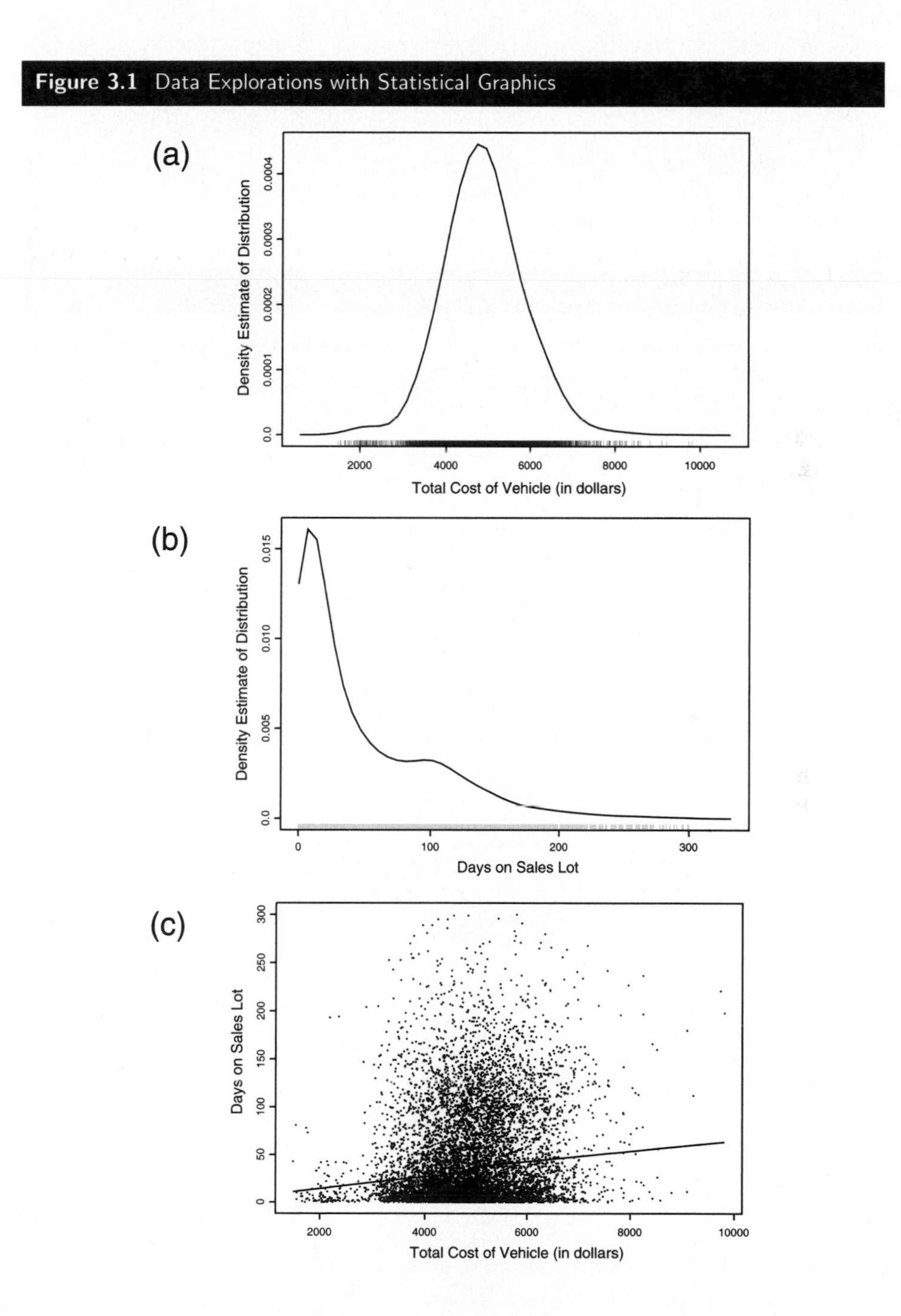

Figure 3.2 A Hexbin Plot of Lot Sale Days by Total Cost

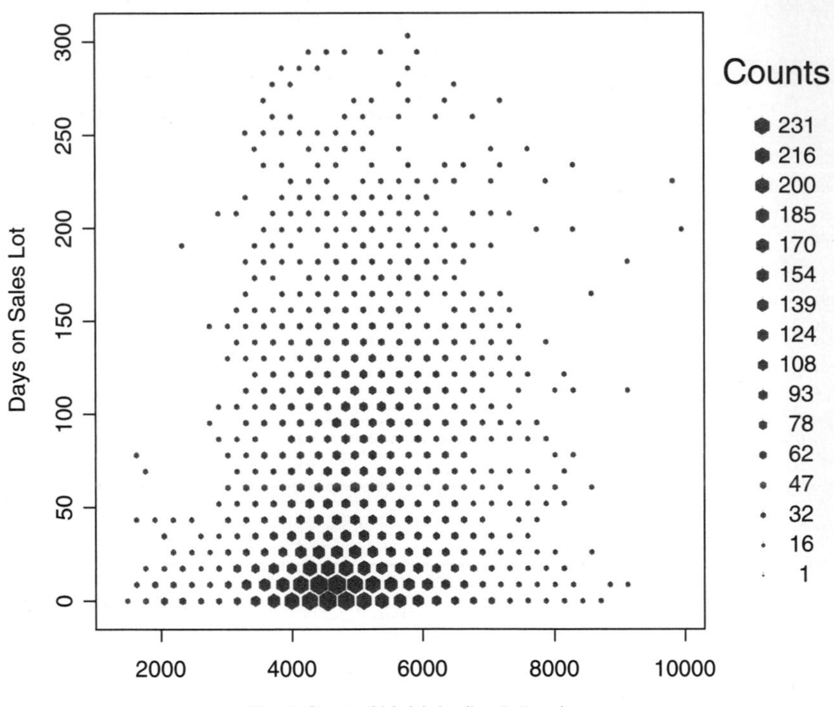

Scatterplot matrices show relationships between many pairs of variables on the same plot. Figure 3.3 shows scatterplots for `LOT.SALE.DAYS`, `TOTAL.COST`, `MILEAGE`, and `VEHICLE.AGE`. To illustrate the method with the large sedan training set, we use a random sample of five hundred vehicles from the set. Smooth curves are plotted through the points to assist in interpreting the relationships between variables.

We can use statistical graphics to examine the distribution of cost across vehicle types for domestics and imports. Figure 3.4 shows the density plots. As expected, luxury cars cost more than large family cars, large family more than medium-sized family, and so on. There is wide variability in the data, as shown by the overlap in the distributions. At the bottom of each panel within this figure, individual vehicles are shown by open circles positioned at their value on the variable `TOTAL.COST`. When there are many vehicles close together in cost, the open circles overlap to form a solid line.

Further explorations lead us to produce a scatterplot trellis. Figure 3.5 shows scatterplots of cost and mileage, conditioned on vehicle age and type; that is, there are three explanatory variables and one response variable on the same plot. Looking across the panels of the trellis from left to right, we see the effect of vehicle age: cost goes down as age goes up. Looking from the bottom row of plots to the top, we see the relationship between cost and vehicle type; cost goes up as we move from smaller economy cars to larger family and luxury cars. With each panel, however, we continue to see wide variability in the response variable cost. The smooth curves fit within panels usually slope down, showing that cost goes down as mileage goes up. But this is not universally true, after controlling for age and vehicle type as we have here. Also, there remains wide variability in cost both within and across the panels of the trellis.

Consider the "probability smooth" in Figure 3.6, which shows the estimated probability of a sedan not being sold within ninety days (overage) plotted against the vehicle's total cost. The row of tick marks at the top of the plot shows individual overage vehicles; the row of tick marks at the bottom shows individual vehicles sold within ninety days. Plots like this are created using smoothing splines or local regression. Probability smooths are easy to understand. We can see from this figure that higher cost vehicles are more likely to be overage vehicles.

Tree-structured methods reviewed in the next section present additional examples of sophisticated data-adaptive models that, when presented with pictures, are easy to understand and implement. Later in the chapter, we see how graphics like receiver operating characteristic (ROC) curves can help us to evaluate classification models. When costs and revenues are known for correct predictions and errors in prediction, we can also plot anticipated costs, revenues, and profit contributions associated with alternative models and decision rules. Such plots are often referred to as lift charts.

Graphics can be useful in evaluating models, both traditional and data-adaptive. There has been extensive development in the area of regression graphics and diagnostics, including dynamic graphics (Cook 1998; Cook and Weisberg 1999; Atkinson and Riani 2000). Dynamic graphics permit the interactive exploration of data. Systems like S-PLUS and R offer brushing, or the capability of using the mouse like a paintbrush to highlight or color groups of observations in one viewing plane, so that these same

Figure 3.3 A Scatterplot Matrix

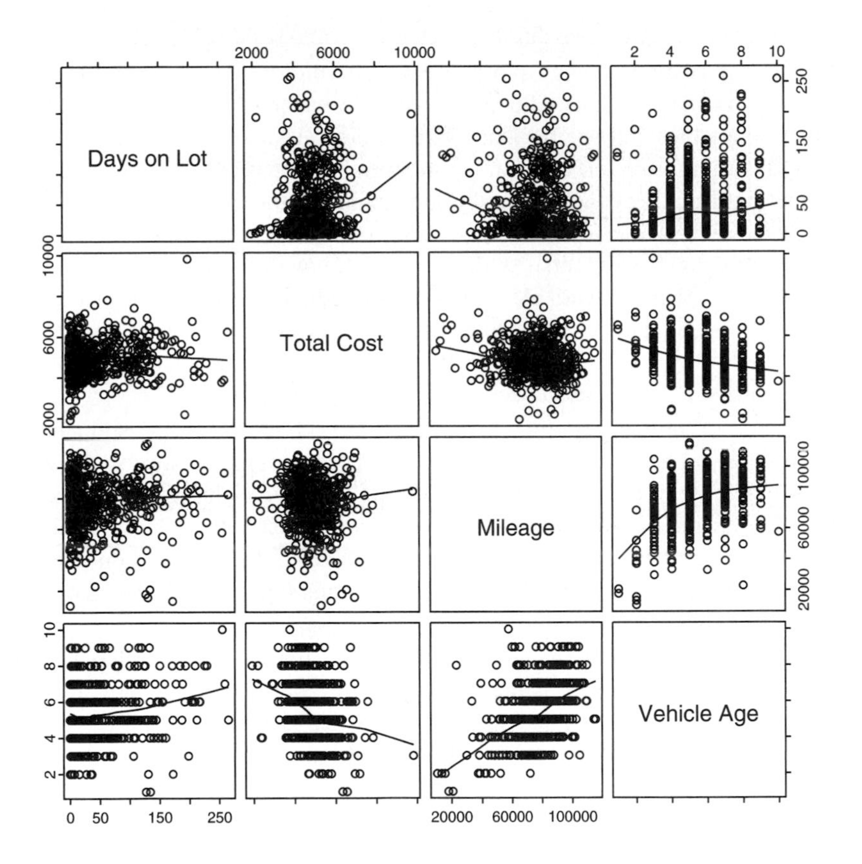

Figure 3.4 Density Estimates of the Distribution of Total Cost by Type of Vehicle

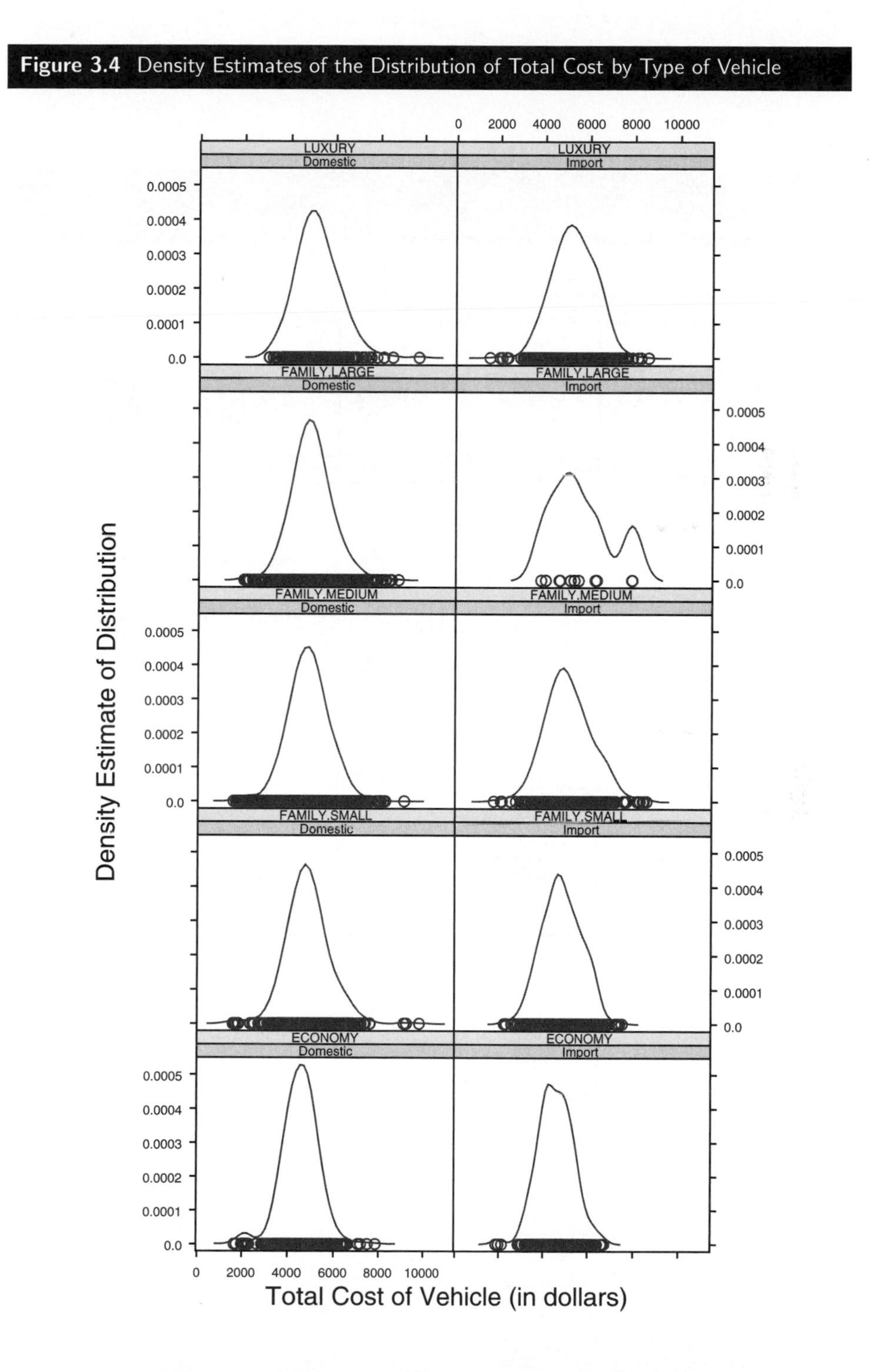

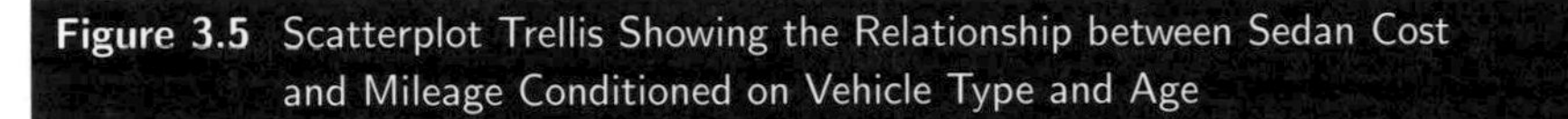

Figure 3.5 Scatterplot Trellis Showing the Relationship between Sedan Cost and Mileage Conditioned on Vehicle Type and Age

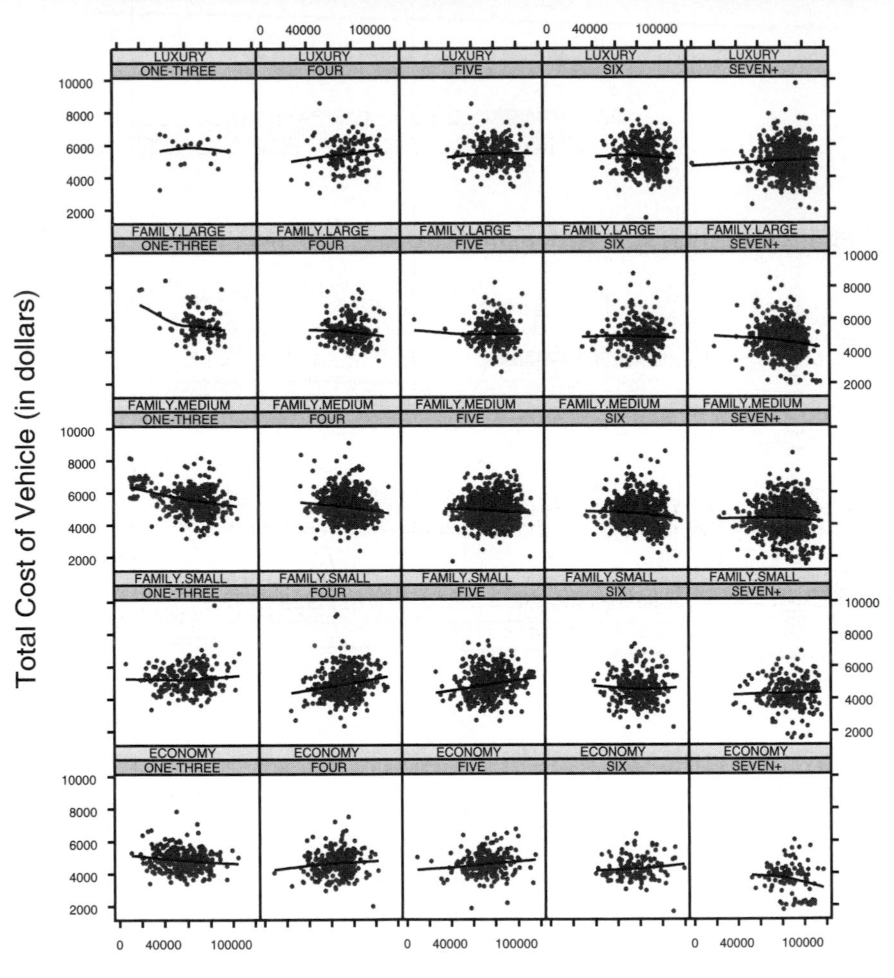

Figure 3.6 A "Probability Smooth" Showing the Relationship between Total Cost and the Estimated Probability of Vehicle Overage

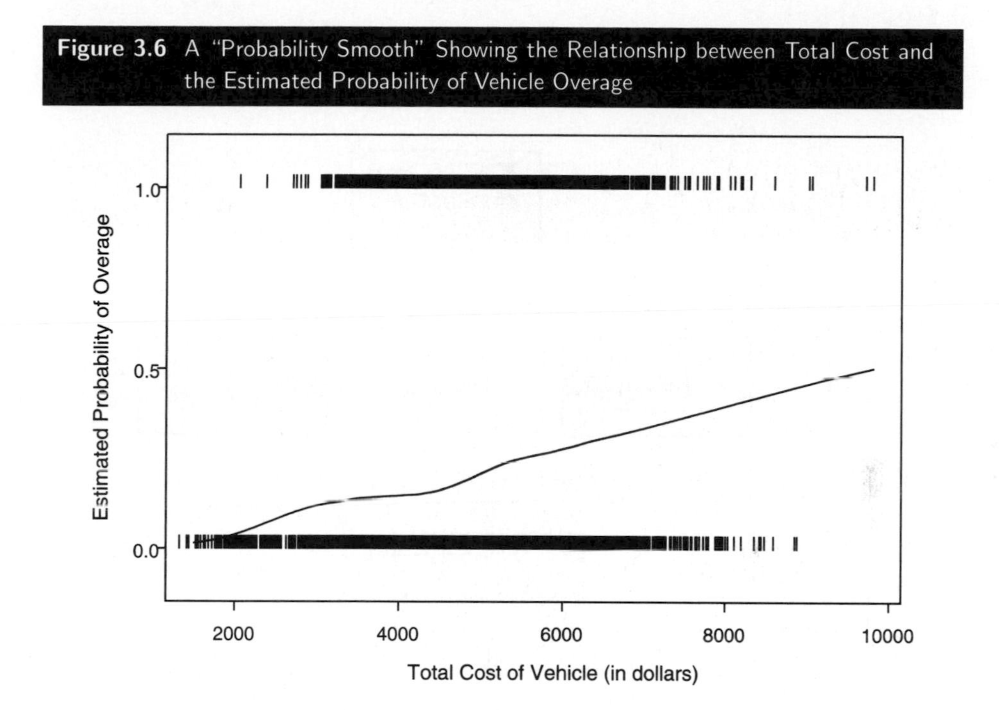

observations may be identified in another viewing plane. Spinning, another common device of dynamic graphics, allows the user to rotate observations around an axis in three-dimensional space, so she can see relationships among three variables at a time. Multivariate dynamic graphics help us to explore high-dimensional data sets, as with the public-domain XGobi system described by Cook et al. (1995) and Swayne, Cook, and Buja (1998).

3.2 TREE-STRUCTURED METHODS

Tree-structured methods involve supervised learning, model fitting guided by knowledge of an observed response. When the response is continuous, we build regression trees. When the response is categorical, we build classification trees.

"Recursive partitioning" is another name for tree-structured methods. The methods involve partitioning or splitting of parent nodes into child nodes, and they are recursive. Parent nodes are split into child nodes. Child nodes become parent nodes and are themselves split into child nodes.

To learn about tree-structured methods, let's draw a simple tree and describe its structure. As we show in Figure 3.7, trees used in data analysis are drawn from the top down, with the top node, the initial parent node in the tree, being the root node. A binary tree splits each parent node into two child nodes. To continue with the language

Figure 3.7 Binary Tree Structure

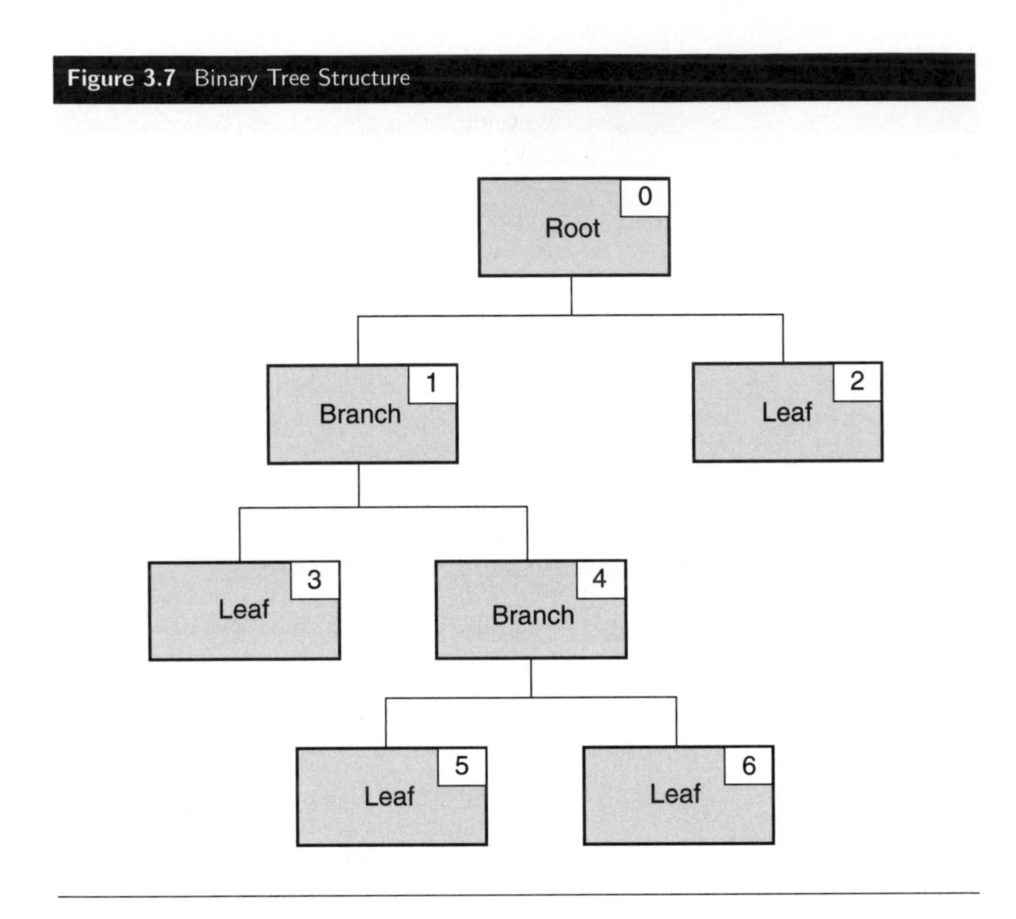

of trees, intermediate nodes are called branches, and terminal nodes are called leaves. In the figure, the root node 0 is split into child nodes 1 and 2. One of those child nodes has children of its own: nodes 3 and 4. And node 4 becomes the parent of nodes 5 and 6. With each split the training set is divided into subsets. In the root node we have the entire training set. As we move down the tree, we work with smaller and smaller subsets of the training set. At each split point, we divide the parent node into two child nodes using one and only one explanatory variable.

3.2.1 Growing and Pruning Binary Trees

A popular approach to tree-structured modeling developed by Breiman et al. (1984) consists of two separate phases: growing and pruning. Tree growing involves splitting parents into child nodes such that each pair of child nodes is as pure as possible in the response; that is, as homogeneous in the response as possible. Tree growing is limited by sample size, node homogeneity, or stopping rules. After the tree has been grown, algorithms are used to prune the tree back. Tree pruning is usually guided by cross-validation within the training data set.

Relying upon splitting rules alone, we could split until we arrive at a node homogeneous in either the response or explanatory variables. When a node is homogeneous in the response (that is, all cases have the same value of the response), then splitting into child nodes offers no possibility for improvement in node purity—all subsequent splits on explanatory variables would be judged of equal value. When a node is homogeneous in all explanatory variables, no further splitting is possible.

With some data sets, it is possible to continue growing a tree until it matches the training data perfectly, providing errorless prediction of the response in the training set. This would be an obvious example of model overfitting. Large trees built to fit the training data precisely often predict poorly in validation or test sets. To avoid overfitting we can employ stopping rules and/or cross-validation strategies.

Stopping rules apply to the tree growing process. For example, we could tell the program not to split a parent node with fewer than ten observations, or we could tell the program not to split a parent node if one of the child nodes were to contain fewer than five observations. This would inhibit tree growing, so that an overly large tree would not be built.

Homogeneity and stopping rules alone provide little protection against building a tree that is too large (a model that is too complex). Often we must prune a tree back in order to have a tree-structured model that we can trust. To arrive at the proper balance between goodness of fit and parsimony, we use internal cross-validation to guide the pruning process. Recognize that we are working only with the training set when we do internal cross-validation. Our goal is to use the training set in a way that helps us to develop and select models that will perform well when tested on test and validation sets.

Figure 3.8 shows how we might do internal cross-validation on the training set. To avoid confusion with "training," "test," and "validation" sets, which we have used when talking about partitioning the full data set, we employ distinct terminology here, referring to "learning" and "assessment" sets. The figure shows a fivefold cross-validation setup. We randomly divide the training set into five folds of approximately equal size. At each iteration, we grow a tree on the four learning folds and assess its goodness of fit on the assessment fold. We grow the trees using the same tree-growing algorithm as we plan to use with the training set. After the fifth iteration, we compile results from the assessment folds to see how well the tree-growing algorithm has performed.

Figure 3.9 shows what we might expect to observe from internal cross-validation-guided pruning. Here we plot the lack of fit against tree size. Lack of fit in cross-validation assessment sets varies with tree size. Larger trees fit better up to a certain point, but after that point, there is evidence of overfitting. We use the cross-validation plot to gauge the size of tree needed for the entire training set. We take the tree that we have fit to the entire training set and prune it to a size consistent with what we have learned works from the assessment sets. We try to select a tree of a size that will perform better than smaller trees and better than larger trees.

Figure 3.8 Internal Cross-Validation

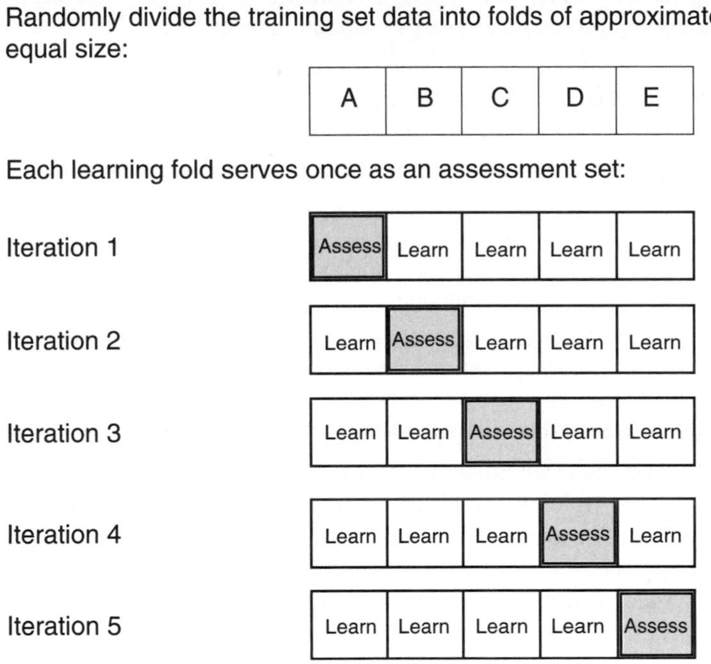

Randomly divide the training set data into folds of approximately equal size:

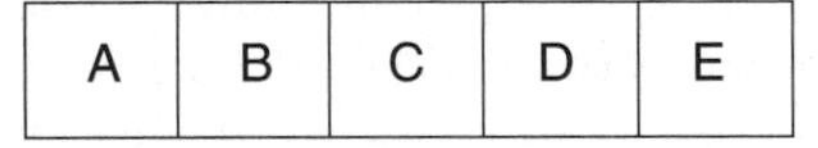

Each learning fold serves once as an assessment set:

Iteration 1	Assess	Learn	Learn	Learn	Learn
Iteration 2	Learn	Assess	Learn	Learn	Learn
Iteration 3	Learn	Learn	Assess	Learn	Learn
Iteration 4	Learn	Learn	Learn	Assess	Learn
Iteration 5	Learn	Learn	Learn	Learn	Assess

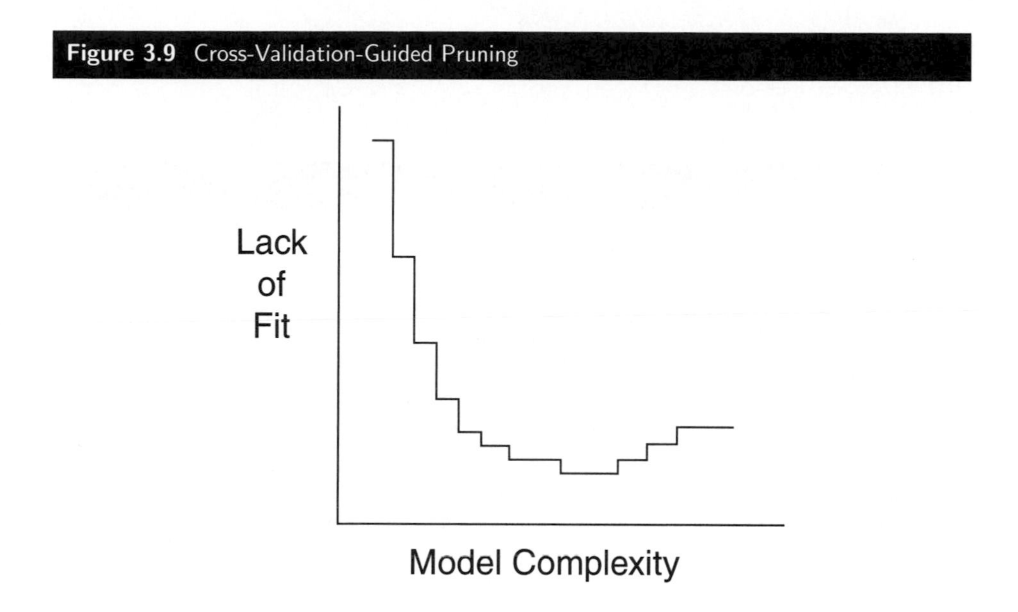

Figure 3.9 Cross-Validation-Guided Pruning

3.2.2 Classification Tree Example

Suppose we want to see what kind of people go to Circus World Museum in the Wisconsin Dells. Working with the Dells training set, we have the binary response variable `circusworld`, which has the code `YES` for those who go to the museum and `NO` for those who don't. This is a classification problem with a binary response and with nine possible explanatory variables, as described in the case description in Appendix A. Building a classification tree from these data yields the result shown in Figure 3.10.

What does the classification tree tell us about visitors to Circus World Museum? The root node shows that 297 of the 1,000 Dells visitors in the training set went to the museum. To find those most likely to visit the museum, we would use explanatory variables such as the number of nights the visitors are staying in the Dells, where they are coming from, the number of adults in the party, age, and income. Those most likely to visit the museum are those staying more than four nights, visiting from Chicago, having one, two, or five or more adults in their party, not being middle-aged, and coming from lower income levels. Numbers at the bottom of the plotted nodes of the tree show the number of `YES` and `NO` responses to the `circusworld` item on the questionnaire. The `YES` and `NO` labels in each plotted tree node show the prediction we would make for that node if we were to use a 0.50 cutoff in making that prediction. Oval-shaped nodes in the figure are root or branching nodes; rectangular nodes are leaves or terminal nodes. The actual predictions we make in using a tree-structured model like this are those in the terminal nodes.

Figure 3.10 Classification Tree for Finding Visitors to Circus World Museum

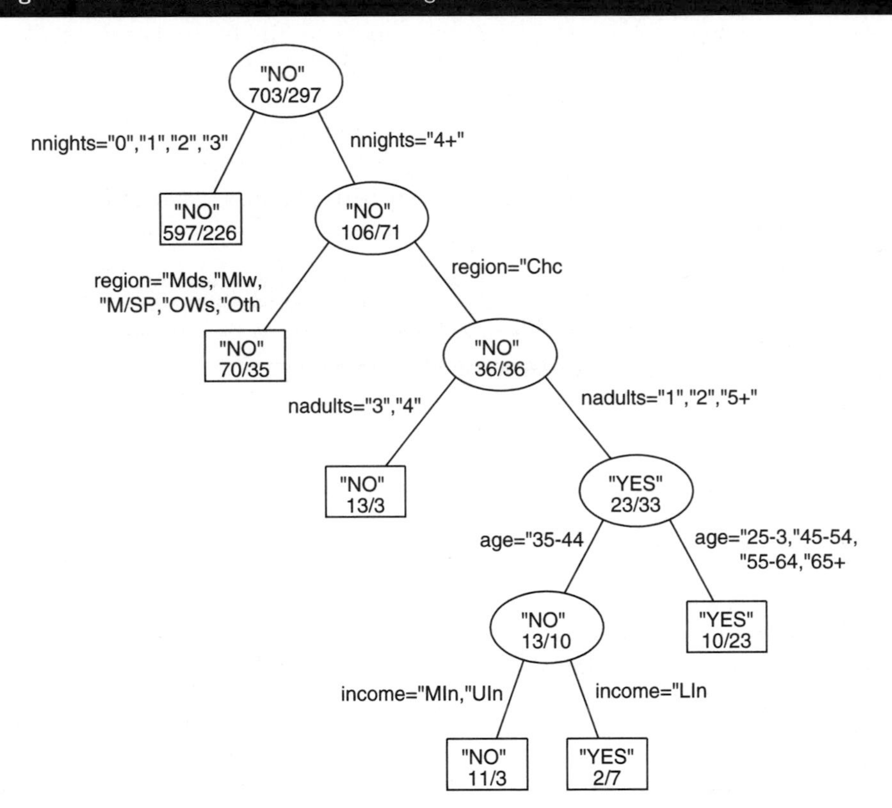

Terminal Node Information:

3.2.3 Regression Tree Example

To provide a regression tree example we return to the problem of predicting the total cost of vehicles in the DriveTime case. For our example, we use the sedan training set. The response variable TOTAL.COST is continuous, while possible explanatory variables are both continuous and categorical. Instead of specifying a model with just four explanatory variables, as we did for multiple regression in the previous chapter, we let the tree growing and pruning algorithm find explanatory variables from a larger set of possible explanatory variables, including MILEAGE, VEHICLE.TYPE, DOMESTIC.IMPORT, VEHICLE.AGE, COLOR.SET, MAKEX, and STATE.

The tree-structured algorithm sorts through the training data and examines all possible explanatory variables and their relationships to the continuous response variable. At each node of the tree, the algorithm finds the very best splitting variable and value from the set of possible explanatory variables. The algorithm grows the regression tree and prunes the tree using tenfold internal cross-validation. The computer does the hard work of building the tree. The result, shown in Figure 3.11, is amazingly simple. Only two explanatory variables are used in the final regression tree: VEHICLE.AGE and MAKEX. The labels in each plotted node show the number of sedans in the node and the average total cost of those sedans. To use the regression tree in predicting total cost, we look to average total cost values in the terminal nodes of the tree.

3.2.4 Applications of Trees

Tree-structured methods are being used increasingly as variable selection tools. In many research settings the number of potential explanatory variables is large. The business researcher, faced with the task of identifying relevant explanatory variables, may find that traditional methods are difficult to use. This is especially true when the functional form relating explanatory variables and the response is unknown, when the functional form is nonlinear or neither strictly increasing or decreasing, or when there are interactions among explanatory variables. Tree-structured models may be used without the prior specification of a functional form relating response to explanatory variables. And, by their very nature, they model interactions among explanatory variables. That is, whenever a tree includes more than one explanatory variable as a splitting variable, the tree is a model of interaction.

Trees have become popular in business applications, especially those involving classification. Managers often find pictures of trees easier to understand than lists of regression or logistic regression coefficients. Classification trees with few branches can be easy to implement in the field. This is not to say that trees are the method of choice for classification problems. In small samples, strong explanatory variables tend to mask effects of weaker explanatory variables (Miller 1998), and trees have limitations as selectors of explanatory variables (Ribic and Miller 1998).

Trees, by their hierarchical structure, are predisposed to find interactions. In other words, any tree involving splits on two or more explanatory variables is an interaction model for the response. Models with interactions can be difficult to understand and explain. Most fitted trees are asymmetric; moving from the root node to the leaves,

Figure 3.11 Regression Tree for Predicting the Total Cost of Sedans

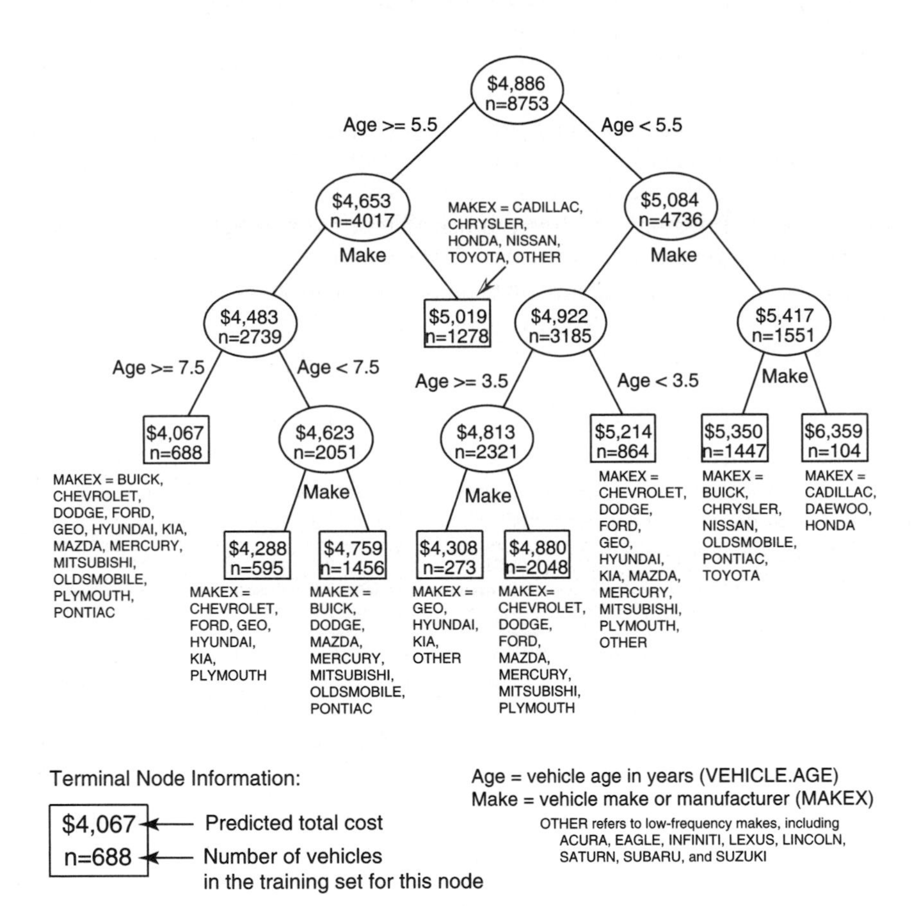

splitting variables and split points differ on the left- and right-hand sides of the tree. Binary trees involve binary splits of continuous and multinomial variables, as well as binary variables. Managers sometimes object to these features of trees.

3.3 SMOOTHING METHODS

We have encountered smoothing methods before when plotting smooth curves through scatterplots. We often use smoothing methods to explore data. They can also be used in modeling work.

Smoothing methods like generalized additive models build upon the structure of linear regression. We write an equation that looks like a linear equation, but instead of using linear functions with constant multipliers of the explanatory variables, we ask the computer to compute smooth functions of explanatory variables. Exhibit 3.1 represents this idea. The function s is a smooth function. We select the type of function we want to use and let the computer fit a model to the data. The smoothing function is usually a smoothing spline or a local regression algorithm.

There are many types of smoothing methods. A generalized additive model, for example, can be used to represent interaction as well as direct (main) effects of explanatory variables by including interaction terms in the model. An alternative to this would be to fit a two-dimensional local regression surface or to use a technique known as multivariate adaptive regression splines.

Smoothing methods are most useful for situations in which we don't care about the precise functional form relating response and explanatory variables. Our interest is in data exploration or discovering relationships, or our interest is in prediction rather than explanation. In other cases, when our goal is to develop prediction formulas relating response and explanatory variables, smoothing methods may be a first step toward finding such formulas. Fitted smooths to scatterplots, for example, often suggest variable transformations that we can use in linear regression models.

3.3.1 Generalized Additive Model Examples

To demonstrate the application of generalized additive models, we continue with our examination of sedan total cost from the DriveTime case. Taking two explanatory variables from the case, `VEHICLE.AGE` and `MILEAGE`, and using smoothing splines, we obtain the model shown in Exhibit 3.2. Jittered tick marks at the bottom of these figures (the "rugs") refer to distinct observations in the sedan training set. Prediction involves summing across the smooths. That is, for each vehicle, we note its age and mileage, compute the smooth of age and the smooth of mileage using the fitted spline functions, and sum the smooths to obtain the predicted total cost.

The fitted smooths in this example point to common problems with generalized additive models. Interpretation can be problematical. Why does the smooth for `MILEAGE` go down, then up, then down? One might think that the relationship between `MILEAGE` and `TOTAL.COST` would be strictly decreasing. Perhaps there is an interaction effect that is not being captured by the additive model. Or there may be omitted explanatory

Exhibit 3.1 From Multiple Regression to Generalized Additive Models

(a) Multiple regression models use linear functions

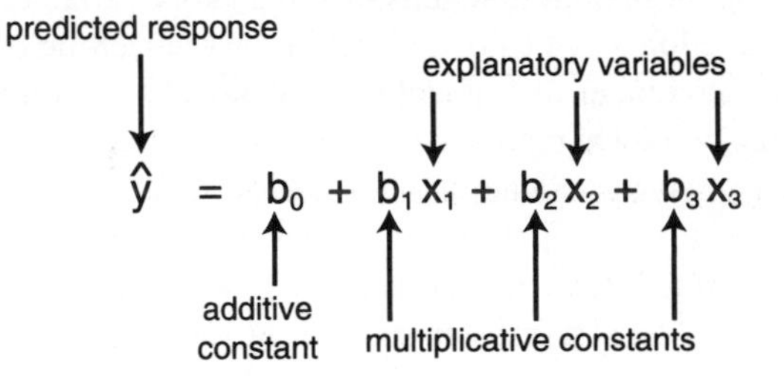

(b) Generalized additive models use smooth functions

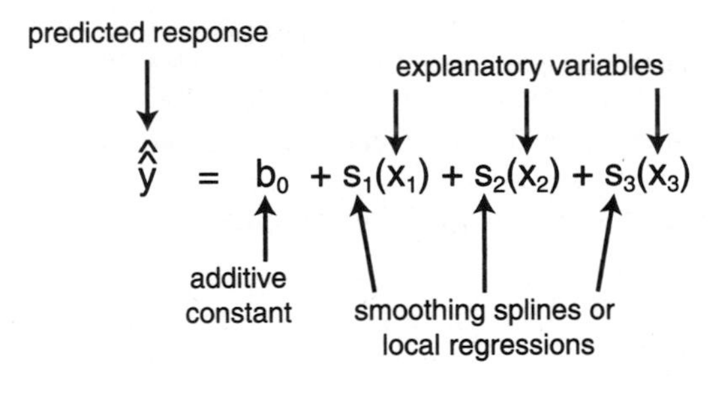

Exhibit 3.2 Generalized Additive Model for Predicting Total Vehicle Cost

$$\text{TOTAL.COST} = b_0 + s_1(\text{MILEAGE}) + s_2(\text{VEHICLE.AGE})$$

(a) Smoothing spline for MILEAGE:

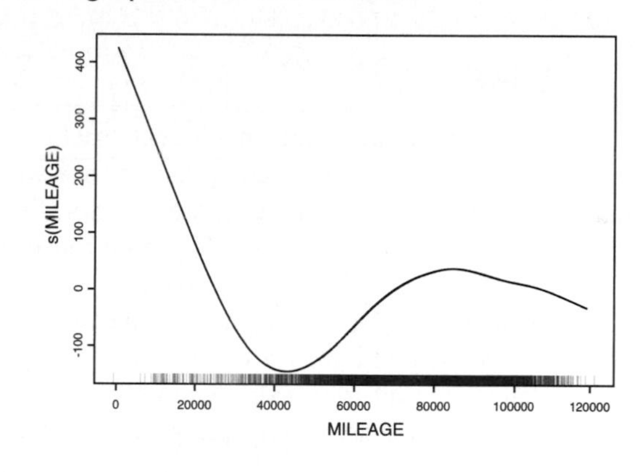

(b) Smoothing spline for VEHICLE.AGE:

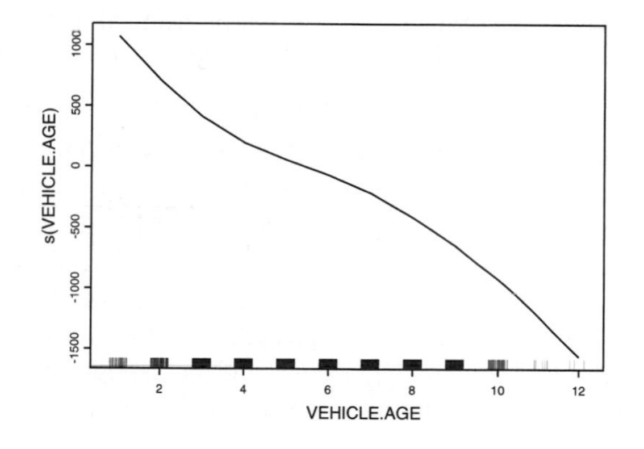

variables—variables we should have included in our model, but did not. It is not always easy to understand or explain the shapes of smooths in generalized additive models; these models are often better predictors than explanatory devices.

Exhibit 3.3 shows a generalized additive model for predicting days on the sales lot (`LOT.SALE.DAYS`). Here we fit smooth splines to three predictors: `TOTAL.COST`, `VEHICLE.AGE`, and `MILEAGE`. Predicted days on the sales lot would be obtained by summing across the three smooths. The plotted smooths seem to be telling a curious story: considering the three explanatory variables in combination, older, high-cost, low-mileage vehicles take the longest to sell. Later in this chapter, we will see that, compared with traditional regression and with other data-adaptive models, this generalized additive model performs very well in predicting days on the sales lot.

3.4 NEURAL NETWORKS

> All our attempts to generate artificially intelligent machines have failed to realize the dreams of the pioneers in computer science who envisioned machines that could "think" faster than us, without error, that never grew old, never got sick, and never got tired.... The main cause of our failure stems from a decision made fifty years ago, when computer science was in its infancy. Rather than carefully define what we meant by an intelligent machine so that we could build such a device from first principles, we set aside such a definition and tried to program a computer to "act like us" in some limited ways. This approach often meant getting computers to perform discrete human activity, such as playing chess, by feeding enormous amounts of knowledge into the computer and having the machine regurgitate that knowledge.... Unfortunately, programming computers to behave like human beings became the central concept of artificial intelligence, setting back our efforts to design truly creative machines for decades. (Fogel 2002, pp. 4–5)

Time and again, artificial intelligence researchers discover that, to imbue computers with intelligence, they must focus upon learning rather than knowledge transfer. To mimic a familiar saying, "Give a computer program a rule, and it will solve a problem; teach a program to learn rules, and it will think for itself." So it is that the discipline of artificial intelligence has changed course. The knowledge engineers and logic programmers of the 1970s and 1980s have been replaced by computer scientists working on machine learning, evolutionary algorithms, and technologies for artificial agents and artificial life. The quest for a thinking machine may be the same, but the methods have changed.

David Fogel's (2002) Blondie24 is a computer program that teaches itself to play checkers. It may not be an IBM supercomputer steeped in content domain knowledge, a Deep Blue of chess grand master caliber, but it is an impressive achievement nonetheless. Blondie24, built upon the parallelism of neural networks and the adaptability of evolutionary algorithms, demonstrates the value of machine learning methods. Surely,

Exhibit 3.3 Generalized Additive Model for Predicting Days on the Sales Lot

$$\text{LOT.SALE.DAYS} = b_0 + s_1(\text{TOTAL.COST}) + s_2(\text{MILEAGE}) + s_3(\text{VEHICLE.AGE})$$

(a) Smoothing spline for TOTAL.COST:

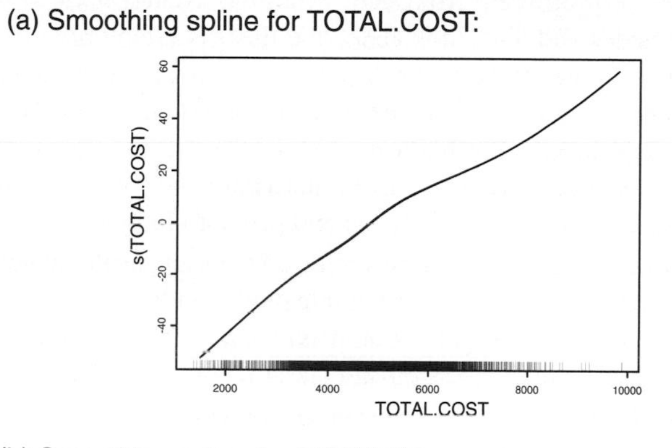

(b) Smoothing spline for MILEAGE:

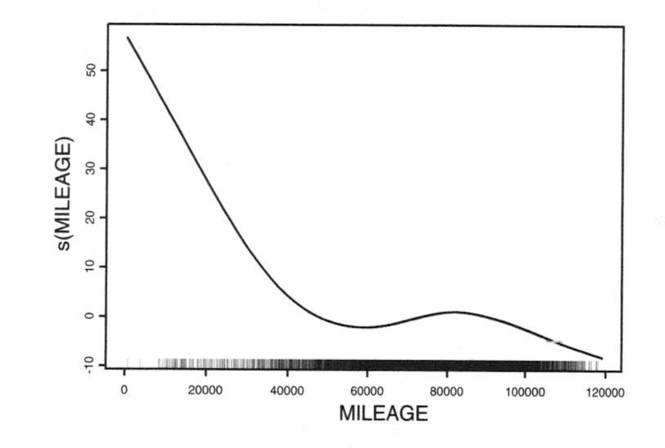

(c) Smoothing spline for VEHICLE.AGE:

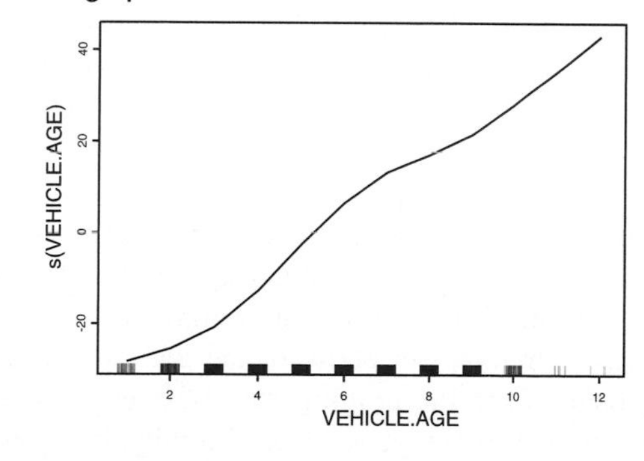

if computer programs can learn the rules of games like tic-tac-toe or checkers, they can be taught to recognize patterns across exploratory and response variables in business research.

Neural networks, like the human brain, exhibit massive parallelism. That is, there are many paths linking input and output nodes. Beyond their massive parallelism, however, neural networks are very different from human brains. Neural networks have simple parallel structures; nodes and links look alike, and there is often only one intermediate layer of nodes between inputs and outputs. The human brain has a complicated structure with many interconnecting layers and neurons of all shapes and sizes. Neural networks have virtual nodes and links. The brain has physical neurons, axons, and dendrites. Neural networks are as reliable as the computer hardware and software from which they are built. The brain, as we know, is unreliable and prone to fatigue.

A neural network, or what is sometimes referred to as an "artificial neural network" to distinguish it from the human brain, is a flexible model built from simple components. Input nodes are the explanatory variables; output nodes are the response variables. Neural networks may be used for both regression and classification problems.

We can think of a neural network as a generalization of other models. Figure 3.12(a) shows a neural network with input and output nodes but no intermediate nodes. With a linear function defining the weights along the links between inputs and outputs, this type of network corresponds to multiple linear regression. Figure 3.12(b) shows a neural network with input and output nodes but with nonlinear weighting functions between input and output nodes. This type of network can represent nonlinear relationships between inputs and outputs. Its structure is similar to a generalized additive model, but the weighting functions have explicit formulas rather than being smooths. It is common to use S-shaped functions as weighting functions. In neural network parlance, weighting functions are also called activation or transfer functions. Figure 3.12(b) shows three weighting functions, one for each input node to the output node.

If we add a layer of intermediate nodes to the neural network, we get a flexible modeling structure, capable of capturing interactions among explanatory variables as well as nonlinear relationships. When we talk about using a neural network for regression or classification, we usually think of a neural network with at least one layer of intermediate nodes, as shown in Figure 3.12(c). This figure shows eight distinct weighting functions, one from each input node to each of two intermediate nodes, and one from each intermediate node to the output node. At each computer iteration, the neural network algorithm adjusts parameters for all weighting functions.

Figure 3.13 summarizes the process of fitting a neural network. We fit a model to the training set while simultaneously evaluating it on the validation set. The neural network adapts to the training data, adjusting its weights with each iteration (generation or epoch). The curve for training set performance goes down across its entire range, showing better and better fit to the training data with each iteration. The curve for validation set performance, however, goes down initially, but eventually turns up. The fact that training and validation set performance diverge indicates that there has been overfitting of the neural network model to the training data.

Figure 3.12 From Regression to Neural Networks

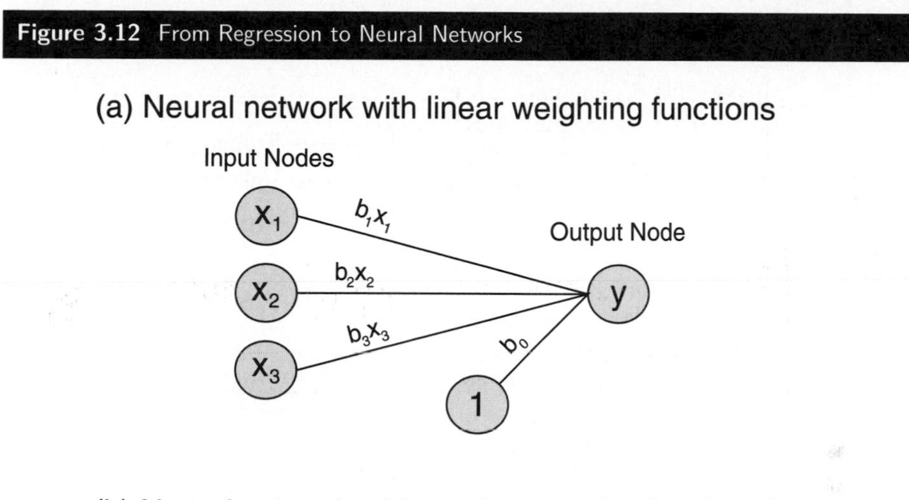

(b) Neural network with nonlinear weighting functions

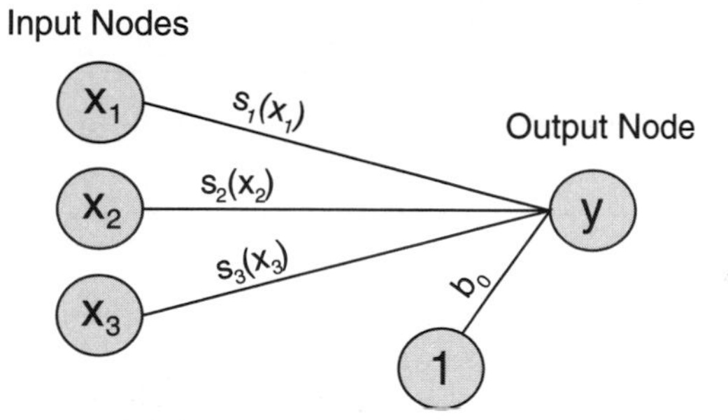

(c) Neural network with nonlinear weighting functions and one layer of intermediate nodes

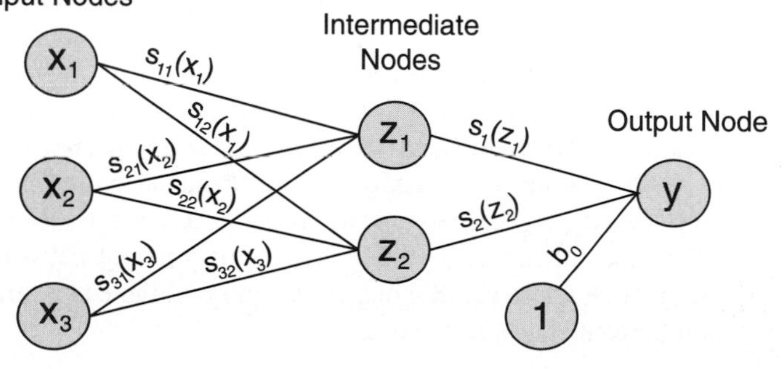

Figure 3.13 Neural Network Learning, Model Selection, and Evaluation

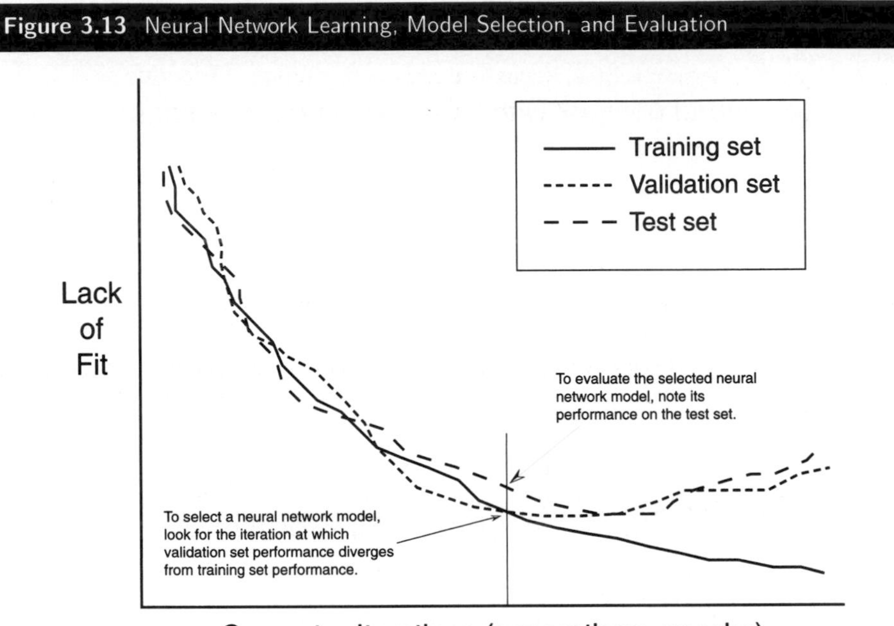

When should we stop training a neural network? What weights should we use for a neural network model? We answer these questions by looking for the point where training and validation set performance diverge. That is, we use the validation set to see when to stop the model fitting process. After a model has been selected, we can evaluate its performance on a separate data set, the test set.

Neural networks are often criticized as being "black box" solutions. We see inputs and outputs but what goes on between the inputs and the outputs is a mystery to many, even to the developers of the networks. This characterization is partially true. If we wanted to peer into the workings of a neural network, to see the weights applied to each input and intermediate node, we could. In order to deploy neural networks, their formulas must be accessible. For most fitted networks, however, the plethora of weights across links and nodes precludes any reasonable interpretation. To understand what a neural network says about relationships among explanatory and response variables (inputs and outputs) we run the network to see what it predicts. Sensitivity analysis is another method for understanding the workings of a neural network; we construct stylized inputs, systematically varying one explanatory variable at a time and observing its effect upon predicted values of the response.

3.5 OTHER DATA-ADAPTIVE METHODS

There are many types of data-adaptive methods, with new methods being added every day. Much recent research has focused upon combinations of methods and models, as well as procedures that involve resampling and rerunning analyses many times. For example, we can use forests of trees or networks of trees as our classification or regression model.

Multivariate adaptive regression splines (MARS), introduced by Friedman (1991), permit flexible modeling of nonlinear relationships and interactions. They have many of the advantages of neural networks but permit more straightforward interpretation of the workings of models. With large data sets and large numbers of potential explanatory variables, some analysts like to explore data, looking for all direct effects and two-way and multi-way interactions. Trees and multivariate adaptive regression splines (MARS) have been used for such data explorations. An analyst can deploy tree-structured or MARS models directly or include identified interactions and nonlinear transformations in the specification of a multiple regression or logistic regression model.

Nearest neighbor methods represent an alternative technology for classification and regression. Nearest neighbors to each observation in the training set may be determined by using distance or dissimilarity measures much like we used for multidimensional scaling and hierarchical clustering analyses. To predict the total cost of a vehicle in the DriveTime case, we can average the total costs of the k nearest neighbors of that vehicle in the space of the explanatory variables.

Bayesian classifiers, also called naive Bayes models, and association rule learning, are data-adaptive classification methods. These methods rely upon Bayes Theorem and rules for conditional probabilities. They require that explanatory variables be categorical; so continuous variables must be recoded into categories representing intervals of values. Rule learning or rule induction involves noting relationships among explanatory and response variable categories. Learned rules are used to make predictions.

Support vector machines represent a viable alternative to neural networks, providing a flexible, data-adaptive technology that relies less upon analyst judgment in the selection of final models (Cristianini and Shawe-Taylor 2000). These have seen extensive application in the area of text categorization, a topic we introduce in the next chapter.

Hybrid models can combine the best features of diverse models. Suppose an analyst observes that trees are doing a better job of representing interactions and regression a better job of representing direct effects. A next step might be to use a hybrid model that adds a tree-structured component to the regression model, or vice versa.

Data-adaptive methods represent a viable alternative to traditional linear models for regression and classification. These methods are data-driven, nonparametric, and computer-intensive. The application of these modern methods involves the specification of algorithms for model development and model evaluation. Model selection is often accomplished within the context of a multifold cross-validation design. In many cases, expert judgment is needed to make decisions among alternative models.

3.6 EVALUATING METHODS AND MODELS

Data-adaptive methods, as their name would suggest, fit models by adapting to data. In particular, they adapt to the data on which they are developed—the training set. We should not be surprised when we see trees, generalized additive models, and neural networks performing better than traditional models in training sets.

What statistical criteria should we use when comparing methods and models? Traditional model selection criteria used for parametric models, such as Akaike and Bayes information criteria, as well as the adjusted R^2, reflect both goodness of fit and parsimony objectives. Nonetheless, we should be wary of indices computed from training data alone.

For an honest appraisal of methods and models, we compute indices of goodness or badness of fit in training, validation, and test sets. For goodness of fit in regression problems, we can use R^2 or the square of the correlation between observed and predicted scores. For badness of fit, we can use the mean squared error of prediction, mean absolute error, or relative squared error. We can also examine distributions of residuals, looking for unusual observations or patterns. To compare the performance of various traditional and data-adaptive models, we examine their performance in validation and test sets. We use validation sets to select the best performing models, and we use test sets to evaluate selected models.

For classification problems the situation is more complex. As we saw in our review of logistic regression, goodness of fit statistics, such as the proportion of cases correctly predicted, vary with the decision rules or cutoffs we employ when making predictions.

3.6.1 Evaluation Example: Regression Models for Days on the Sales Lot

Referring again to the DriveTime case, we consider the problem of predicting the number of days that a vehicle will be on the sales lot. For this example, we use `LOT.SALE.DAYS` as the response and `TOTAL.COST`, `VEHICLE.AGE`, and `MILEAGE` as explanatory variables. We fit models to the sedan training set and select models that perform well in the sedan validation set. Finally, we evaluate selected models using the sedan test set.

Exhibit 3.4 shows a linear regression model fit by ordinary least squares. All explanatory variables contribute significantly to the regression. Nonetheless, we should be cautious about using such a model. In Figure 3.14(a), a plot of residuals against predicted values reveals identifiable patterns, calling into question the specification of the linear regression model. There is larger variability in residuals for higher-valued predictions than for lower-valued predictions; this is known as heteroscedasticity, a violation of an assumption underlying linear regression. Looking at Figure 3.14(a), we see that predicted values can be negative, which is impossible for a count of the number of days on the sales lot. And the normal probability plot in Figure 3.14(b) shows obvious departure from normality. For these reasons, we would not use linear regression in this problem.

A statistical theorist would argue that Poisson regression, a generalized linear model, is an appropriate traditional method for this problem. He would say that the number of days on the sales lot is a count, a variable that has meaningful magnitude but takes

Exhibit 3.4 Linear Regression for Predicting Days on the Sales Lot

```
Residuals:
   Min    1Q Median   3Q Max
 -92.6 -35.2  -17.1 26.4 245

Coefficients:
              Value Std. Error t value Pr(>|t|)
(Intercept) -49.038   4.359    -11.249   0.000
 TOTAL.COST   0.013   0.001     21.437   0.000
    MILEAGE   0.000   0.000     -2.901   0.004
VEHICLE.AGE   7.305   0.360     20.279   0.000

Residual standard error: 51 on 8749 degrees of freedom
Multiple R-Squared: 0.074
F-statistic: 232 on 3 and 8749 degrees of freedom, the p-value is 0


Analysis of Variance Table
Response: LOT.SALE.DAYS
Terms added sequentially (first to last)

              Df Sum of Sq Mean Sq F Value     Pr(F)
 TOTAL.COST    1    633418  633418     245 0.0e+000
    MILEAGE    1    106833  106833      41 1.4e-010
VEHICLE.AGE    1   1063595 1063595     411 0.0e+000
  Residuals 8749  22626763    2586
```

Figure 3.14 Diagnostic Plots for the Linear Regression Predicting Days on the Sales Lot

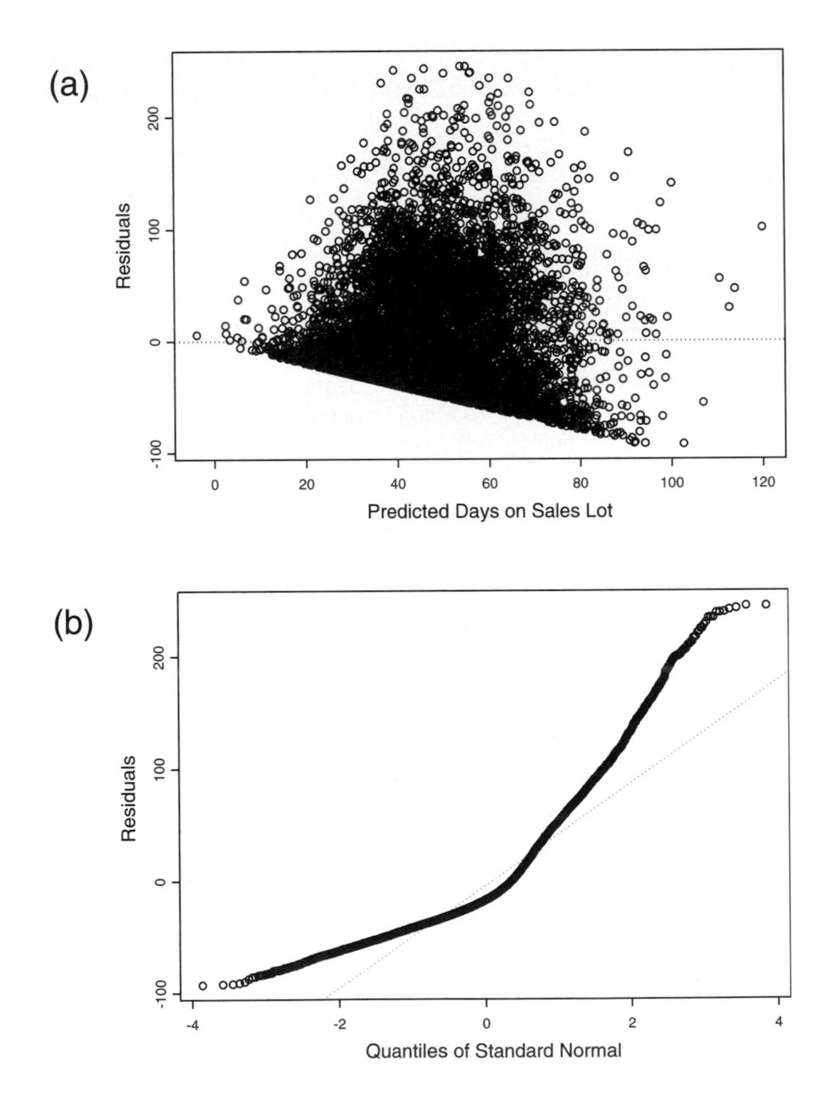

Exhibit 3.5 Poisson Regression for Predicting Days on the Sales Lot

```
Deviance Residuals:
 Min    1Q Median   3Q Max
 -15 -6.7    -3.2 3.6  25

Coefficients:
                Value Std. Error t value
(Intercept)  1.887771   1.2e-002     153
 TOTAL.COST  0.000261   1.6e-006     158
    MILEAGE -0.000002   1.0e-007     -20
VEHICLE.AGE  0.147016   9.9e-004     148

Analysis of Deviance Table
Poisson model
Response: LOT.SALE.DAYS
Terms added sequentially (first to last)

            Df Deviance Resid. Df Resid. Dev Pr(Chi)
       NULL                  8752     465440
 TOTAL.COST  1    13319      8751     452121       0
    MILEAGE  1     2187      8750     449934       0
VEHICLE.AGE  1    21352      8749     428582       0
```

nonnegative integer values only. Exhibit 3.5 shows a Poisson regression for the training data. Given the large size of the sedan training set, all explanatory variables contribute significantly to the Poisson regression. Poisson regression employs a log transformation; to predict lot sale days from the resulting generalized linear model, we use an exponential function of the linear predictor. Poisson regression is well suited to analyzing counts; the mathematics of the method guarantee that we will never predict a negative value for days on the sales lot.

There are many potential data-adaptive methods for this problem, including generalized additive models, regression trees, and neural networks. Exhibit 3.3, presented earlier in the chapter, showed the generalized additive model. For regression trees, we can use distinct stopping rules to grow initial trees of various sizes and then use internal cross-validation within the training set to guide the pruning of trees. For this problem, the process of growing and pruning trees yields regression trees with three, six, and twenty-four terminal nodes, which we refer to as "very small," "small," and "large" trees. Finally, for neural networks, we build networks with three or ten nodes in a single layer of intermediate (hidden) nodes.

Exhibit 3.6 Evaluation of Regression Models for Predicting Days on the Sales Lot

	Mean Squared Error of Prediction in Sedan Data Sets		
	Training (n = 8,753)	*Validation (n = 4,377)*	*Test (n = 4,376)*
Linear Regression	2,585	2,564	2,663
Poisson Regression	2,608	2,591	2,690
Generalized Additive Model	2,553	2,526	2,635
Regression Tree (Very Small)	2,663	2,635	2,713
Regression Tree (Small)	2,590	2,576	2,685
Regression Tree (Large)	2,487	2,558	2,645
Neural Network (3 Hidden Nodes)	2,635	2,600	2,704
Neural Network (10 Hidden Nodes)	2,637	2,600	2,701

Our evaluation of models in this problem is based upon the mean squared error of prediction. Smaller values of error are better. Exhibit 3.6 presents a table of the results; Figure 3.15 shows the corresponding dot plot trellis. Across all methods and models used for this problem, the generalized additive model is the best performer; it has the lowest mean squared error in both the validation set and the test set. We see little evidence of overfitting with most of the methods. Only the large tree shows a substantial increase in mean squared error when moving from the training to the validation set or from the training set to the test set.

Which method and model should we select for predicting days on the sales lot? If we were to use validation set performance as our guide, we would choose the generalized additive model. But there are other considerations in model selection. We should ask which of the models is the easiest to understand and to explain to management. And we should consider ease of implementation and deployment.

An argument could be made for selecting the Poisson regression model. Although the mathematics behind the method may be hard to explain to management, the model is easy to implement. Deployment in the field would be accomplished by giving Drive-Time purchasing agents a programmable calculator or spreadsheet with the formula for

Figure 3.15 Dot Plot Trellis for Evaluating Regression Models for Predicting Days on the Sales Lot

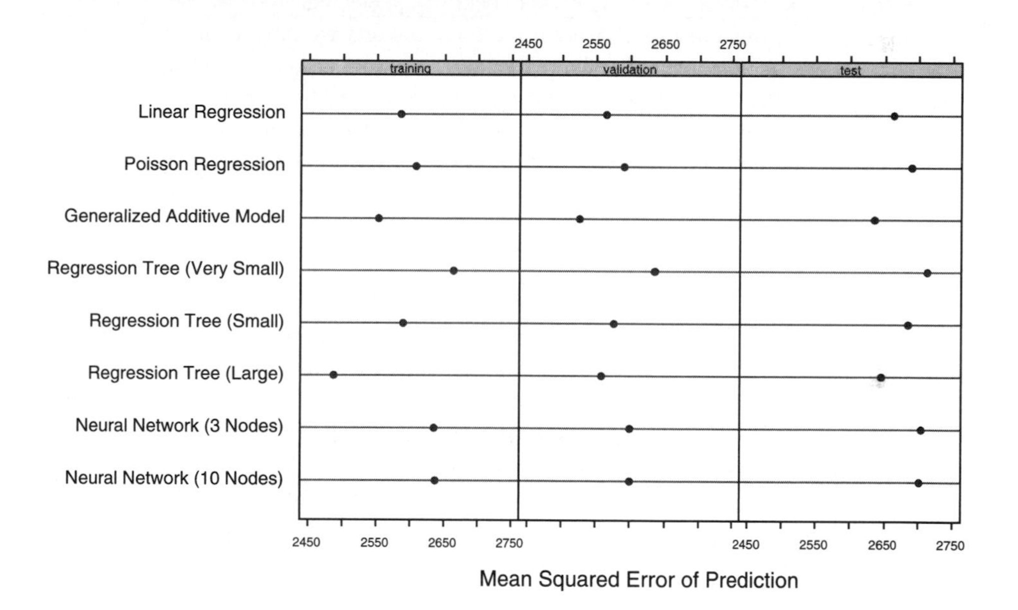

predicted days on the sales lot. But Poisson regression has a higher error rate than the generalized additive model.

Another possible choice of model would be the small tree, which is shown in Figure 3.16. Rectangular boxes in this figure represent terminal nodes. Values in each terminal node box show the predicted number of days on the sales lot and the number of vehicles in the sedan training set. In the validation set, the small tree has a lower error rate than Poisson regression and the neural networks. The small tree would be easy to explain to management. We could tell DriveTime purchasing agents to avoid older, higher-cost vehicles because they take longer to sell. The tree also reveals an interesting interaction among explanatory variables. Note that in this problem there is a small group of low-mileage, late-model-year vehicles (fifty-seven vehicles in the training set) that take much longer to sell than other vehicles. These, too, should be avoided when purchasing vehicles for DriveTime. Field deployment of the tree-structured model is simple: we give purchasing agents a picture of the tree.

What sort of performance would we expect from selected models? We look to the test set to answer this question. Among the three models we have examined in detail (Poisson regression, generalized additive model, and small tree), the generalized additive model would be the best performer. But the generalized additive model would be the most difficult to implement. The small tree performs better than Poisson regression and is the easiest to implement. Choices among models often involve tradeoffs such as these: predictive performance versus interpretability or predictive performance versus ease of implementation and deployment.

3.6.2 Receiver Operating Characteristic (ROC) Curves

The way we talk about prediction for binary responses draws upon language from the fields of medical research (epidemiology and diagnostic testing) and electronics (signal detection theory). The true positive rate or sensitivity is the number of true positive predictions divided by the number of actual positives. The false positive rate is the number of false positive predictions divided by the number of actual negatives. The true negative rate or specificity is the number of true negative predictions divided by the number of actual negatives; this is equal to one minus the false positive rate. These and other quantities for binary classification problems are defined in Exhibit 3.7.

Exhibit 3.7 shows the 2×2 table for a binary classification problem. Correct predictions are true positives (predict `YES` when the actual situation is `YES`) and true negatives (predict `NO` when the actual situation is `NO`). Incorrect predictions come in two flavors; there are false positives (predict `YES` when the actual situation is `NO`) or false negatives (predict `NO` when the actual situation is `YES`). The 2×2 table for observed and predicted binary responses has the curious name "confusion matrix." The exhibit shows some of the quantities that can be computed from this table. We use the true positive and false positive rates, for example, to obtain the receiver operating characteristic (ROC) curve.

The ROC curve provides a picture of prediction performance of a binary classification task. In particular, it plots the true positive rate against the false positive rate across

Figure 3.16 Small Tree for Predicting Days on the Sales Lot

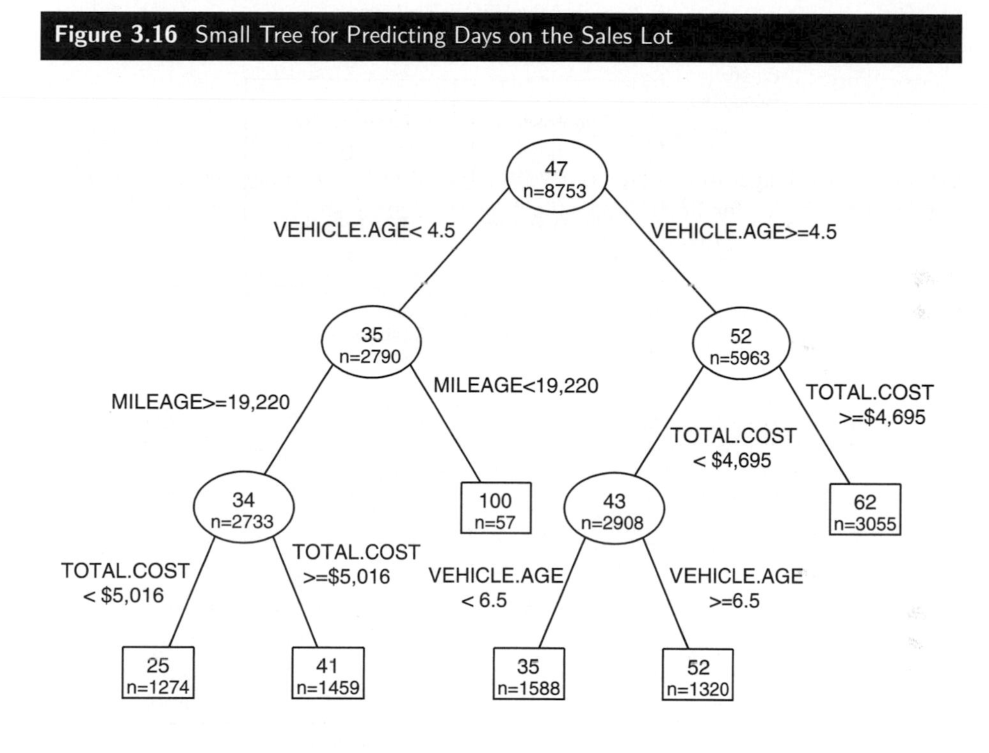

Terminal Node Information:

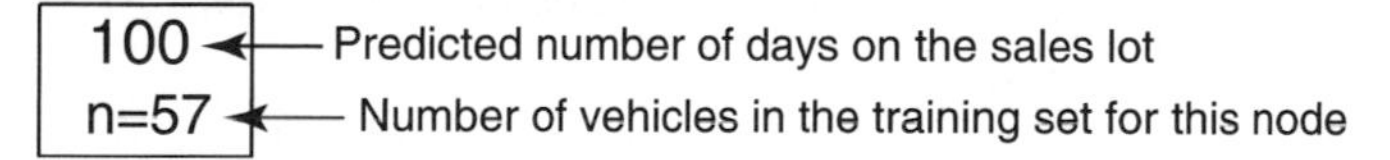

Exhibit 3.7 Evaluating Binary Classifiers: Performance Indices and the ROC Curve

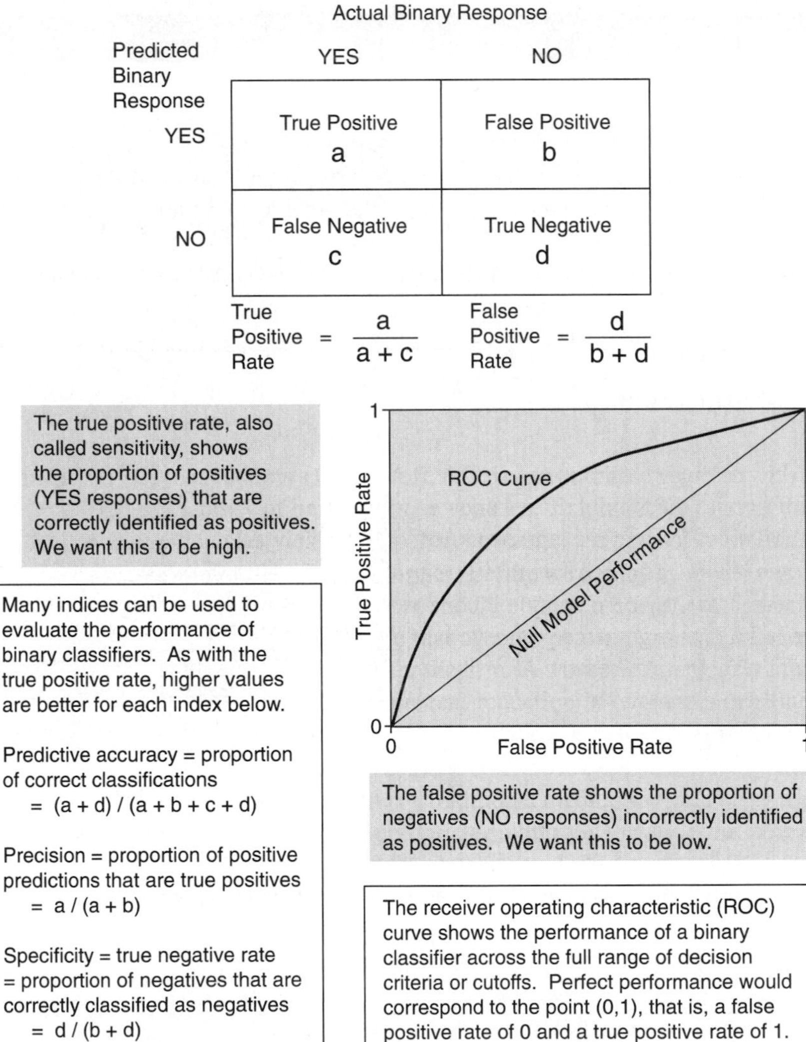

the range of possible decision rules (cutoffs from zero to one). Each classification model has its own ROC curve. When using a null model (no model at all) true positive and false positive rates are equal regardless of the cutoff rule. This corresponds to the diagonal line on the ROC curve. If we always predict NO, then true and false positive rates are zero, and we are on the lower left-hand corner of the plot. If we always predict YES, then true and false positive rates are one, and we are on the upper right-hand corner of the plot. All ROC curves, like the null model, go through the lower left-hand corner and the upper right-hand corner of the plot.

What do we want from binary predictors? We want true positive rates to be as high as possible and false positive rates to be as low as possible. We want to see ROC curves that go up and to the left. A perfect predictor will have a true positive rate of one and a false positive rate of zero; this corresponds to the upper left-hand corner of the ROC plot. Real life binary classifiers in business and social research are far from perfect. But all ROC curves share a common characteristic across the full range of decision or cutoff rules: as the true positive rate goes up (which is good), the false positive rate also goes up (which is bad).

We can use ROC curves to compare models across the complete range of decision rules (estimated probability cutoffs from zero to one). Models with predictive value must, of course, do better than the null model; these models will have ROC curves that lie above the diagonal line for the null model. Models that have ROC curves falling anywhere below the null model diagonal are suspect. If the ROC curve for one model lies above the ROC curve of another model across the entire range of false positive rates, we choose the dominant model, the model with the higher ROC curve. In many situations, however, one model will be better under high false positive rates and the other will be better under low false positive rates. In those situations we should consider the domain of false positive rates that is most relevant to the business problem at hand. Additional criteria could be used to choose between models. A method favored by some data miners is to compare areas under ROC curves. For each model being considered, we compute the area between its ROC curve and the null model diagonal; then we choose the model with the largest area under its curve.

The ROC curve may be thought of as a type of lift chart. That is, using a classification model "lifts" one above the null model diagonal or what we would expect to observe without using the model. To be useful, a classification model must have lift. It must lift the curve above the null model diagonal. In comparing classification models, we look for the one with the highest lift.

Other lift charts speak directly to the goals of business managers, showing the benefit of using classification models in dollars and cents. If we know about the costs and revenues of individual outcomes, then we can plot anticipated costs, revenues, and profit contributions associated with alternative models and decision rules. Using the resulting lift charts, we can determine optimal decision rules and cutoffs. We can examine candidate models and choose the one that has the highest expected profit contribution. Lift charts speak directly to the goals of business managers. The Veterans Organization Direct Marketing case from Appendix A provides a detailed example.

3.7 FURTHER READING

Modern, data-adaptive methods have the advantage of being flexible. They work with continuous and categorical response and explanatory variables. They do not require the prior specification of a functional form relating response and explanatory variables. They are useful for modeling, exploratory data analysis, and model checking. Furthermore, for analysts who prefer to deploy traditional models, data-adaptive methods can assist in the definition of traditional models, model checking, and diagnostics.

Comprehensive reviews of data-adaptive methods have been provided by Cherkassky and Mulier (1998), Hand, Mannila, and Smyth (2001), Hastie, Tibshirani, and Friedman (2001), and Han and Kamber (2001). Breiman et al. (1984), Miller (1994, 1996, 1998, 1999), Ribic and Miller (1998), and Zhang and Singer (1999) discuss tree-structured methods. Reviews of smoothing methods may be found in works by Simonoff (1996) and Bowman and Azzalini (1997). There are also specific references to generalized additive models (Hastie and Tibshirani 1990; Chambers and Hastie 1992), multivariate adaptive regression splines (Friedman 1991), and adaptive generalized linear models (Clarkson et al. 2002). For a review of the field of machine learning, as seen by computer scientists, see Langley (1996). Quinlan (1993) provides examples of methods for association rule learning.

There is an extensive literature surrounding neural networks. Caudill and Butler (1990) provide a conceptual introduction; Bishop (1995) and Haykin (1999) provide general overviews. For a discussion of the most commonly applied forms of neural networks, the reader can refer to Ripley (1996) and Reed and Robert (1999). Most neural network problems involve supervised learning with a goal of predicting a continuous response or a choice, much like we would do with traditional methods of regression and classification. Kohonen (2001) networks or self-organizing maps, on the other hand, represent unsupervised neural networks useful for clustering and segmentation problems.

There is a large and growing literature dealing with artificial life and agent-based technologies. Relevant analytical methods, as reviewed by Mitchell (1996) and Kennedy and Eberhart (2001), include cellular automata, evolutionary computation, genetic algorithms, and evolving neural networks. Genetic algorithms are general-purpose optimization routines that find their way into many types of models. Edited volumes demonstrate applications within the fields of economics and finance (Luna and Stefansson 2000; Luna and Perrone 2001).

There are many excellent references for learning about statistical graphics and data visualization. Basic principles of visualization and graphical display are discussed by Wainer (1997), Wilkinson (1999), and Tufte (1990, 1997, 2001). Classic references for exploratory data analysis with graphics are Tukey (1977) and Mosteller and Tukey (1977). Statistical graphics in S have been reviewed by Chambers et al. (1983), Cleveland (1993), Krause and Olson (2002), and Heiberger and Holland (in press). Cleveland (1994) provides examples of trellis graphics.

CHAPTER 4 TEXT MINING

> Looking specifically at data mining, we see that the greatest need is not to enlarge our knowledge bases, however desirable that may be, but to be able to access in them the specific knowledge we need, whether or not we know it exists or even what it is.... We will design better data miners only if we remember that the scarce factor is not information but human attention, and that the task of the data miner is to conserve it for its most important uses. (Simon 2002, p. xvii)

Kim goes to the library looking for a book called *Management Consulting: A Guide to the Profession*. She searches an electronic catalog for the title. A Library of Congress call number identifies the book. A map points to the section of the library where the book is located. Shelves of books are neatly labeled with call number ranges. Each book spine has a unique call number. Kim's book search is easy because she knows what is relevant (the title), has a way to find it (an index or catalog), and has a well-organized place to find it (the library).

What if there were no obvious organization for the library's books? Imagine a library with hundreds of thousands of books and no electronic catalog, no titles or author names, no call numbers, no labels on shelves and book spines. How long would it take Kim to find a particular book? How long would it take to find relevant sources of information? This is the situation with much information in business.

The text mine of many firms is an unstructured collection of documents. Aside from files stored within functional areas—customer transactions under sales or order entry, new product ideas under research and development, complaints under customer support, litigation with the comptroller or legal counsel—there may be little to aid the employee in search of information. What does an employee need to do to get relevant information? Go to the functional area, find someone with experience in the area, ask relevant questions, and hope for the best.

Much of business information is text. There are internal memos, facsimiles, electronic mail messages, written contracts, and letters to and from suppliers and customers. What exists is raw text, paper documents in file cabinets and archive boxes, scanned text with no obvious way to find it, electronic files without an index. Few firms maintain text databases. Fewer still would know what to do with a text database if they had one.

Data mining is today's job. Business databases beg for analysis. Many data fields are numeric or can be easily recoded as numeric. Data are organized into rows and columns. Databases have structure; there are keyed fields that point to relevant information.

Text mining is the job of the future. It begins with raw, unstructured text lacking the organization of a traditional database. Rather than being divided into discrete records and fields of numeric data, dates, or character strings, raw text is a string of characters separated by spaces and punctuation marks. There is no data dictionary or index to guide us to the relevant information—no dictionary or index until we create one. The tools of text mining help us to move from raw text to something that can be searched for answers to business questions.

This chapter introduces text mining and defines the major tasks of text mining. It reviews applications under the general headings of text categorization, information retrieval, and text measurement. For firms willing to invest time and money in the technology, text mining offers many benefits. Text mining is on the information frontier—a key to future success in a knowledge-based economy.

4.1 WHAT IS TEXT MINING?

Text mining is the automated or partially automated processing of text. It involves imposing structure upon text and extracting relevant information from text.

People read documents. Computers read documents. People write and provide answers to questions. Computers print and provide answers to questions. In between the reading and the writing, we hope that there is human intelligence when people do the work and human-like intelligence when computers do the work.

Text mining deals with words. Words, millions of words transcribed and stored in electronic files, represent raw data for analysis. Internal documents, external publications, and the words of consumers and business buyers beg for analysis. Overwhelming quantities of text come to us unstructured. To make sense out of textual data, we must impose structure.

Classifying text documents, analyzing syntax, identifying relationships among documents, understanding a question expressed in natural language, extracting meaning from a message, summarizing the meaning—these are nontrivial tasks involving more than the mere matching of words in text. To do a thorough job of text mining requires technologies from computational linguistics and pattern recognition, as well as traditional and data-adaptive modeling tools.

Some suggest that text mining concerns itself with large quantities of textual data. Our definition of text mining, like our definition of data mining, is not dependent upon the size of the database or document collection. We view text mining as a process, an approach to doing research that begins with words rather than numbers. Text mining methods are relevant to small document collections as well as large document collections.

Major business applications of text mining fall under the general categories of text categorization, information retrieval, and measurement. Categorization has organization as its initial objective. Information retrieval relates to searching, finding the proverbial "needle in the haystack." Measurement and the definition of text measures involve converting textual information into numeric information, so that it may be analyzed like other business data.

Text mining has business value. Firms with efficient mechanisms of information retrieval have a competitive advantage. Text produced in the form of memos and reports in one area of a company may be relevant to other areas of the company. Business intelligence, both internal and external, is important to corporate survival. Many companies are in the process of building data or knowledge warehouses with the objective of making information more widely available to knowledge workers. Text mining can foster collaboration and the sharing of expertise within a firm.

Measurement or text scoring, less well understood by the proponents of computational linguistics and text mining, flows from the work of text categorization. Research respondents listen to interviewer questions; they answer questions. Focus group participants talk about their experiences and feelings about products. User group participants type questions and comments into online message boards and chat rooms. Buyers send messages to sellers by electronic mail. To the extent that measures or scores can be extracted from these text sources, text mining holds promise as a business research tool.

4.2 WORKING WITH TEXT

> The ingredients of language are words and rules. Words in the sense of memorized links between sound and meaning: rules in the sense of operations that assemble the words into combinations whose meaning can be computed from the meanings of words and the way they are arranged. . . . We have digital minds in an analog world. More accurately, a part of our minds is digital. We remember familiar entities and their graded, crisscrossing traits, but we also generate novel mental products by reckoning with rules. It is surely no coincidence that the species that invented numbers, ranks, kinship terms, life stages, legal and illegal acts, and scientific theories also invented grammatical sentences and regular past-tense forms. Words and rules give rise to the vast expressive power of language, allowing us to share the fruits of the vast creative power of thought. (Pinker 1999, pp. 269, 287)

We have, as Pinker (1994) describes it, a "language instinct." The structure of sentences, the words we use—these are the observables of the speech act. Underlying the words and sentences is meaning—call it a latent message. It is the meaning or latent message that matters. "I have strong feelings for you. You touch my heart. You complete me. Deeply moved am I by the very sight of you. I can't bear to lose you. Let's stay together forever." Depending upon the context in which they are spoken, these sentences could be thought of as carrying the same meaning: "I love you." We may not be the best writers or speakers (or lovers), but we can understand the meaning of all manner

Figure 4.1 Natural Language Processing and Text Mining

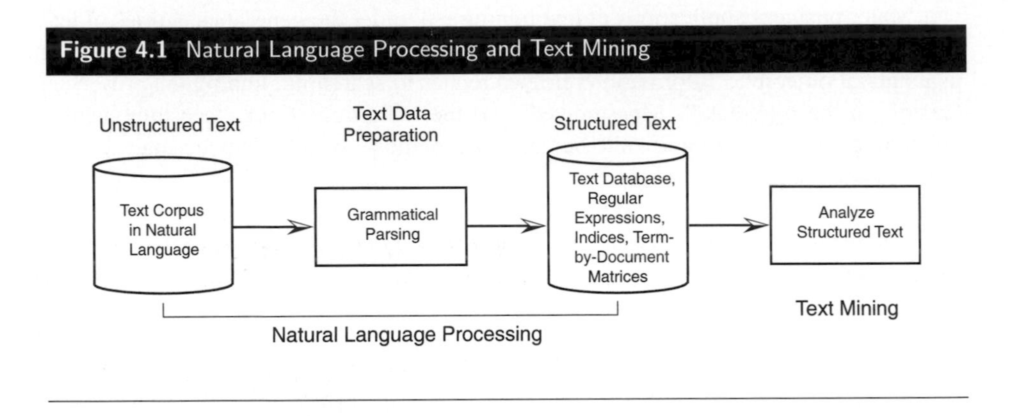

of messages. We speak and listen with ease, recalling Juliet's words from Shakespeare: "What's in a name? That which we call a rose by any other name would smell as sweet."

People are good at processing small quantities of unstructured text. Computers are good at processing large quantities of structured text. To do the work of text mining—to process large quantities of unstructured text—we must either give an enormous amount of time to people or a modicum of intelligence to computers. Because people's time is better spent in other ways, we try to give intelligence to computers. We find ways to structure text so that it can be understood by computers. This is the work of natural language processing, a preliminary to text mining. As illustrated in Figure 4.1, natural language processing involves parsing unstructured or grammatically structured natural language, creating regular expressions that are more easily analyzed by computer.

Text mining begins with a document collection, sometimes referred to as a "corpus." Compared with a traditional database, a document collection is unstructured, raw text. It is in the natural language, rather than a specialized computer language or set of codes. Documents contain paragraphs, paragraphs contain sentences, and sentences words. Natural language follows grammatical rules, with many ways of conveying the same idea and with many exceptions to rules. Words and the rules of grammar comprise the linguistic foundations of text mining as shown in Figure 4.2.

Linguists study natural language, the words and the rules that we use to form meaningful utterances. "Generative grammar" is a general term for the rules; "morphology," "syntax," and "semantics" are more specific terms. Computer programs for natural language processing use grammatical rules to mimic human communication and convert natural language into structured text for further analysis.

A corpus or document collection usually represents a particular content domain or publishing venue. All articles published in *The Wall Street Journal* in 2002 would be a corpus. The units of analysis, the documents, would be the individual articles. Each document has attributes—date of publication, newspaper section, page number, and length—that could be coded as "tags," alphanumeric data or search codes associated with the article. The meaning of a document, what it actually says, is reflected by its

Figure 4.2 Generative Grammar: Linguistic Foundations of Text Mining

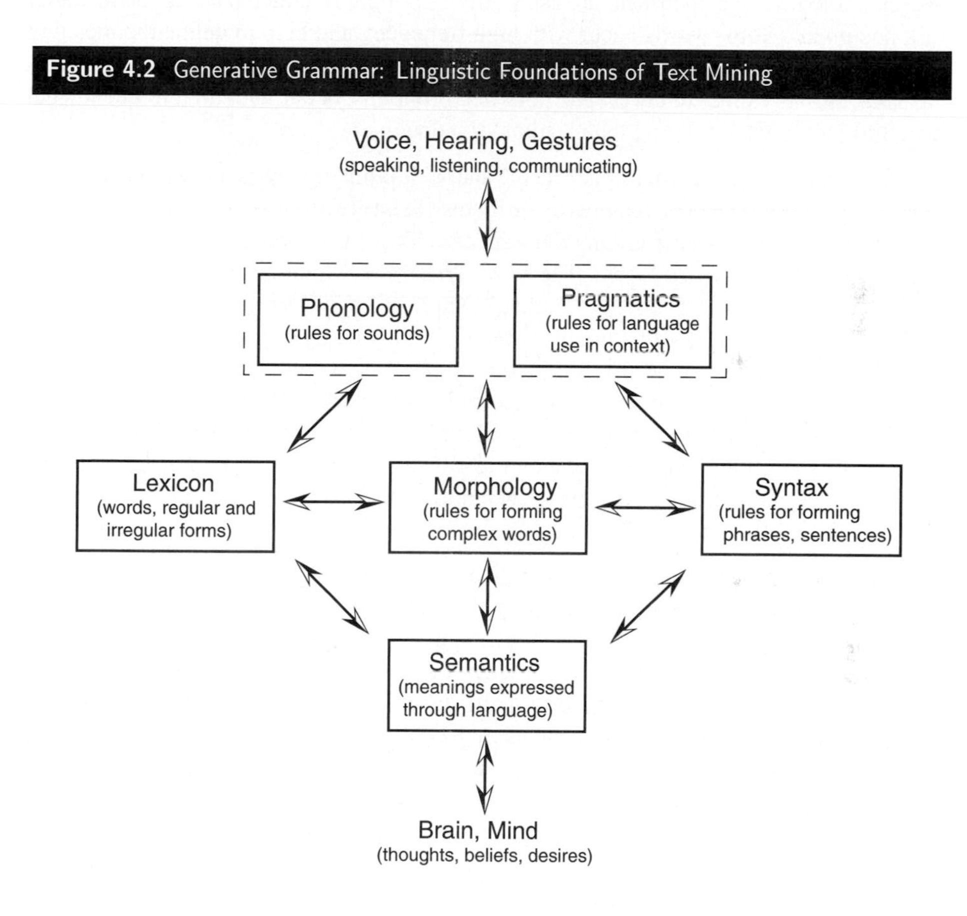

Source: Adapted from Pinker (1999).

words. Discovering the meaning and coding that meaning are the hard parts of text mining.

The location of words in sentences is a key to understanding text. Words follow a sequence, with earlier words often more important than later words, and with early sentences and paragraphs often more important than later sentences and paragraphs. Words in the title of a document are especially important to understanding the meaning of a document. Some words occur with high frequency and help to define the meaning of a document. Other words, such as the definite article "the" and the indefinite articles "a" and "an," as well as many prepositions and pronouns, occur with high frequency but have little to do with defining the meaning of a document.

What makes text unstructured from the analyst's point of view is the fact that features of text must be defined. The features or attributes of text are often associated with terms—collections of words that mean something special. There are collections of words relating to the same concept or word stem. The words "marketer," "marketeer," and "marketing" build on the common word stem "market." There are syntactic structures to consider, such as adjectives followed by nouns and nouns followed by nouns. Most important to text mining are sequences of words that form terms. The words "New" and "York" have special meaning when combined to form the term "New York." The words "financial" and "analysis" have special meaning when combined to form the term "financial analysis." We talk of "stemming," which is the identification of word stems, dropping suffixes (and sometimes prefixes) from words. More generally, we are parsing natural language text to arrive at structured text.

Terms identified in the document collection act as variables in text mining. After coming up with a list of unique terms from the document collection, we can sort the list based upon frequency of occurrence. Additional structure may be imposed upon textual data by creating a term-by-document matrix (sometimes called a lexical table). The rows of this data matrix correspond to word stems from the document collection, and the columns correspond to the documents in the collection. Terms constitute a subset of the most important (or highest frequency) terms. The entry in each cell of a term-by-document matrix could be a binary indicator for the presence or absence of a term in a document, a frequency count of the number of times a term is used in a document, or (more likely) a weighted frequency indicating the importance of a term in a document. Exhibit 4.1 illustrates the process.

Typical text mining applications have many more terms than documents, resulting in sparse rectangular term-by-document matrices. To obtain meaningful results for text mining applications, analysts examine the distribution of terms across the document collection. Very low frequency terms, those used in few documents, may be dropped from the term-by-document matrix, reducing the number of rows in the matrix. After the term-by-document matrix has been refined, text mining turns into data mining. We have numbers suitable for analysis using a variety of traditional and data-adaptive methods, including principal components (singular value decomposition), cluster analysis, classification and regression trees, and support vector machines.

Exhibit 4.1 Creating a Term-by-Document Matrix

An initial step in text mining applications, such as information retrieval and text categorization, is the formation of a term-by-document matrix. The drawing below illustrates the process. The first document comes from Steven Pinker's *Words and Rules* (1999, p. 4), the second from Richard K. Belew's *Finding Out About* (2000, p. 73). Terms correspond to stems of words that appear in the documents. In this example, each matrix entry represents the number of times a term appears in a document. We treat nouns, verbs, and adjectives similarly in the definition of stems. The stem "combine" represents both the verb "combine" and the noun "combination." Likewise, "function" represents the verb, noun, and adjective form "functional." An alternative system might distinguish among parts of speech, permitting more sophisticated syntactic searches across the set of documents. Once created, the term-by-document matrix is like an index, a mapping of document identifiers and terms (keywords or stems). For information retrieval systems or search engines we might also retain information regarding the specific location of terms within documents.

Pinker (1999)

> People do not just blurt out isolated words, but rather *combine* them into phrases and sentences, in which the meaning of the combination can be inferred from the meanings of words and the way they are arranged. We talk not merely of roses, but of the red rose, proud rose, sad rose of all my days. We can express our feelings about bread and roses, guns and roses, the War of Roses, or days of wine and roses. We can say that lovely is the rose, roses are red, or a rose is a rose is a rose When we combine words, their arrangement is crucial: *Violets are red, roses are blue*, though containing all the ingredients of the familiar verse, means something very different.

Belew (2000)

> The most frequently occurring words are not really about anything. Words like NOT, OF, THE, OR, TO, BUT, and BE obviously play an important functional role, as part of the syntactic structure of sentences, but it is hard to imagine users asking for documents about OF or about BUT. Define function words to be those that have only a syntactic function, for example, OF, THE, BUT, and distinguish them from content words, which are descriptive in the sense that we're interested in them for the indexing task.

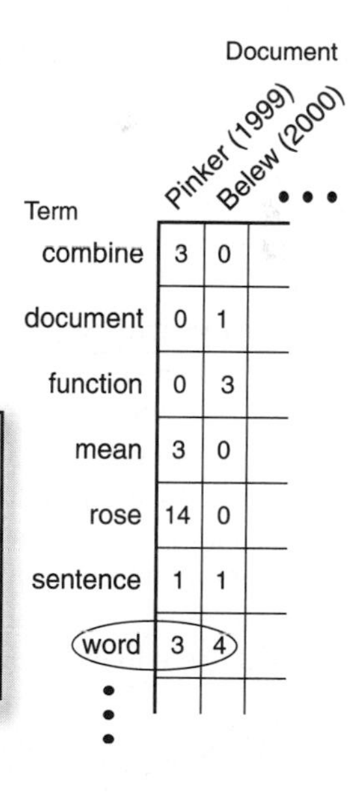

Figure 4.3 Selecting Documents for the Document Collection (Corpus)

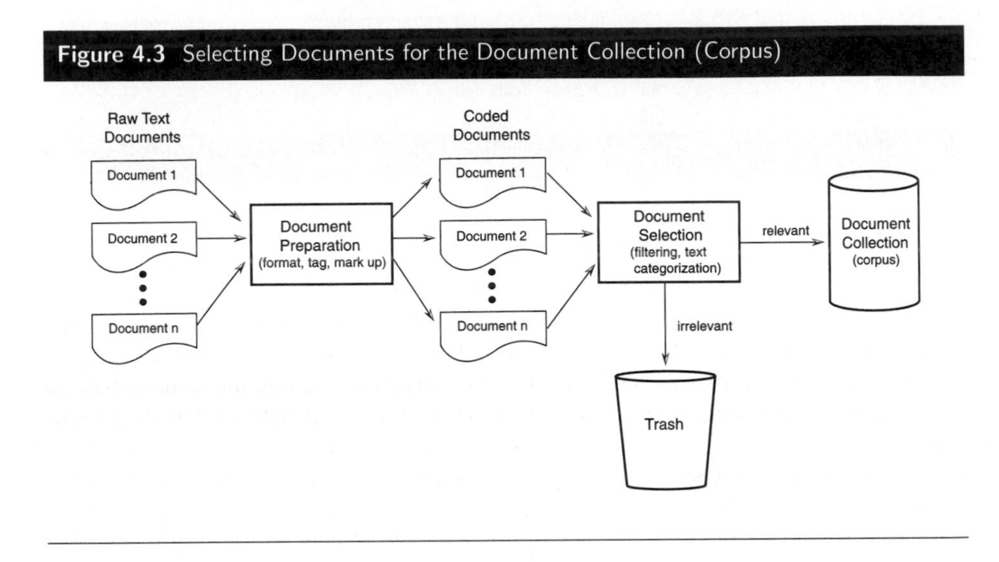

Textual data, often overwhelming quantities of textual data, come to us unstructured. To make sense out of text, we impose structure. Forming the term-by-document matrix is often the beginning of the process of imposing structure. Note that the term-by-document matrix is specific to the document collection from which it is derived. When we add documents to the document collection, we must add columns to the matrix. When many documents are added, we should consider redefining the set of terms (the rows of the matrix). For large text mining systems, updating of the term-by-document matrix and subsequent analysis of the matrix may be carried out periodically as a batch operation.

4.3 TEXT CATEGORIZATION

Text categorization involves identifying common features across documents and organizing those documents into groups based upon the common features. Text categorization is an important component of many text mining applications, including those involving information retrieval and text measures. Text categorization is also a common first step in data mining. We categorize documents according to their relevance to the document collection or corpus. This is a filtering process, as shown in Figure 4.3. Relevant documents go into the document collection, irrelevant documents go into the trash.

4.3.1 Example: E-Mail Classification

A text categorization problem that most of us can relate to is the junk e-mail problem. For active e-mail users, thousands of messages are received each month. Separating the good messages from the junk can be a time-consuming process as users painstakingly review their in-boxes. Because the distinction between good and junk messages varies from one user to the next, standard e-mail classification programs, such as those for identifying spam, fall short of providing the kind of facility that many users require.

We can use text categorization programs to automate the process of sorting e-mail messages into good and junk piles. The binary response, defined by an individual user, is the classification of the message as good or junk. Each message or document may be described by its sender, subject text/terms, message length, and message text/terms. The E-Mail Text Categorization from Appendix A illustrates the types of explanatory variables that could be used in such problems.

Suppose an individual user, Daniel, reviews one thousand e-mail messages. For each message, he decides whether it is good (he clicks on the message to read it) or junk (he ignores or deletes the message without reading it). A computer program records Daniel's behavior, noting the disposition of messages. Logs from the one thousand messages, with information about explanatory variables and responses, constitute a training set for the e-mail classification problem.

In going from e-mail text to continuous and categorical explanatory variables and a binary response, we have converted our text mining problem to a data mining problem. With Daniel's training set, we have a supervised learning problem. To build a classification model, we can use a variety of methods, including logistic regression, classification trees, neural network classifiers, and support vector machines. Subsequent observation of Daniel's behavior can provide a validation set for evaluating the performance of alternative methods and models. Further observation could provide a test set for evaluating the performance of the selected model.

Why should we develop a text classification for e-mail? Because it can improve productivity of office workers. Deployment of the system could take the form of an intelligent e-mail agent customized for each office worker. Figure 4.4 depicts an office worker's life before and after the introduction of an e-mail agent.

4.3.2 Example: Electronic Business Library

Turning to the problem of business information management, we note that business libraries, like libraries in general, have changed with information technology. The physical library of books, periodicals, and corporate reports is being overtaken by a plethora of online information sources, both internal and external to the firm. As the amount of machine retrievable information grows daily, the need for efficient indexing and cataloging grows with it. Technologies for text categorization can help information specialists to build electronic libraries that serve user needs.

Recognize that the generic text categorization problem is a series of binary classification problems. That is, each document has the potential of being classified under many topical categories. Suppose the pharmaceutical firm Pfizer sends a letter to the drug retailer Walgreens. The letter reviews pricing policies as well as recommended pharmacist warning labels to be distributed to consumers of an ethical drug XYZ. Walgreens scans the letter and stores it as a document in its electronic library. The document could be classified under "Pfizer," "pricing," "pharmacist warnings," and "XYZ," among

Figure 4.4 An Electronic Mail Agent with Text Categorization

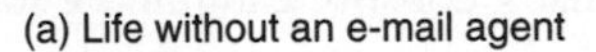

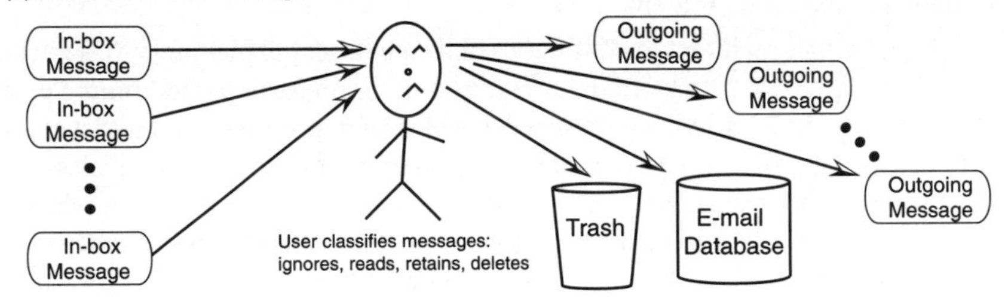

(b) Life with an e-mail agent

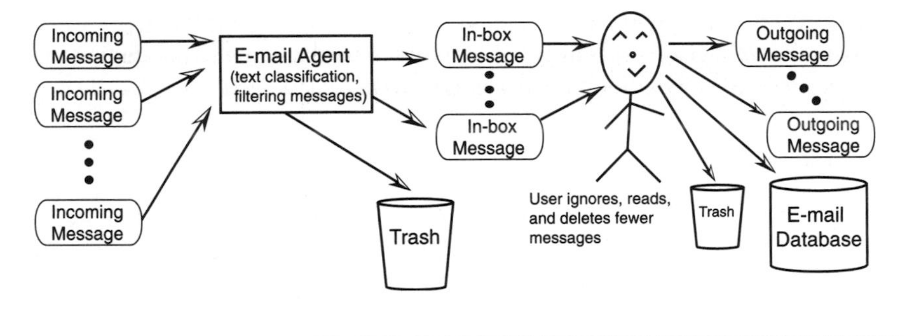

other indexing keys. Initial indexing and categorizing work is the job of clerical workers, information specialists, or business librarians; it is a manual process.

To automate the process of maintaining an electronic library, business information specialists must first devise an index or categorization scheme. They should rely upon an understanding of the information flows into and out of the organization and of the information needs of library users, including employees, suppliers, and customers. The index or categorization scheme should be comprehensive, so that every document may be assigned at least one key, and it should provide sufficient detail to accommodate the information retrieval needs of users.

After an index has been defined, information specialists or corporate librarians can build training, validation, and test sets of documents, assigning appropriate keys to each document. A letter from Pfizer gets the key "Pfizer" but not the key "Johnson & Johnson." It gets the key "XYZ" but not the key "aspirin." And so on. The set of training documents should be sufficiently large to have multiple instances of every indexing key.

Indexing keys serve the role of binary response variables. Automated text categorization utilizes classification models fit to the text data (represented by a term-by-document matrix, for example). Using the set of training documents, we fit a separate model for each of the keys in the index. Like the e-mail versus junk mail problem, supervised learning methods may be used for the classification models.

4.3.3 Example: Managing Information Overload

The text categorization examples of e-mail classification and business libraries presume supervised learning environments in which training documents are categorized by human experts. Now we consider a generic unsupervised learning problem.

Suppose that a support engineer for a software firm is asked to monitor the activity in a user chat room. In particular, she is asked to observe user discussions for a month and prepare a summary report for management identifying primary discussion threads or themes.

Hundreds, perhaps thousands, of chat room messages are logged each month as users, both satisfied and dissatisfied, express their opinions about the firm's software products. Reading the entire transcript from the chat room could take many hours. Identifying primary threads or themes could be a difficult task. The support engineer wonders whether it might be possible to use text mining tools to organize, explore, and summarize the domain of user opinion in the chat room.

Think of chat room messages as entries in a document collection or corpus. Construct a term-by-document matrix. Identify or define attributes that may be used to differentiate among documents, such as document length, word choice, or other text measures. Augment the term-by-document matrix by adding rows for these measures. The columns of the augmented term-by-document matrix represent numeric vectors describing the documents; these constitute input data for unsupervised learning methods.

Just as we can use multivariate methods like principal components and multidimensional scaling to develop product positioning maps from consumer surveys, we can use multivariate methods to develop semantic maps from chat room text. Berry and Browne

(1999), for example, describe how singular value decomposition may be used to analyze rectangular term-by-document matrices. Lebart (1998) shows how the multivariate technique of correspondence analysis converts frequency counts in a term-by-document matrix into maps of terms and documents, providing a visualization of textual data.

Just as we can use cluster analysis to identify product classes or consumer segments, we can use cluster analysis to identify semantic clusters or groups of documents with common themes. Messages within a cluster are more like one another than to messages in other clusters. If we can identify messages at the center of each cluster, we may be able to provide examples of prototypical chat room messages, those most descriptive of the major threads or themes of discussion.

The support engineer's job in this example—reading, organizing, and summarizing a large body of text—is not unlike the job of many knowledge workers. Unsupervised learning methods for text categorization, properly employed, help people to cope with the problem of information overload. Furthermore, knowledge workers can use unsupervised learning methods without preconceived notions about the nature of the information. They let the text define the categories and the structure of the summary.

Automatic text summarization is another area of research and development that can help with information management. Imagine a text analysis program with the ability to read each document in a collection and summarize it in a sentence or two, perhaps quoting from the document itself. To our hypothetical e-mail agent, categorizing messages as spam or normal messages, we add a component that reads the normal messages, summarizes them, and organizes them for review by management. Wishful thinking? Perhaps. But, given developments in the area of automatic text summarization (Mani and Maybury 1999), intelligent systems like this are becoming a reality.

4.4 INFORMATION RETRIEVAL

Users of the Internet and World Wide Web are familiar with search engines that look across the expansive domain of the World Wide Web to find matches for user queries. This is an information retrieval operation.

Information retrieval systems are search engines. Figure 4.5 shows the typical structure of an information retrieval system. The fundamental task involves matching user queries with documents. If the user query is in natural language, the system must first convert the user query into a structured query; this is a grammatical parsing or "query binding" operation, as it is sometimes called. The information retrieval system also relies upon the prior text processing of the corpus, converting natural language documents into structured text.

We want search engines to have high recall, identifying all documents relevant to an information request. Search engines with high recall may also retrieve documents that are irrelevant or only indirectly related to the information request. A search engine that retrieves only documents that are relevant to an information request is said to have high precision. When using a high precision engine, however, we run the risk of missing relevant documents. Witten, Moffat, and Bell (1999) note that the tension between

Figure 4.5 Components of an Information Retrieval System

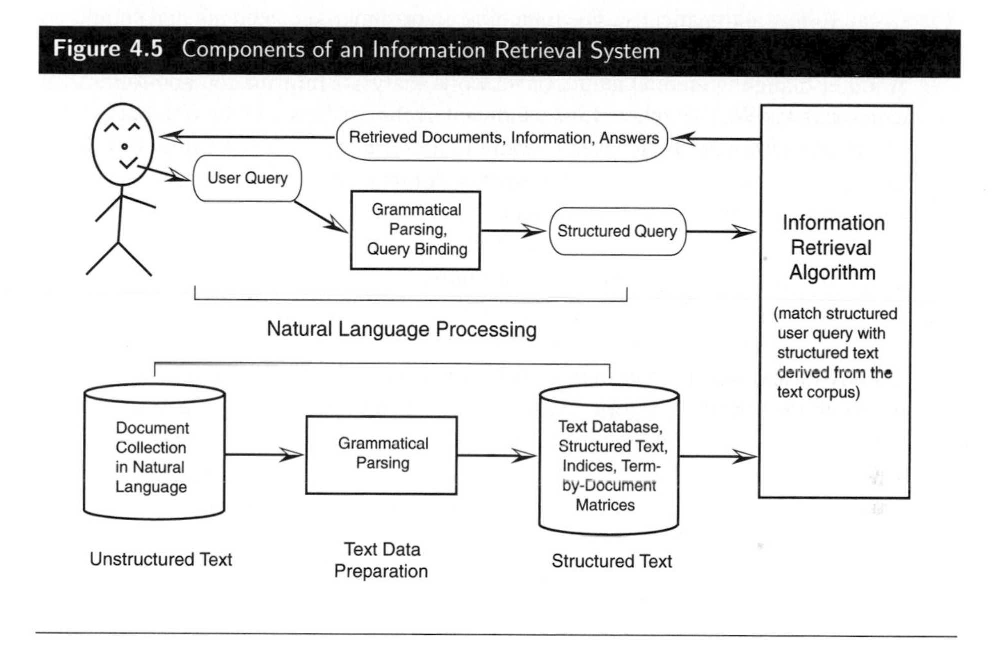

the dual objectives of high recall and high precision has been an enduring theme in information retrieval research.

Information retrieval systems or search engines perform a matching function; they attempt to match the words used in a user's query with words used in documents. Various methods may be used to accomplish the matching. Each user query may be thought of as a vector of search terms which may be compared with vectors of terms for documents being searched. A simple Boolean or logical method involves a matching of terms used in the user's query with terms used in documents. Some search engines complement Boolean matching with references to knowledge bases, dictionaries, or patterns in user queries. Vector space models and various text classification algorithms can facilitate the search.

What about the information retrieval or matching algorithm itself? Is is necessary to compare the user's structured query with the structured text of each and every document? No. We can build upon methods of text categorization as reviewed in the previous section to simplify the information retrieval and matching process.

Text categorization and methods that assess document affinities or similarities are useful preliminaries to information retrieval. When a user asks for information, her query, along with the documents of the corpus, may be parsed, categorized, or positioned within the semantic space of the corpus. Documents in the same text category as the user's query or close in space to the user's query are those most likely to satisfy the user's information needs. Retrieve one document in a class of documents, and the others can follow automatically. Retrieve one document, and nearby documents (in the semantic space) can follow automatically. The matching algorithm, then, need not and should not entail a document-by-document comparison with the user query.

Another matching method is link or network analysis. Information about links can be incorporated in Web searches. Links show interrelationships among Web pages; they help us to find additional Web pages relevant to a user query. Hub and authority pages, for example, play special roles in Web searches. A hub page points to many other pages, and an authority page is pointed to by many other pages.

Information retrieval is an active area of research and development. We should expect more efficient search engines in the future, as natural language and text mining algorithms find their way into commercial offerings. Future systems are likely to employ interaction between search engines and user analysts. There will be natural language capabilities on the user side in the parsing of queries and on the database side in the organization and analysis of text. Insightful's InFact system, for example, permits the user to enter requests as natural language queries and employs technologies from computational linguistics.

Search engines like Google and AltaVista are based upon simple word matching operations, importance coding, or the linking of the documents or Web pages across the World Wide Web. We need to go beyond the capabilities of today's search engines. To quote Herbert Simon:

> Our search engines must become more intelligent so that they can select and filter from the forests of information the particular items our eyes need to see. They must not only be able to respond to our specific requests, but also to use broader knowledge of our needs to retrieve important information we have not asked for and may be surprised by. (Simon 2002, p. xvii)

In the future we will see intelligent applications and agents that perform syntactic processing and meaning-based Web searches. Syntactic modeling provides the ability to do relationship searches in addition to keyword searches. For most modern languages the order or configuration of words within a sentence is important to understanding the meaning of the sentence.

In English it is customary to place the subject before the verb and the object after the verb. In English verb tense is important. The sentence "Tom carries the Apple computer," can have the same meaning as the sentence "The Apple computer is carried by Tom." "Apple computer," the object of the active verb "carry" is the subject of the passive verb "is carried." Understanding that the two sentences mean the same thing is a first step in the direction of building intelligent search engines.

Programs with syntactic processing capabilities, such as Insightful's InFact, provide a glimpse of what search engines may become in the future. Such programs perform grammatical parsing with an understanding of the roles of subject, verb, object, and modifier. They know parts of speech (nouns, verbs, adjective, adverbs). And, using identified entities, representing people, places, things, and organizations, they can perform relationship searches. Working with a syntactic processing program and a business news database, for example, a user might ask to identify all activities (verb forms) relating

Coke and Pepsi. Retrieved documents could be quite useful as sources of competitive intelligence.

Facilitated by standards for information interchange like XML, the World Wide Web holds promise as a public information store, a vast repository of machine-retrievable and machine-understandable data. In the future we will be "spinning the Semantic Web," as described by Daconta, Obrst, and Smith (2003) and Fenzel et al. (2003). Text mining methods will be important in this information-rich environment, as we move from information retrieval to knowledge discovery.

4.4.1 Example: Searching a Document Archive

Text categorization and information retrieval often go hand in hand. The objective is to use the power of the computer to organize large bodies of text (text categorization) and to find answers from the text (information retrieval). In writing their book about the marketing research and information services industry, Miller and James (2004) had access to the electronic archive of *Inside Research*, a monthly newsletter about the marketing research industry written by Jack J. Honomichl and Laurence N. Gold. There were basic questions to be answered. How had the marketing research industry changed in recent years? What had been the history of mergers and acquisitions? What could be learned about factors of production? What about sales revenues and the demand for research and information services? The authors wondered whether answers could be found in the archive.

Searching the entire *Inside Research* archive for answers seemed a daunting task given the amount of detail and lack of structure in the original documents. The archive contains articles of interest to buyers and sellers of marketing research and information services. The archive available to Miller and James (2004) began with the first issue from January 1990 and continued through December 2003. Originally distributed as a set of Microsoft Word files, one for each year of publication, the *Inside Research* archive contained more than two thousand printed pages and a million words of text. A small body of text by text mining standards, *Inside Research* presented an interesting technical challenge because of its organization as many individual news items covering a wide range of content in each monthly issue. For the most part, documents were unstructured. Some paragraphs and sections of documents had titles; others did not. There was no comprehensive index for the archive.

The first step in analyzing the *Inside Research* archive was to organize the document collection into discrete units for analysis. Miller and James (2004) used text editors and a Perl program to convert the original Microsoft Word files, organized as newsletters, into ASCII text documents. Some documents represented long articles on selected marketing research topics. Others were short, such as one-sentence paragraphs about events affecting individuals and firms in the marketing research industry. Graphics were not part of the archive, but documents could include tables as well as paragraphs of text. Extensive text editing yielded a document collection of around seven thousand ASCII text documents.

How could one extract meaning from the *Inside Research* document collection? Faced with the task of reviewing large quantities of textual information, Miller and James (2004) turned to text categorization and information retrieval tools developed by Insightful Corporation. When the authors wanted to find documents related to pricing, they searched the document collection for "pricing." When they wanted to find news items about the ACNielsen company, they searched the collection for "ACNielsen." The text categorization system provided an efficient mechanism for finding and verifying facts about individuals and companies, as well as for finding feature articles on selected topics.

An interesting feature of the system employed by Miller and James (2004) was its ability to learn from user feedback. With each request for information, the system returns what its algorithms indicate are the most relevant documents. Then the analyst has the opportunity to rate documents according to her own judgment of their relevance. Analyst ratings are then available to the text categorization program, so they can be used in future information requests. Relevancy feedback, interaction between computer algorithms and human judgment, offers considerable promise for the future of text mining.

4.4.2 Example: Web Spiders for Competitive Intelligence

The Society of Competitive Intelligence Professionals (SCIP) provides this definition of competitive intelligence (CI):

> A systematic and ethical program for gathering, analyzing, and managing external information that can affect your company's plans, decisions, and operations. Put another way, CI is the process of enhancing marketplace competitiveness through a greater—yet unequivocally ethical—understanding of a firm's competitors and the competitive environment. (Society of Competitive Intelligence Professionals 2003)

Competitive intelligence professionals ask questions. Who is the competition, and what are they like? What is their financial position? What is their market share? What about business objectives? Do they have strategic alliances with other firms? What products and services do the competitors offer? What are their prices? Are there new competitors on the horizon? Competitive intelligence professionals answer these questions by gathering and analyzing information from public sources.

The Internet and World Wide Web have transformed the landscape of competitive intelligence by providing a vast store of publicly available information. Corporate Web sites and online reports, user chat rooms, news articles, and reports about products and prices from online shopping sites are sources of competitive intelligence. It is easy to retrieve information about competitors and competitive products. The challenge is to sort through mounds of retrieved information, identifying the most relevant documents for management.

Web spiders, also called crawlers, wanderers, Webbots, or bots, are software programs that search the Web for relevant information. They do this by following universal resource locator (URL) links from one Web page to another. Spiders usually work in conjunction with scrapers, which gather information from Web pages. The general idea is to replace manual searching by analysts with automated searching by computer.

An exemplary Web spider for competitive intelligence is the CI Spider program developed by Chen, Chau, and Zeng (2002). To use the CI Spider, the researcher provides a starting list of Web addresses, such as home page URLs of known competitors. The researcher enters search terms, such as "products" and "prices," and constraints, such as limiting the search to commercial sites, excluding education and government sites.

Working from the initial list of Web addresses and employing a breadth-first algorithm that searches widely across sites before it searches deeply within sites, the CI Spider follows all possible links, finding Web pages that match the researcher's search terms and constraints. The search stops after the spider has identified a specified number of relevant Web pages. The result of the search is the list of URLs for these Web pages. The researcher can click on the URLs to view complete content of the pages.

In experiments with student users, Chen, Chau, and Zeng (2002) observed that the CI Spider program performed better than both Lycos searches constrained by Internet domain and analyst-driven, within-site searches. CI Spider is one of many programs for automatic Web searching (Rasmussen 2003; Zhong, Liu, and Yao 2003; Bar-Ilan 2004; Chen and Chau 2004; Hemenway and Calishain 2004). Sullivan (2000) discusses text mining methods for competitive intelligence research, referring to a number of commercially available programs. General reviews of the competitive intelligence landscape have been provided by Fuld (1994) and Bergeron and Hiller (2002).

4.5 TEXT MEASURES

What are text measures? They are scores on attributes that describe text. Each document in a collection can be assigned scores. Measurement, in its most basic sense, is the assignment of numbers to attributes according to rules. Text measures can be used to assess personality, consumer preferences, and political opinions, just as survey instruments can. The difference between text measures and survey instruments is that text measures begin with unstructured text as their input data, rather than forced-choice questionnaire responses.

The term "text measures" may be new, but many examples of this type of text analysis exist, going under names such as content analysis, and thematic, semantic, and network text analysis (Roberts 1997; Popping 2000). Text analysis has seen a wide range of application within the social sciences, including the analysis of political discourse. West (2001) notes growing interest in the field of content analysis in recent years.

An early computer implementation of content analysis is found in the General Inquirer program (Stone et al. 1966; Stone 1997). Buvač and Stone (2001) describe a recent version of the program, which provides text measures based upon word counts across numerous semantic categories. Some of the more popular categories relate to bipolar dimensions identified in Charles Osgood's semantic differential research (Osgood, Suci, and Tannenbaum 1957; Osgood 1962), including positive–negative, strong–weak, and active–passive dimensions. A more recent example of computerized content analysis is

Figure 4.6 Components of a Text Measurement System

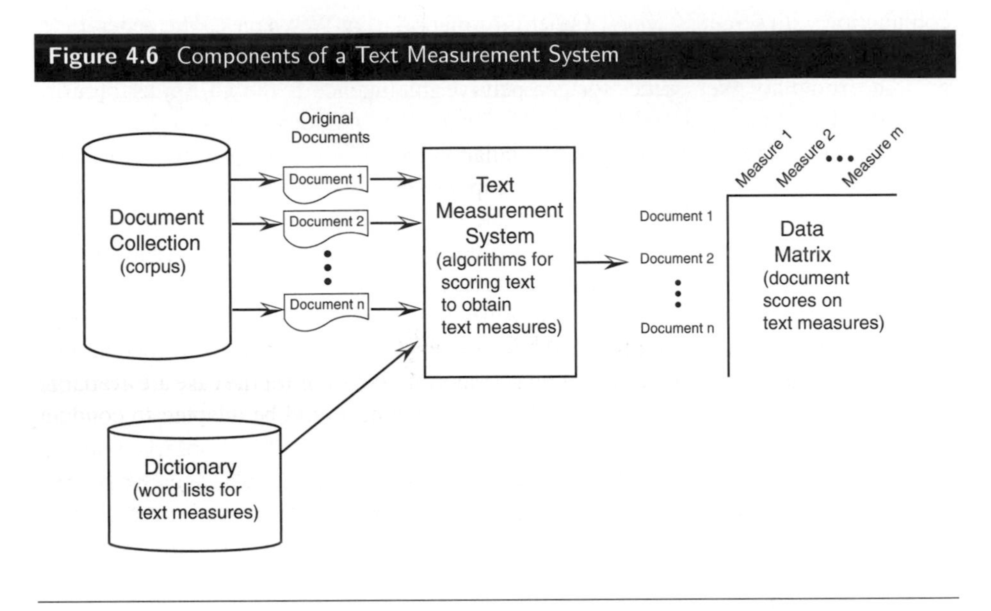

the DICTION program (Hart 2000b; Hart 2001) for analyzing the tone of text messages, as discussed in an example below.

Text measures involve a scoring of documents based upon predefined measurement categories or methods. Figure 4.6 shows a generic text measurement system. Text measures flow from a measurement model (algorithms for scoring) and a dictionary, both defined by the researcher or analyst. A dictionary in this context is not a traditional dictionary; it is not an alphabetized list of words and their definitions. Rather, the dictionary used to construct text measures is a repository of word lists, such as synonyms and antonyms, positive and negative words, strong and weak sounding words, bipolar adjectives, parts of speech, and so on. The lists come from expert judgment about the meaning of words. The text measurement system scores documents from the collection by using scoring algorithms and the dictionary.

Popular, but perhaps overly simplistic, examples of text measures are the "What sucks? What rocks?" programs for gauging public opinion through Web searches. Jon Orwant and Steve Lidie offered "What Languages Suck" programs, referring to programming languages. Don Marti developed what he called an "Operating System Sucks-Rules-O-Meter" that runs daily over the Web. A review of the logic behind these systems is provided by Dan Brian (2003).

"What sucks? What rocks?" systems utilize search engines like Google or AltaVista to gather text examples of the items being evaluated. Then they employ grammatical parsing programs, often written in Perl, to convert the natural language in the text examples into regularized expressions for analysis. Finally, text measures are employed; that is, the text examples for each item being evaluated are scored for the number of hits associated with sets of bipolar verbs or adjectives, such as sucks-rules, bad-good, stupid-brilliant, and so on. The public-domain systems on the Web gather data on a regular, usually daily, basis and report summary data (usually frequency counts) for the items or objects being judged.

Nothing is to prevent us from using similar mechanisms for doing serious consumer and public opinion research. We can refine bipolar text scoring methods so the resulting measures are more trustworthy. We can use a series of bipolar adjectives to develop multivariate text measures or profiles for objects being judged. In addition, we can establish norms for text measures so that objects may be judged relative to other objects within the same category, and we can compare text measures across objects and time. The Web Text Mining case in Appendix A provides an exercise along these lines. Written in the Perl language, natural language and text scoring programs for the case are available in the public domain. With a little work these programs could be adapted to conduct meaningful business and market research.

A related area of text analysis (and a research stream with a long and storied history) concerns document word counts, literary styles, and authorship identification (Zipf 1949; Oakman 1980; Mosteller and Wallace 1984). While the objectives of historical and literary studies have little to do with contemporary business applications of text mining, methods of linguistic and literary analysis contribute to our general understanding of text mining methods. Characteristic of these studies is the scoring of documents, the creation of text measures.

4.5.1 Example: Text Measures for a Political Document Collection

To get a feeling for what text measures can provide, we examine the political research of Roderick P. Hart (Hart 2000a) in the book *Campaign Talk: Why Elections Are Good for Us*. To conduct this research, Hart had to prepare a representative text database, identifying political documents and storing them in electronic form. He also had to develop text measures, constructing dictionaries for the scoring of documents.

As with many data and text mining applications, the hard part, the time-consuming part, is data and text preparation. Preparing the document collection for Hart's (2000a) research was a monumental task. His research covered the thirteen U. S. presidential campaigns from 1948 to 1996. He collected text from press releases (7,309 documents) and broadcast media (1,219 documents), transcripts of campaign speeches (2,357 documents), political advertisements (553 documents), and letters to the editor from newspapers (6,126 documents). Documents were converted to electronic media and organized by time (election and campaign cycle), candidate, and political voice (people, politicians, and press).

Print media text came from *The New York Times*, *Washington Post*, *Christian Science Monitor*, *Atlanta Constitution*, *Chicago Tribune*, and *Los Angeles Times*, as well as from Associated Press and United Press International reports. Text for the broadcast media was gathered from photocopies of scripts and transcripts of audiotapes from the nightly news. News bureaus from ABC, CBS, NBC, CNN, and PBS were represented. Campaign speeches included all nationally broadcasted addresses during general elections as well as selected campaign stump speeches. Political advertisements represented a sampling of advertisements across seven of the thirteen campaigns in the study. Finally, letters to the editor were drawn from newspapers representing twelve major cities across the United States.

The text measurement system for Hart's research draws upon the DICTION program and a dictionary of around ten thousand words arranged in thirty-three disjoint lists (Hart 2000a, 2000b, 2001). The scoring algorithm relies upon simple word counts. It assumes semantic independence, counting each word occurrence equally, regardless of context or grammatical role.

Five general text measures summarize the tone of documents along dimensions called certainty, optimism, activity, realism, and commonality (shared values). Each measure depends upon counting words that correspond to selected word lists. Some words receive positive weights, others negative weights. The optimism measure, for example, assigns positive weights to words relating to praise, satisfaction, and inspiration, while recording negative weights for words relating to blame, hardship, and denial. The realism measure draws upon the concept of familiarity. A text measure in its own right, familiarity is computed with reference to a dictionary of forty-four words that are regarded as the most common words in the English language.

Hart's research demonstrates how text measures may be used to understand large and diverse text sources. Reviewing the voices of the three main groups (politicians, press, and public), he observed increasing complexity (lower familiarity scores) over time. Across the entire period of the study, the voice of the press was decidedly negative in tone (low in optimism), compared with politicians and the public. Normalcy in speech, if not in policy, is rewarded in American politics. Among political candidates, centrist speakers, those who spoke in common parlance, were more successful than non-centrist candidates.

Judging from the text sources used in Hart's studies, there is great variability in the way people talk about politics. Hart (2000a) identified three general groups of political speakers: (1) "pundits," who focus upon campaign dynamics, (2) "traditionals" concerned about national values, and (3) "functionals," the largest group, who avoid both pundit and traditional language in order to focus upon community problems.

Hart's contribution to the analysis of political discourse lies in his reliance upon original text sources. Whereas many political analysts spend their time putting a "spin" on what people say, Hart lets people speak for themselves. While many analysts rely upon political polls to assess public opinion, Hart relies upon the actual words of the people. Reviewing his work with content analysis over the years, Hart (2001) writes,

> I have found virtually every stereotype about computerized content analysis to be untrue. It is alleged to be mechanical, but I have found it to be creative. It has been decried as oafish, but I am fascinated by its subtlety. It is said to be reliable but not valid, and yet I see its validity as its greatest strength. It is said to be reactive, colorless, and arcane; I have found it to be heuristic, exciting, and altogether normal. (Hart 2001, p. 43)

4.5.2 Text Measures and Qualitative Research

Qualitative research is currently a labor-intensive enterprise. Whether conducting in-depth interviews or focus group discussions, the moderator participates in a conversation. Talking and listening take time. Spoken words, recorded on video or audio tape, are often transcribed into text, another time-consuming process. The analysis of qualitative data is equally labor-intensive, with the researcher reviewing tapes and transcripts and turning the unstructured words of others into a coherent story, a report of research findings.

Many software tools designed for the qualitative data analyst assist in the organization process. They help the analyst to keep track of the details of text analysis and to restructure an analysis quickly when new text categories or theories become apparent. Tools such as Atlas/ti and NUD.IST are analyst-driven. They automate the clerical aspects of analysis, the tasks of data organization and record keeping, but are not text mining tools. Reviews of such tools have been provided by others (Kelle 1995; Weitzman and Miles 1995; Fielding and Lee 1998; Popping 2000; Weitzman 2000). Geisler (2004) discusses text data preparation and issues involved with the manual coding of transcripts from qualitative research.

Much qualitative research is small-sample research, which is not surprising given the time it takes to collect and analyze text. This situation could change as software tools emerge that automate the process of qualitative data collection and analysis. Miller and Walkowski (2004) suggest possibilities with focused conversations and qualitative research online. When we have large bodies of qualitative data focused upon the same subject, then we have an opportunity to explore additional possibilities of text mining.

Text measurement holds promise as a technology for understanding consumer opinion and markets. Just as political researchers a la Hart (2000a) can learn from the words of the public, press, and politicians, business researchers can learn from the words of consumers, press, and competitors. Commercial advertisements can be analyzed just as political advertisements. User group postings can be analyzed just as letters to the editor in newspapers.

The work of content analysts and qualitative researchers in the social sciences can serve as a model for business and marketing research. We are encouraged to understand consumers in their own words, to understand the competitive landscape in the words of competitors, and to use the power of the computer to do the work of text analysis.

Words and numbers—that's what we have. Ideas about the business world are expressed in words. Through measurement we find ways to convert words to numbers. Data analysis, traditional and data-adaptive, converts millions of numbers to thousands of numbers, and thousands to a few. At the end of analysis we look at summary numbers and models fit to the data, and we turn those numbers and models into words, interpreting results, telling a story to managers. This is, of course, an oversimplification of the research process. But it is interesting to think of research in terms of numbers and words. It helps to put data and text mining into perspective. Quantitative researchers go from words (theories and survey instruments) to numbers and from numbers to words (reports of results). Qualitative researchers, by contrast, deal almost entirely with words.

4.6 FURTHER READING

Data mining is quantitative research—a numbers game. Text mining is also a numbers game, but with words rather than numbers as the raw input. As computers, natural language processing, syntactic modeling, and text analysis algorithms become more capable, we will see new and exciting applications of text categorization, information retrieval, and text measures.

For those interested in learning more about text mining, reviews may be found in Trybula (1999), Witten, Moffat, and Bell (1999), Meadow, Boyce, and Kraft (2000), Sullivan (2001), Feldman (2002), and Sebastiani (2002). Hausser (2001) gives an account of generative grammar and computational linguistics. Statistical language learning and natural language processing are discussed by Charniak (1993) and Manning and Schütze (1999). The writings of Steven Pinker (1994, 1997, 1999) provide insight into grammar and psycholinguistics. Maybury (1997) reviews data preparation for text mining and the related tasks of source detection, translation and conversion, information extraction, and information exploitation. Detection relates to identifying relevant sources of information; conversion and translation involve converting from one medium or coding form to another.

Meadow, Boyce, and Kraft (2000) and the edited volume by Baeza-Yates and Ribeiro-Neto (1999) provide comprehensive reviews of computer technologies for information retrieval. Belew (2000) and Berry and Browne (1999) discuss technologies relevant to Web search engines, and Huberman (2001) reviews patterns of Web user activities. Merkl (2002) provides discussion of clustering techniques, which explore similarities among documents and group documents into classes. These can be quite useful to analysts and managers facing a glut of textual information. Dumais (2004) reviews latent semantic analysis and statistical approaches to extracting relationships among terms in a document collection.

The edited volume by Denzin and Lincoln (2000) provides an overview of qualitative research methods. Antecedents of text measures may be found in the text analysis methods of qualitative researchers, as described in Schrott and Lanoue (1994), Roberts (1997), and Silverman (2000, 2001). Also relevant are works dealing with applications and methods of content analysis, including computer-assisted methods (Popping 2000; Neuendorf 2002; West 2001).

Pfeifer (2003) reviews information retrieval systems based upon the public-domain language Perl. For those interested in programming for text preparation and text processing, Perl is often the language of choice. Introductory Perl references include Christiansen and Torkington (2003) and Schwartz and Phoenix (2001). For more advanced programming ideas, the reader can refer to Wall, Christiansen, and Orwant (2000), Conway (2000), Cross (2001), Quigley (2002), and Schwartz and Phoenix (2003). The online Perl community (`http://www.perl.org`) and *The Perl Journal* are excellent sources of Perl programs and lore. Edited volumes by Jon Orwant (2003a, 2003b) contain articles from *The Perl Journal*. Perl is often used for dynamic Web applications (Radcliff 2002), including those involving XML (Ray and McIntosh 2002; Riehl and Sterin 2003) and Web services (Ray and Kulchenko 2003).

CHAPTER 5

AND IN CONCLUSION...

> Welcome to the Information Age, an age of instant access to the most diverse and arcane knowledge at almost no cost, and where electronic signals are starting to replace in value the bulky manufactured goods that used to define the wealth of nations, companies, and individuals. And this is just the beginning. Impressed as we are with what we now see, in a few years it will seem quaint and outdated when compared to the wonders that cyberspace will bring to most people on this earth. (Huberman 2001, p. 2)

We are near the end of our introduction to data and text mining. Our focus has been the organization and analysis of the numbers and words for business and market research. Our focus is justified by the availability of systems for processing numbers and words. Discussion of graphical, video, and audio information processing—the mining of multimedia information stores—must await future technological developments and the wonders of cyberspace and the information age, to echo Huberman's (2001) words.

We have mentioned many methods only briefly, focusing upon cross-sectional data and text. It remains for others, as cited in "Further Readings," to provide detail, mathematical derivations, and depth and breadth of coverage, including discussion of data sets with time and spatial dimensions. We expect new methods to emerge in the coming years, and we will see a diversity of applications explored as business analysts become familiar with this exciting approach to research.

What is this approach to research we call data and text mining? It is a flexible but disciplined approach to research. Much in the tradition of exploratory data analysis, we begin with data and text, not theory. We must have data and text. Without them, we have nothing to do and nothing to talk about. We are flexible, confronting problems with an open mind and a willingness to learn from data.

There are many methods and models from which to choose. For any given problem, many models may perform equally well. We recognize that model building and model selection are as much art as science. Just the same, we can avoid major problems by following a disciplined approach to research, as described by the list of basic principles below.

- **Work in a Team.** No individual should be expected to know the details of business problems, as well as analysis methods. Teams of managers, business analysts, statisticians, modelers, database specialists, and information systems professionals need to work together in solving business problems and deploying data and text mining solutions.

- **Prepare for Research.** Work with management to understand the business problem. Work with information systems personnel to understand data sources. Carefully prepare data prior to modeling. Look for outliers and unusual observations, patterns, or clusters in the data. Use good judgment and statistical principles in addressing missing data problems.

- **Explore Data.** Use graphics to explore modeling alternatives. Examine plots of residuals across training and test sets. Look for patterns in the residuals. Use the power of the computer to plot smooth curves through the data; look for nonlinearities. Inspect trellis plots, conditioning upon potential explanatory variables, and identify possible interactions among explanatory variables. Graphics are often the key to finding a better model.

- **Employ a Validation Plan.** Partition the data set prior to modeling. Use a training set to build models. Compare and evaluate models by looking at validation and test set performance, not training set performance.

- **Balance Fit and Parsimony.** Remember that the art of modeling is a balancing act between fit and parsimony. Models should fit the data, yielding small errors of prediction and classification. Models should be as simple as possible because simple, parsimonious models are easier to understand and use than complex models. When analysts strike the proper balance between fit and parsimony, they develop models with explanatory power.

- **Demonstrate Business Value.** Evaluate models in terms of their business value as well as their statistical performance. Deployed models should contribute to profit. The modeling effort itself should yield positive return on investment.

- **Conduct Research in a Legal and Ethical Manner.** Privacy is an area of concern for those who work with large customer databases. The more data we collect about individuals, the more careful we must be in using those data and in protecting them from being misused. It is important to protect people's privacy and to honor our commitments to maintain the confidentiality and anonymity of research participants. Appendix B provides a review of privacy issues in business research. Another area that demands special care on the part of researchers is protection of copyright. See Borrull and Oppenheim (2004) for a review of legal copyright issues as they relate to data collected from the World Wide Web.

Data-adaptive methods teach us to be skeptical. We don't trust models that are developed and evaluated on the same data set. Classical significance tests, p-values, Akaike and Bayes information criteria, as well as R^2 and adjusted R^2 statistics, when computed (as they usually are) from the training data alone, are of limited value in gauging the utility of models. Classical significance tests and p-values are especially suspect when working with large data sets. It is difficult to select among models when all models are statistically significant. It is a challenge to choose explanatory variables when all variables have a statistically significant relationship with the response.

Turning away from the training-set-only methods of classical and Bayesian statistics, data miners choose a more rigorous and straightforward approach to model validation. This approach, illustrated by numerous examples in the book, involves partitioning data into training, validation, and test sets. Data miners build models on the training set using a variety of methods. They compare methods and models in terms of their performance in the validation set; they choose the method and model that works best with the validation set. Finally, they evaluate the performance of the selected model in the test set. Does statistical significance matter? No. What matters is that the selected model, the deployed model, works with new data.

What kind of research is needed? This will depend upon management and its needs. Research can serve various purposes, including exploration, searching for structure or explanations, and prediction. For business managers, the results of data and text mining are more important than the methods. It is not enough to gather, organize, and reduce data. It is not enough to reduce data through the application of traditional and data-adaptive methods. Analysts must also translate their analyses into meaningful information and knowledge. There are important questions to answer in this regard: What can be done to make data-adaptive, data-driven systems easier to use? How can data and models be made accessible to managers? How can managers ensure that good models are deployed? What can be done to demonstrate positive return on investment for data and text mining projects?

Most data and text mining projects fall within the domain of observational research. We take data as they come to us and try to make sense out of them. Samples can be biased, measures invalid, and data, however plentiful, inadequate for the research purpose. Furthermore, the integrity of data depends upon the due diligence of those collecting, coding, entering, and maintaining those data. Business analysts are well advised to work closely with information systems professionals to learn about data specifications.

Large databases, powerful computers, sophisticated algorithms, and flush budgets are nice when we have them. But to trust the results of studies, we need good design, valid and relevant measures, and careful execution of research plans. When it comes to research, good thinking and good science win over technological prowess and brute force. Data and text miners, properly schooled, are flexible in their approach to problems and rigorous in their evaluation of results. They explore with rude abandon but deploy with care.

APPENDIX A
CASES AND DATA SETS

Cases show real data and address actual business problems. Each case below includes sufficient data to permit the application of traditional and data-adaptive methods. Case documentation, data files, S-PLUS, Insightful Miner, R, and Perl programs are available on the Web site for this book. Miller (2004) provides additional cases and discussion. Here is a brief description of the cases:

- **AT&T Choice Study.** The consumer data for this case are distributed by Insightful Corporation as part of its S-PLUS system. Common carrier choice may be predicted from customer demographic and telephone usage data.
- **Boston Housing Study.** Originally intended as a study of the environmental impact of air pollution upon housing prices, this case provides an opportunity to develop market response pricing models using traditional and data-adaptive methods. Versions of the case data have been used in many published studies in statistics.
- **DriveTime.** Data relating to used car and truck characteristics, costs, and sales may be used to guide inventory decisions. Vehicle cost and time-to-sale models may be developed.
- **E-Mail Text Categorization.** E-mail message data collected at Hewlett-Packard Laboratories provides a text categorization problem. The task of the modeler is to classify messages as true e-mail or spam based upon variables that describe the message text.
- **Movie-Going Surveys.** Nationwide surveys of consumers help us to understand movie-going behavior and attitudes. A small data set by data mining standards, this case provides an opportunity to demonstrate various traditional and data-adaptive methods. Data are available from telephone interviews and online surveys, permitting comparisons across research modalities.

- **Musicnotes.com.** Musicnotes.com is an online retailer of digital sheet music. The company wants to learn from customer order data. Are there identifiable customer segments that may be used in future direct marketing efforts? Is it possible to build reliable sales forecasting models from customer order data? With a data set that contains orders across the first three years of the firm's operations, the case provides the opportunity to explore models and methods for database marketing.

- **U. S. Census of Population and Housing.** This case describes a data set containing complete population and economic data from the 2000 U. S. Census of Population and Housing. The data are organized by five-digit ZIP codes, providing a rich information source for geo-demographic segmentation. Selected data items may also serve as ZIP-code–linked explanatory variables for use with other cases.

- **Veterans Organization Direct Marketing.** A U.S. veterans organization uses direct marketing to solicit contributions from past donors. Mailings to the entire database would be expensive given the number of past donors. Administrators wonder whether a targeted mailing to donors most likely to contribute would be more cost effective. The organization's database may be used to build models identifying donors most likely to contribute.

- **Web Text Mining.** This case is an exercise in collecting text data over the Web, parsing those data, and analyzing the parsed data to tell a story to management. The exercise relies upon programs written by the author to gather and analyze Web text data.

- **Wisconsin Dells.** Face-to-face interviews with visitors to the Wisconsin Dells provide demographic and activity data for consumers. The data are useful in explorations of market structure, product positioning, and market segmentation methods.

A.1 AT&T CHOICE STUDY

Following its breakup in 1986, AT&T wanted to identify factors relating to customer choice of long-distance carriers. The firm collected respondent data from telephone interviews, household service and billing information from corporate databases, and census data linked to household addresses. Exhibit A.1.1 shows variable names and definitions. Given data from one thousand long-distance telephone customers, is it possible to develop a model for predicting telephone customer choices? Could such a model be used in targeted marketing?

Exhibit A.1.1 Variables for the AT&T Choice Study

Variable	*Description and Coding*	
pick	Customer choice of long-distance service: (AT&T or OCC = Other common carrier)	
income	Income level of the household (in thousands of dollars)	
moves	Number of times the household moved in the last five years	
age	Age level of the respondent in years (18–24, 25–34, 35–44, 45–54, 55–64, 65+)	
education	<HS = Less than high school	HS = High school graduate
	Voc = Vocational school	Coll = Some college
	BA = College graduate	>BA = Graduate school
employment	D = Disabled	F = Full-time
	H = Homemaker	P = Part-time
	R = Retired	S = Student
	U = Unemployed	
usage	Telephone usage (average minutes per month)	
nonpub	Does the household have an unlisted telephone number?	
reach.out	Has the household participated in the AT&T "Reach Out America" telephone service plan?	
card	Does the household have an AT&T calling card?	

 This case is intended to serve as the basis for student learning and discussion rather than to illustrate either effective or ineffective research design and analysis. The original data for this case were provided by James W. Watson and distributed as part of Insightful's S-PLUS system. The details of the study were discussed in Chambers and Hastie (1992).

A.2 BOSTON HOUSING STUDY

The Boston Housing Study is a market response study of sorts, with the markets being 506 census tracts in the Boston metropolitan area. The objective of the study was to examine the effect of air pollution upon housing prices, controlling for the effects of other explanatory variables. The response variable is the median price of homes (in 1970 dollars) in the census track. Exhibit A.2.1 shows variables included in the case. Short variable names correspond to those used in previously published studies.

Exhibit A.2.1 Boston Housing Study Variables

Variable Name	*Description*
neighborhood	Name of the Boston neighborhood location of the census tract
mv	Median value of homes in dollars
nox	Air pollution (nitrogen oxide concentration)
crim	Crime rate
zn	Percent of land zoned for lots
indus	Percent of business that is industrial or nonretail
chas	On the Charles River (1) or not (0)
rooms	Average number of rooms per home
age	Percentage of homes built before 1940
dis	Weighted distance to employment centers
rad	Accessibility to radial highways
tax	Tax rate
ptratio	Pupil/teacher ratio in public schools
lstat	Percentage of population of lower socio-economic status

 This case is intended to serve as the basis for student learning and discussion rather than to illustrate either effective or ineffective research design and analysis. The original data from the Boston Housing Study (Harrison and Rubinfeld 1978) were published by Belsley, Kuh, and Welsch (1980) in their book about regression diagnostics. In subsequent years, versions of these data have been used by statisticians to introduce and evaluate regression methods, including classification and regression trees (Breiman et al. 1984), treed regression (Alexander and Grimshaw 1996), and monotone regression (Dole 1999). Introducing a split-sample simulation design for statistical research, Miller (1999) used the data to explore sample size requirements for a number of modern data-adaptive regression methods. Data provided for this case represent an updated version of the original data, following the suggested revisions of Gilley and Pace (1996).

A.3 DRIVETIME

DriveTime is an automobile dealership and financing firm with seventy-six dealerships in eight states. DriveTime sells used vehicles and provides financing for those vehicles, processing about ten thousand credit applications and selling about four thousand vehicles a month. Virtually all sales are financed. Its stated mission is: "To be the auto dealership and finance company for people with less than perfect credit."

DriveTime generates traffic at its dealerships through television and radio advertising, referrals from other dealerships, and its Web site (www.drivetime.com). Customers who need financing in order to purchase vehicles are run through a custom credit risk scorecard, which uses both credit bureau and application information to determine the credit worthiness of applicants. A generated risk score is used to determine the proper deal structure and credit policy for each applicant.

DriveTime purchases most of its vehicles at auctions and from wholesalers. Vehicles include many makes and models of cars and trucks. DriveTime uses an information service known as Experian Autocheck to ensure that vehicles have the correct odometer reading, have not been previously "totaled" (i.e. evaluated as having no value after an accident), and have no other significant negative history. Vehicles that fail the Experian check are rejected and sent back to sellers. Those that pass the Experian check are sent to a DriveTime reconditioning and inspection center, where they are put through additional checks and repaired as necessary. Vehicles are then delivered to the dealerships for sale.

Normal dealer sales occur within 90 days of delivery to the dealership. If a vehicle does not sell within 90 days, it is called an "overage" vehicle, meaning that it is too old to generate normal dealer profits. Each overage vehicle has its sales price reduced in order to encourage a sale within the ensuing 91- to 119-day period. Profits on vehicles sold within the 91- to 119-day period are much lower than profits on vehicles sold within the normal 90-day period. Furthermore, if an overage vehicle is not sold within 120 days, the vehicle is taken off the lot and sold at auction. DriveTime takes a loss on vehicles sold at auction.

Exhibit A.3.1 provides a hypothetical example, showing how normal and overage sales translate into business profits or losses for DriveTime. This example suggests the profit implications of using a statistical model to select vehicles for sale. Profit contributions in the example represent hypothetical gross profit contributions rather than net profit contributions. In other words, they do not account for operating costs, overhead costs, or taxes.

Exhibit A.3.2 describes variables in the DriveTime vehicles database. Included are variables relating to vehicle features, costs, and sales history. Four types of variables appear in the database: (1) string variables are character strings used to identify transactions; (2) date variables, which represent calendar dates by month/day/year, are used to compute selected numeric variables; (3) numeric variables have meaningful magnitude relating to durations of time, counts, or U. S. dollars; and (4) categorical variables relate

 This case is intended to serve as the basis for student learning and discussion rather than to illustrate either effective or ineffective research design and analysis. Special thanks go to DriveTime for providing the case data.

to vehicle or sales transaction features that do not have meaningful magnitude. Certain numeric and categorical variables may be useful in developing vehicle cost and time-to-sale models for vehicle selection. Desirable vehicles, those with newer model years and lower mileage, for example, can be expected to sell faster. Research may show that there are many factors relating to time-to-sale.

Like many databases used for data mining, the DriveTime vehicles database represents a transactions database. Each database record relates to a unique vehicle transaction, a car or truck sold and financed by DriveTime within the second half of 2001. These sales were made across the eight states in which DriveTime operates: Arizona, California, Florida, Georgia, Nevada, New Mexico, Texas, and Virginia.

The DriveTime database for this case includes the amount of the loan associated with each transaction. The database does not include the retail sales price. We can assume that prices for vehicles sold within 90 days are marked up, so that the company recovers all costs associated with purchasing, repair, operations, and interest, and makes an appropriate profit on normal dealer sales.

Information about typical used car and truck prices is available in published sources such as the *Blue Book Used Car Guide*, published by the Kelly Blue Book Company, Irvine, California, and the *NADA Official Used Car Guide–Consumer Edition*, published by the National Automobile Dealers Association (NADA), Costa Mesa, California. Kelly offers online used car pricing information on its Web site (www.kbb.com), and NADA offers information on its Web site (NADAguides.com). Note that a number of categorical variables in the DriveTime vehicles database correspond to NADA vehicle codes.

Exhibit A.3.1 Hypothetical Profits from Model-Guided Vehicle Selection

The table below reflects hypothetical profits associated with DriveTime vehicle sales, given an average total cost per vehicle of $5,000, a 20 percent markup for normal dealer sales, 10 percent markup for overage dealer sales, and 20 percent loss for overage vehicles sold at auction. Of the approximately four thousand vehicles sold each month, this example assumes that about 85 percent are normal dealer sales, 10 percent overage dealer sales (within the 91- to 119-day period), and 5 percent overage auction sales.

	Type of Sale			
	Normal Dealer	*Overage Dealer*	*Overage Auction*	*Monthly Totals*
Unit total cost	$5,000	$5,000	$5,000	
Unit price	$6,000	$5,500	$4,000	
Unit margin profit (loss)	$1,000	$ 500	($1,000)	
Units sold	3,400	400	200	4,000
	(85%)	(10%)	(5%)	
Profit (loss)	$3,400,000	$200,000	($200,000)	$3,400,000

Suppose that analysts are able to develop a model that is reasonably accurate in predicting vehicle time-to-sale. Suppose further that, by using this model to guide inventory decisions, DriveTime is able to increase normal dealer sales from 85 percent to 90 percent, with corresponding declines in overage vehicle sales. Assuming no change in vehicle costs or prices, what would be the effect upon profits? The following table suggests that monthly profits would increase by $220,000. Twelve months of sales of this type would contribute more than $2.6 million in profit a year. This demonstrates the value of using statistical models to guide business decisions.

	Type of Sale			
	Normal Dealer	*Overage Dealer*	*Overage Auction*	*Monthly Totals*
Unit total cost	$5,000	$5,000	$5,000	
Unit price	$6,000	$5,500	$4,000	
Unit margin profit (loss)	$1,000	$ 500	($1,000)	
Units sold	3,600	280	120	4,000
	(90%)	(7%)	(3%)	
Profit (loss)	$3,600,000	$140,000	($120,000)	$3,620,000

Exhibit A.3.2 DriveTime Vehicle Database

Variable Name	*Type*	*Description*
PRIMARY.KEY	string	Unique vehicle ID
DEALER	categorical	Dealership where vehicle was sold
REGION	categorical	Region of dealership where vehicle sold
SALE.DATE	date	Date of vehicle sale
BASE.COST	numeric	Cost of vehicle purchased
REPAIR.COST	numeric	Cost of repairs put into vehicle before being delivered to dealership
TOTAL.COST	numeric	Total cost of vehicle (base cost + repair cost + other costs)
VEHICLE.CATEGORY	categorical	Manual classification of vehicle (Example: FAM/L is a large family car)
YEAR	numeric	Year vehicle made (1990, etc.)
MAKE	categorical	Make of vehicle (Ford, Chevrolet, etc.)
MODEL	categorical	Model of vehicle (Escort, Taurus, etc.)
MILEAGE	numeric	Mileage on vehicle at time of sale
VEHICLE.AGE	numeric	Age of vehicle in years (year of sale minus model year)
MILES.PER.YEAR	numeric	Miles driven per year at time of vehicle sale
LOAN.VALUE	numeric	Loan value of vehicle at time of purchase
RATIO.BCLV	numeric	Base cost divided by loan value
RATIO.TCLV	numeric	Total cost divided by loan value
RATIO.RCTC	numeric	Repair cost divided by total cost
RATIO.RCBC	numeric	Repair cost divided by base cost
RECEIPT.DATE	date	Date vehicle received from vendor (auction or wholesaler)
DEALER.DATE	date	Date vehicle received at dealership from inspection center
RECEIPT.LOT.DAYS	numeric	Days from receipt of vehicle from vendor to delivery of vehicle to dealership
LOT.SALE.DAYS	numeric	Days from vehicle delivery to dealership to sale of vehicle (time-to-sale response variable for models)
RECEIPT.SALE.DAYS	numeric	Days from receipt of vehicle from vendor to sale of vehicle
PURCHASE.REGION	categorical	Region where vehicle purchased
VENDOR.TYPE	categorical	Type of vendor (AUCTION, WHOLESALER, etc.)
MAKE.NADA	categorical	Make of vehicle per NADA conversion (Ford, Chevrolet, etc.)
TRUCK	categorical	Truck flag per NADA conversion
STYLE.TYPE.NADA	categorical	Style of vehicle per NADA conversion (COUPE, PICKUP, etc.)
DOORS.NADA	categorical	Number of doors on vehicle per NADA conversion (2DR, 4DR, etc.)
DRIVE.NADA	categorical	Drive type on vehicle if available per NADA conversion (2WD or 4WD)
SERIES.NADA	categorical	Model of vehicle per NADA conversion (Escort, Taurus, etc.)
ENGINE.TYPE.NADA	categorical	Engine type on vehicle if available per NADA conversion
REGION.NADA	categorical	Region where vehicle made per NADA conversion
COLOR	categorical	Color of vehicle per NADA conversion
DOMESTIC.IMPORT	categorical	Domestic or import flag
COUNT.REPAIRS	numeric	Number of repairs performed on vehicle before delivery to dealership

A.4 E-MAIL TEXT CATEGORIZATION

This case concerns the automatic detection of junk e-mail or spam. Spam is unsolicited and unwanted commercial e-mail, such as advertisements for products, get-rich schemes, chain letters, and adult erotic literature. Spam is usually sent to people on mailing lists and newsgroups. This type of e-mail activity is considered unethical because the full cost of sending the messages is not borne by the senders and because recipients have not agreed to receive the messages.

E-mail text categorization is important to business. As reported by *InformationWeek* in August 2003, levels of spam reached epidemic proportions as spam-promoting viruses and worms attacked e-mail applications and servers on the Internet. Overrun by the number of bogus messages, many organizations were forced to shut down their e-mail systems. Interest grew in software products designed for spam filtering and spam blocking, as well as software patches to server systems to prevent further security violations.

We can use the text characteristics of e-mail messages to identify spam versus normal e-mail. Indicators of spam could be words relating to money, a preponderance of capital letters, or special characters that are used to garner the reader's attention. Indicators of normal e-mail include personal names, work-related terms, and work-related numbers, such as telephone area codes for business contacts.

The data for this case consist of descriptors of 4,601 e-mail messages collected at Hewlett-Packard Laboratories in 1999. Of these messages, 1,813 (39.4 percent) were classified as spam. There are fifty-seven potential explanatory variables, all continuous, described in Exhibit A.4.1. The response variable is the binary classification of the message as spam or normal e-mail.

The fundamental problem in the case concerns the development of a model for classifying e-mail messages. Many methods may be explored, both traditional and data adaptive. What type of method works best? How shall we select an appropriate model, and how shall we test its performance?

 This case is intended to serve as the basis for student learning and discussion rather than to illustrate either effective or ineffective research design and analysis. According to Hormel Foods Corporation (`http://www.spam.com`), the use of the word "spam" to describe unsolicited commercial e-mail resulted from a Monty Python skit in which Hormel's meat product SPAM (spelled with all capital letters) was featured. In the skit a group of Vikings sang a chorus of "spam, spam, spam," drowning out other conversation. By analogy, unsolicited commercial e-mail can drown out good e-mail. For additional background on e-mail spam, see Cranor and LaMacchia (1998) and the *InformationWeek* online site (`http://information.week.com/spam`). Ethical issues regarding spam, including research uses of spam, are discussed on Web sites for the Interactive Marketing Research Organization (`http://www.imro.org`) and the Council of American Survey Research Organizations (`http://www.casro.org`). The original data for this case were generated by Mark Hopkins, Erik Reeber, George Forman, and Jaap Suermondtat at Hewlett-Packard Laboratories. George Forman donated the data to the Machine Learning Repository at the University of California–Irvine, thus placing it in the public domain. Exemplary analyses of these data may be found in Hastie, Tibshirani, and Friedman (2001). Complete data sets may be found at the case Web site (`ftp://ftp.ics.uci.edu/pub/machine-learning-databases/spambase/`).

Exhibit A.4.1 E-mail Text Categorization Variables

Variable Name	*Description*
make	Percentage of words or character strings in the message that correspond to `make`
address	Percentage of words or character strings in the message that correspond to `address`
all	Percentage of words or character strings in the message that correspond to `all`
. . .	Forty-five additional percentage-of variables follow the structure above, with variable names associated with the following words and strings: `3rd` `our` `over` `remove` `internet` `report` `addresses` `free` `business` `email` `you` `credit` `your` `font` `000` `money` `hp` `hpl` `george` `650` `lab` `labs` `telnet` `857` `data` `415` `85` `technology` `1999` `parts` `pm` `direct` `cs` `meeting` `original` `project` `re` `edu` `table` `conference`
semicolon	Percentage of characters in message that match the semicolon character `;`
openparen	Percentage of characters in message that match the open parenthesis character `(`
openbracket	Percentage of characters in message that match the open bracket character `[`
exclamation	Percentage of characters in message that match the exclamation point `!`
dollarsign	Percentage of characters in message that match the dollar sign character `$`
pound	Percentage of characters in message that match the pound or number character `#`
avecaprun	Average length of uninterrupted sequences of capital letters
maxcaprun	Maximum length of uninterrupted sequences of capital letters
totcap	Total number of capital letters in the message
spam	Classification of the e-mail (1 = spam, 0 = normal e-mail)

A.5 MOVIE-GOING SURVEYS

The Chicago office of Mintel International Group, Ltd. conducts periodic surveys of consumer behavior in a variety of areas. Movie-going behavior is one of those areas. Advertisers, retailers, and entertainment service providers are interested in consumer movie-going behavior. What kinds of people go to the movies? How often do they go to the movies? What do they expect to spend on a night out at the movies? Are there identifiable segments of moviegoers? Does movie-going behavior vary from one part of the country to the next?

In the spring of 2001 Mintel was interested in exploring possibilities for using online surveys of consumer behavior. Previous research made extensive use of telephone interviewing, but online research was seen as having substantial cost advantages. By running parallel studies using online and telephone surveys, Mintel hoped to assess comparability across modalities. Mintel worked with The NPD Group to collect online data, while at the same time working with International Communication Research to collect telephone interview data. Common questions about movie going were used in the online and telephone surveys.

Although both online and telephone respondent groups were chosen to be representative of the U. S. population of adult consumers at least eighteen years of age, Mintel researchers were concerned about possible differences between online and telephone groups on selected demographic variables. Seven key demographic variables were identified: age, sex, income level, educational level, marital status, presence of children under the age of eighteen in the household, and census region. Exhibit A.5.1 shows demographic variable names and codes as they appear in the case data. Exhibits A.5.2 and A.5.3 show survey instructions and variable names for survey items.

For firms like Mintel engaged in tracking opinions of consumers within product and service categories, there is a need for consistent, trustworthy measures from one year to the next and from one survey to the next. Mintel management wondered if there were differences between online survey and telephone interview results. If there were differences, management wanted to know if it would be possible (using statistical case weighting perhaps) to adjust online survey results to more closely resemble telephone interview results. Exhibit A.5.4 provides a summary of this type of comparability testing and its implications for research management.

 The author thanks Bill Patterson and his associates in the Chicago office of Mintel International Group, Ltd. for providing consumer survey data for this case.

Exhibit A.5.1 Movie-Going Survey Demographic Variables

Variable	*Description and Coding*
age	Age of respondent in years
sex	Sex of respondent 1 = Male 2 = Female
income	Annual household income level 1 = Less than $25,000 2 = $25,000–$49,999 3 = $50,000–$74,999 4 = $75,000–$99,999 5 = $100,000 or more
education	Educational level of respondent 1 = Less than high school graduate 2 = High school graduate (or technical school) 3 = Some college 4 = College graduate 5 = Graduate school or more
mstatus	Marital status 1 = Married 2 = Widowed 3 = Divorced/separated 4 = Single/never married 5 = Domestic partnership
children	Presence of children under 18 in the household 1 = YES 2 = NO
region	U.S. census region of respondent's household 1 = New England 2 = Middle Atlantic 3 = East North Central 4 = West North Central 5 = South Atlantic 6 = East South Central 7 = West South Central 8 = Mountain 9 = Pacific

Exhibit A.5.2 Movie-Going Survey Instructions and Variable Names (Part 1)

```
Now, thinking about movie theaters . . .

    MT1.     How often do you attend films at
                  an indoor or outdoor theater?
    (DO NOT READ)

        1    Once a week or more (four or more times per month)
        2    Two to three times a month
        3    Once a month
        4    Once every couple of months
        5    Less than once every two months
        N    Never            SKIP TO QMT-5
        D    Don't know
        R    Refused

    MT2.     When you go to the movie theater, how much would you expect
      to spend in total on a ticket and refreshments per person?
    (INSERT $ AND CENTS.  GET BEST ESTIMATE.  DO NOT ACCEPT RANGE.
       IF MORE THAN $20, CLARIFY "Is that per person?"
     IF RESPONDENT INDICATES "IT VARIES,"
    ASK FOR THEATER VISITED MOST OFTEN)

       INSERT AMOUNT   $ _ _ . _ _

       DD  (DO NOT READ) Don't know
       RR  (DO NOT READ) Refused

    MT3.     Would you say that you regularly, occasionally, seldom,
                 or never buy refreshments at movie theaters?

       4    Regularly
       3    Occasionally
       2    Seldom
       1    Never
       D    Don't know
       R    Refused
```

Exhibit A.5.3 Movie-Going Survey Instructions and Variable Names (Part 2)

```
MT4.    Please tell me whether or not you agree with the following
   statements about refreshments at movie theaters.
        Do you agree or disagree
        (ASK FOR EACH STATEMENT)

        1   YES, Agree
        2   NO, Disagree
        D   Don't know
        R   Refused

        ROTATE
        a.  If prices on refreshments were raised,
        you would stop purchasing them.
        b.  You would buy more refreshments if they were less expensive.
        c.  You would like to see healthier food options at the
        movie theater.

    MT5a--MT5e.  And now, which of the following statements
    do you agree with?

        Do you agree or disagree
        (ASK FOR EACH STATEMENT)

        1   YES, Agree
        2   NO, Disagree
        D   Don't know
        R   Refused

        ROTATE
        MT5a.   You enjoy video/DVD rentals,
        but they don't replace movie theaters.
        MT5b.   You usually go to a discount theater
        or attend movies offering discount tickets.
        MT5c.   You feel that movie tickets are reasonably priced.
        MT5d.   You would rather attend a multi-screen theater
        than a single-screen.
        MT5e.   You would be willing to pay higher prices
        for better theater facilities
            (i.e., stadium seating, higher quality sound system).
```

Exhibit A.5.4 Comparability Testing and Its Implications for Research Management

More than fifty years ago survey researchers asked whether telephone interviews were comparable to face-to-face interviews. Today we ask whether online surveys are comparable to telephone and mail surveys. In recent years, we have seen substantial growth in the use of online research. Many studies involve multimethod research—research that uses more than one method of data collection.

Suppose that a researcher gives the same questions to two groups of respondents. One group receives an online survey and the other a telephone interview. Observing significant differences between online and telephone results, the researcher asks the comparability question: "Arc differences in survey response due to the method of administration or to demographic differences between respondent groups?"

The figure below illustrates how the comparability question relates to management decisions about research. When survey responses are comparable across methods or modalities, we can use either method. When differences in survey response are due to known demographic differences between groups, we can adjust for demographic differences and use either method. In many situations, however, we don't know why survey responses are different. We must conduct further research to understand the source of differences.

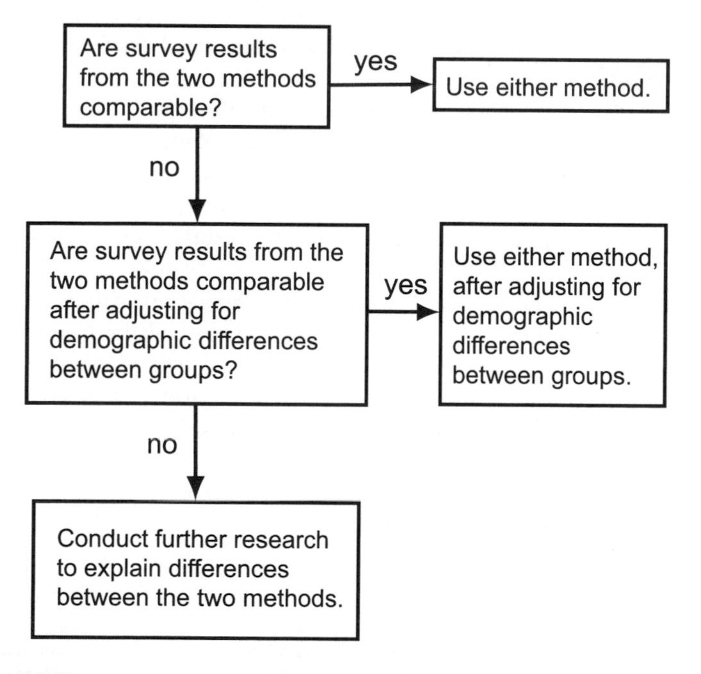

Source: Miller (2002).

A.6 MUSICNOTES.COM

Musicnotes.com is a digital music publisher located in Madison, Wisconsin. Its main product is digital sheet music, which is delivered to its online customers over the Internet. The firm sells content and respects copyright. Musicnotes.com has long-term content contracts with Warner Brothers, BMG, Viacom, and others, and a distribution contract with AOL.

The existing print sheet music market is $1 billion, but it is very inefficient. Sheet music customers include musicians and teachers and students of music. These customers go to stores whose primary business is the sale of musical instruments. They search store shelves for specific pieces of sheet music for specific instruments. They often search in vain because individual stores are forced to carry a limited selection of sheet music. Not finding the sheet music on the shelves, customers place special orders for the items they desire and wait for delivery of printed copies of sheet music.

Musicnotes.com offers an attractive alternative for buying sheet music—digital sheet music on demand. Customers order online and receive immediate downloads of sheet music to their personal computers and printers. Many pieces of sheet music are accompanied by digital-audio files that show how the music sounds when played by professional musicians.

Financed by a small group of investors, Musicnotes hopes to someday be a multimillion dollar business. During its first three years of operation, the firm has generated encouraging sales through online marketing initiatives. Sales are expected to grow as customers embrace the convenience of digital downloads and discover the value added by online digital files.

Musicnotes managers want to expand marketing efforts in order to increase awareness of the firm and drive traffic to the Web site (`www.Musicnotes.com`) and to the Web sites of its distribution partners. Marketing initiatives could include direct mailings, catalog efforts, e-mail campaigns, targeted advertising, and trade show exhibits. Information from sales to current customers could be useful in generating and executing marketing plans.

With a data set that contains orders across the first three years of the firm's operations, ample opportunity should exist to explore models and methods in database marketing. The company wants to learn from customer order data. Are there identifiable customer segments that may be used in future direct marketing efforts? Is it possible to build reliable sales forecasting models from customer order data?

 This case is intended to serve as the basis for student learning and discussion rather than to illustrate either effective or ineffective research design and analysis. The author thanks Kathleen Marsh, John Higgins, and Tim Reiland of Musicnotes.com for their help in providing background information for this case.

A.7 U. S. CENSUS OF POPULATION AND HOUSING

Aggregated data from the 2000 U. S. Census of Population and Housing, available in the public domain, represent a rich source of information about consumers and markets. Many businesses are interested in identifying potential customers by geo-demographic segment. The popular book *Latitudes and Attitudes* (Weiss 1994) heralds the importance of geo-demographics in business and marketing research.

Commercial firms like Acxiom, Claritas, ESRI, Experian, and MapInfo offer segmentation solutions based upon census data (McManus 2003). Claritas, for example, offers segmentation solutions under the product names PRIZM and MicroVision. Drawing upon 1990 Census data, PRIZM had identified sixty-two clusters across fifteen social groups, whereas MicroVision identified forty-eight segments across nine social groups. Web acccss to an application called ClaritasExpress allows individuals to enter their five-digit ZIP codes and get information about the kinds of people most likely to live in those ZIP codes. Weiss (2000) provides a detailed description of lifestyles associated with the sixty-two PRIZM clusters, which go by interesting names such as "blue blood estates," "country squires," "young literati," "pools and patios," "young influentials," "gray power," "towns and gowns," and "red, white, & blues."

For those who want to develop their own geo-demographic clusters, information from the 2000 U. S. Census of Population and Housing is available in the public domain. Census data may be obtained at various geographical levels, including data for nationwide, statewide, and metropolitan areas. Data are available for census tracks and block groups. Most convenient for marketing purposes, however, are data organized by ZIP codes. That is because prospect and customer lists for targeted marketing campaigns usually include mailing addresses with ZIP codes.

The complete ZIP-code data file for the 2000 U. S. Census of Population and Housing consists of 33,179 rows, corresponding to five-digit U. S. ZIP codes, and 16,603 columns of information, corresponding to demographic, houschold, and economic variables. Because few analysts want to work with 16,603 variables, filtering, also called "variable extraction" or "feature selection," is important to census data analysis. We can choose subsets of variables by using (1) expert judgment about the meaning of the variables and their relevance to business and marketing research, (2) statistical criteria for variable selection, or (3) a combination of expert judgment and statistical criteria.

Census data are often used to supplement data from other sources. In conducting telephone surveys, for example, a marketing researcher may ask for a person's five-digit ZIP code in lieu of asking personal questions about income and household ownership. Then the researcher may go on to use ZIP-code–linked data as explanatory variables in building consumer response or segmentation models.

 This case is intended to serve as the basis for student learning and discussion rather than to illustrate either effective or ineffective research design and analysis. The author thanks Dan Verloff of the Applied Population Laboratory at the University of Wisconsin–Madison for his help in processing census data. Complete census data and documentation are available through the Web site for the U. S. Census Bureau (`http://www.census.gov`).

A.8 VETERANS ORGANIZATION DIRECT MARKETING

A nonprofit organization that offers programs and services to U. S. veterans is interested in developing more efficient direct marketing campaigns. With an internal database of more than thirteen million records from past donors, the organization is one of the largest direct mail fund raisers in the United States. This case concerns a 1997 marketing campaign involving a direct mailing to 3.5 million past donors. Extensive data are available for a subset of 100,000 donors.

Potential response variables include whether or not a past donor makes a contribution to the 1997 campaign and the dollar amount of that contribution. Classification models are used to predict whether a donor makes a contribution. Regression models are used to predict the dollar amount of a contribution. There are hundreds of potential explanatory variables in the database. These relate to promotional events and donor-giving histories, as well as to household demographics. A key modeling challenge in this case is to determine which variables to include in models for predicting responses to the campaign.

Evaluation of alternative classification models may be accomplished with receiver operating characteristic (ROC) curves or lift charts. To understand the concept of lift, think about how it applies to a direct marketing campaign. For each marketing campaign, managers must decide how many direct mail pieces to send and to which past donors to send. Sending to no one will result in no contributions. With a 1 percent hit rate, sending to the entire database of 3.5 million people would result in 35,000 responses or hits. A typical mailing goes to 100,000 past donors. If the organization chooses 100,000 target recipients at random, given a 1 percent hit rate, there will be only 1,000 responses or hits. That is, the null model hit rate is 1 percent, and the null model hits would be 1,000 for a typical mailing.

But suppose the organization uses a classification model developed from logistic regression, tree-structured methods, or a classification neural network. Using a classification model, the organization could target its mailing to past donors judged to be most likely to respond. If the organization is able to increase its hit rate to 5 percent with this targeted mailing, it will have a 4 percent lift in hit rate. With a mailing to 100,000 past donors, it will get 5,000 contributions—a 4,000 lift in hits. Given case information about the cost of sending direct mail and the average dollars received from donors that respond to direct mail, it is also possible to estimate lift in terms of profit contribution.

As with ROC curves, estimates of lift (hit rate, hits, or profit contribution) may be plotted across alternative decision rules (cutoff criteria) and classification models. The resulting lift charts can be used to determine optimal decision rules and to select among alternative classification models. In comparing models, we look for the one with the highest lift.

 Original case documentation and data were part of the 1998 KDD Cup competition sponsored by the Knowledge Discovery and Data Mining Special Interest Group of the Association for Computing Machines. Maintained at the University of California–Irvine, the KDD Cup archive (`http://kdd.ics.uci.edu/databases/kddcup98/kddcup98.html`) contains extensive data and documentation relating to this case.

A.9 WEB TEXT MINING

This case is an exercise in text data collection and analysis. The document collection includes text collected from the Web using Google, a popular search engine. A sample program written by the author parses the collected data and computes text measures based upon lists of bipolar adjectives.

The student's job is to choose a category of products and list specific objects within that category. Take soft drinks, for example. The category is well defined and a frequent topic of conversation on the Web. Listed objects could be Coke, Pepsi, A&W Root Beer, 7UP, Mountain Dew, and many others. Objects can be described in terms of their brand names and can be more than one word in length. Synonyms for the same object, such as Coke and Coca-Cola, are placed on the same line, separated by commas. The list does not have to be exhaustive, but items listed on distinct lines should be mutually exclusive. The student enters the list when prompted by the program.

Next, the student has the option of (1) using a default text measure developed along the lines of the semantic differential (Osgood, Suci, and Tannenbaum 1957; Osgood 1962) or (2) developing a customized text measure. If the student chooses to develop a customized measure, then additional information about adjectives must be entered by the student when prompted by the program. Synonyms for the same end of a binary attribute are entered on a single line, separated by commas, following much the same procedure as used for object names. The program provides examples of valid input for creating text measures.

Recognizing that text measures obtained from Web searches may have considerable variability across time, the student is encouraged to collect and score text across a number of days or weeks. Text samples can be gathered, parsed, and scored each day or week to provide a time-series of text measures for subsequent analysis. Summary statistics can be used in the analysis of these data. Furthermore, it is possible to store the collected text samples in a document collection, so that a variety of text measures may be computed.

The student's job is to describe the measurement procedure employed. Is the measurement process reliable? Does it offer a valid portrayal of public opinion or, at least, the opinions of Web users? What about sampling issues? Are Web users representative of all users or consumers, or, more to the point, are the developers of Web content representative of all users or consumers? What can be done to build reference samples or norms to assist in the interpretation of results?

 This case is intended to serve as the basis for student learning and discussion rather than to illustrate either effective or ineffective research design and analysis. Perl programs for conducting the research draw upon programs and discussion by Dan Brian (2003). Sample programs are available on the Web site for this book. Students with Perl programming experience can modify these programs or develop their own Web spiders and scrapers. Hemenway and Calishain (2004) show how to develop Web spiders in Perl, and Burke (2002) provides a useful set of modules for working on the Web.

A.10 THE WISCONSIN DELLS

Wisconsin Dells, a sprawling vacation and entertainment center in South Central Wisconsin, is one of the Midwest's favorite vacation destinations. The Dells area is a mixture of beautiful valleys, canyons, hills, forests, and recreational businesses nestled around an interlocking series of lakes and rivers. Wisconsin Dells is an hour north of Madison, Wisconsin (the state capital), three to four hours from Chicago, and four hours from Minneapolis/St. Paul. The Dells offers a wide variety of activities. In summer, people come for its water parks and amphibious tours. In winter, people come for cross-country skiing and snowmobiling. Indoor attractions are open year-round.

In the summer of 1995 Wisconsin Dells business owners were developing plans for drawing visitors to their attractions. They had many questions about their customers and potential future customers. To answer these questions, business owners, represented by the Wisconsin Dells Visitor and Convention Bureau, enlisted the aid of Chamberlain Research Consultants, a marketing research firm headquartered in Madison.

From the end of June 1995 to the beginning of September 1995, Chamberlain Research Consultants conducted 1,698 in-person interviews with visitors to Wisconsin Dells. These interviews took place on the main street of Wisconsin Dells and at the area water parks, hotels, restaurants, and other area attractions. Interviewers obtained demographic and vacation trip information from visitors. Exhibit A.10.1 shows visitor variables and their coding. Interviewers also asked visitors whether they had participated in or were likely to participate in any of a number of activities around the Wisconsin Dells. Binary activities variables, listed in Exhibit A.10.2, relate to Wisconsin Dells attractions. Exhibit A.10.3 describes a few of these attractions.

Taking the role of a Dells business owner or a representative of the Wisconsin Dells Visitor and Convention Bureau, we have many questions to answer. What can we learn about the people who visit the Dells? Are there discernible patterns in visitor activities? Is it possible to identify consumer segments among the visitors? What kinds of activities would we recommend for visitor groups identified by demographics or type of visiting party?

A majority of current Dells advertising takes the form of brochures and pamphlets placed at various attractions in the Dells. Business owners would like to target advertising to those people most likely to visit attractions. What can we learn from the Dells data to help business owners in their advertising and marketing activities?

 The authors thank the Wisconsin Dells Visitor and Convention Bureau and Chamberlain Research Consultants for making the survey data available.

Exhibit A.10.1 Dells Survey Data: Visitor Characteristics

Variable	*Interview Item and Coding*
nnights	Length of stay (number of nights) (Coded as five ordered categories: 0, 1, 2, 3, 4+)
nadults	Number of adults in the party, including the respondent (Coded as five ordered categories: 1, 2, 3, 4, 5+)
nchildren	Number of children under 18 in the party (Coded as six ordered categories: None, 1, 2, 3, 4, 5+)
planning	How far in advance the vacation was planned One month or more ago This month (between two and four weeks ago) This week
sex	Sex of respondent (coded by sight and sound of voice)
age	Age category of respondent (in years) Less than 25, 25–34, 35–44, 45–54 , 55–64, 65+
education	Highest level of education completed by respondent High school graduate or less Some college College graduate Attended or completed graduate school
income	Level of total household annual income Lower income ($50,000 or less) Middle income (between $50,000 and $100,000) Upper income ($100,000 or more)
region	ZIP code recoded into one of six regions Chicago, Milwaukee, Madison, Minneapolis/St. Paul, Other Wisconsin, Other

Exhibit A.10.2 Dells Survey Data: Visitor Activities

Variable	*Activity (Binary Coding: No or Yes)*
shopping	Shopping
antiquing	Antiquing
scenery	Driving to look at scenery
eatfine	Eating out at fine restaurants
eatcasual	Casual theme restaurants
eatfamstyle	Family-style restaurants/buffets
eatfastfood	Fast-food restaurants
museums	Going to museums/indoor activities
indoorpool	Relaxing in indoor pool areas where staying
outdoorpool	Relaxing in outdoor pool areas where staying
hiking	Hiking
gambling	Gambling
boatswim	Boating/swimming/outdoor sports
fishing	Fishing
golfing	Golfing
boattours	Boat tours
rideducks	Riding The Ducks
amusepark	Amusement or theme park
minigolf	Miniature golf
gocarting	Go-carting
waterpark	Water park
circusworld	Circus World Museum
tbskishow	Tommy Bartlett's ski show
helicopter	Helicopter rides
horseride	Horseback riding
standrock	Stand Rock Ceremony
outattract	Outdoor attractions (not an amusement park)
nearbyattract	Nearby area attractions
movietheater	Movie theater
concerttheater	Concert/theater/evening entertainment
barpubdance	Bars, pubs, dancing
shopbroadway	Shop, browse on Broadway
bungeejumping	Bungee jumping

Exhibit A.10.3 Wisconsin Dells Attractions

The Wisconsin Dells offers many popular tourist activities and attractions. Here are some of the more popular attractions:

- **Tommy Bartlett's Thrill Show.** Started in 1952, this is one of the most famous of the Dells attractions. The Tommy Bartlett show is a combination of on-stage performances (including juggling, tumbling, and music) and a water-skiing show. The water show has highly choreographed stunts, including a three-tier human pyramid on water skis. The Thrill Show auditorium holds five thousand people, and there are three performances daily from Memorial Day to Labor Day.

- **The Ducks.** When people talk about "The Ducks in the Dells," they are not talking about waterfowl. These Ducks are amphibious vehicles built by the U.S. Army during World War II as a means of transporting soldiers over land and water. In Wisconsin Dells, Ducks are used to give tours of the natural wonders of the area. Dells Duck Tours take visitors up hills, down into valleys, across rivers, and through lakes. Along the way, visitors see all manner of intriguing rock formations and beautiful scenery. Dells Duck Tours run from March through October, weather permitting.

- **Circus World Museum.** Wisconsin Dells is located just north of Baraboo, Wisconsin, former home of the famous Ringling brothers, founders of the Ringling Brothers and Barnum & Bailey Circus. Owned by the State Historical Society of Wisconsin, Circus World Museum celebrates the history of the circus with exhibits, circus performances, variety shows, clown shows, animal shows, and a petting menagerie. The museum is open year-round with extended hours during the summer.

- **Boat Tours.** The Dells area stretches along the Wisconsin River and includes several lakes. An alternative to the Duck Tours are the boat tours, which stick to the waterways and attractions along the shorelines.

- **Stand Rock.** The Dells has fascinating natural rock formations, originating from upper layers of rock being more resilient to erosion than underlying layers. Stand Rock is an unusual formation, with a large, round, table like rock supported by a far narrower column. This formation is near another tall rock formation with a gap in between. To commemorate a famous leap across the gap, the tour of this site includes a dog leaping from rock to rock. Stand Rock is accessible by boat.

- **Water Parks.** The Dells area is home to several water parks, including Noah's Ark, which is reportedly the largest water park in the nation.

- **Gambling.** Ho-Chunk Casino is located one mile south of downtown Wisconsin Dells. This Indian casino features slots, video poker, blackjack, and various forms of entertainment.

Other attractions in the area include a wax museum, numerous campgrounds, many shopping opportunities, go-carts, a fifties revival show, golf courses, nature walks, a UFO and science fiction museum, a motor speedway, fishing trips, riding stables, laser tag facilities, movie theaters, and various other museums, attractions, and shows.

APPENDIX B

BUSINESS RESEARCH AND PRIVACY PROTECTION

Since the late 1990s, laws regarding the privacy of personal information have become increasingly forceful, largely in response to public demand. Federal, state, and international measures now affect how researchers are able to contact potential respondents as well as how they can disseminate consumers' personal data. Researchers must comply with consumers' requests to opt-out, and in some cases opt-in, to being interviewed and sharing their information. Some state legislatures have enacted do-not-call legislation, restricting telephone access to consumers. Although directed at telemarketers, these laws have a dampening effect upon market and public opinion research. Many consumers believe that, when included on do-not-call lists, they should receive no unsolicited calls.

As a lobbying organization for the industry, the Council for Marketing and Opinion Research (CMOR) currently monitors some fifteen thousand federal and state legislative bills (compared to four thousand bills in 1996) that could have a negative impact on telephone and online research capabilities (Bowers 2002b). On the regulatory front, agencies such as the Federal Trade Commission and Federal Communications Commission have introduced restrictions to protect individual consumer information within specific industries, including the financial and health care sectors.

Privacy laws in other countries, which are generally broader-reaching and more restrictive than legislation here, also affect research activities in the United States, particularly if data are shared across borders. Complying with state, federal, and international measures requires "outside expertise, legal guidance, and a comprehensive awareness of the complex and pervasive laws and regulations that govern the acquisition, storage, and dissemination of personal information" (Bowers 2002c, p. 115).

The Council of American Survey Research Organizations (CASRO) launched a program in January 2003 that assists research firms in meeting the tests of privacy compliance required for all current and anticipated future privacy regulations. The component documents of the CASRO Privacy Protection Program include model privacy

---

Reprinted from Miller and James (2003, pp. 45, 48–52) with permission from Research Publishers LLC.

policies and statements, model contracts and agreements, sample letters, forms, and language, as well as a resource for verification, certification, and complaint resolution (Bowers 2002b).

Privacy concerns and regulation have been the subject of numerous books and magazine articles (Lyon 1994; Cate 1997; Garfinkel 2000; McHugh 2000; Rosen 2000b; Gardyn 2001; Paul 2001; Herold 2002). Legislative developments in this area could have a profound effect upon the way research data are collected in the future. Survey costs are likely to increase with regulation, as research firms must conform to do-not-call and opt-in requirements. Samples obtained by random digit dialing are likely to be replaced by opt-in panels of respondent volunteers, raising questions about the representativeness of survey respondent groups. What follows is a brief discussion of the most important legislative and regulatory issues affecting research and their implications for the industry.

B.1 DATA PRIVACY

European nations have led the development of laws to protect the privacy of personal information. In 1998, the European Union issued the European Union Directive on Data Privacy, prohibiting the transfer of personal data to non-E.U. nations that do not meet the European "adequacy" standard for privacy protection (Bowers 2002c). To protect consumer privacy, the European Union relies on comprehensive legislation that requires the creation of government data protection agencies, registration of databases with those agencies, and in some cases, prior approval before personal data processing may begin (Herold 2002). The United States, on the other hand, has relied primarily on a self-regulatory approach, and is deemed by the European Union to be without "adequate" privacy protections.

To provide a means for U.S. organizations to comply with the E.U. Directive, the U.S. Department of Commerce, working with the European Commission, developed "safe harbors" or a set of principles that meets the specified "standard of adequate privacy protection" for the transfer of information from participating countries to the United States. The European Commission approved the Safe Harbor Privacy Principles in Summer 2000. U.S. organizations that decide to participate in the program, which is voluntary, can either join a self-regulatory privacy program that adheres to the Safe Harbor requirements or form their own privacy program. They must publicly declare their compliance on an annual basis. Enforcement occurs within the United States, primarily by the private sector.

Meanwhile, on the domestic front, researchers must contend with regulation that restricts the collection and use of personal data within certain industries. While marketing research companies are not mentioned in these laws, they are nonetheless directly affected as third-party providers to the covered institutions. The recent regulations provide protection of personal information for health care patients (Health Insurance Portability and Accountability Act); financial customers (Gramm-Leach-Bliley Financial Services Modernization Act); and telephone customers (FCC's Opt-in, Opt-Out Rule).

Exhibit B.1.1 Summary of CASRO Code of Standards and Ethics

This summary of research standards and ethics was provided by Diane Bowers (2002c), on behalf of the Council of American Survey Research Organizations (CASRO). The CASRO Web site provides a more complete listing of the *CASRO Code of Standards and Ethics for Survey Research* (Council of American Survey Research Organizations 2003).

1. Research organizations must give notice of their identity and purpose and use of the data collected. They must also include information about how individuals can contact the organization with inquiries or complaints.

2. Research organizations must give (or ensure their clients have given) respondents an opportunity to opt-out or opt-in, depending on the regulation or sensitivity level of the information, to research. (For instance, health care patients must opt-in, while financial customers opt-out of sharing their personal information.)

3. Research organizations must sign legal agreements with their clients, specifying and ensuring the purpose for which they collect personal information about their customers and the ways in which they will use and protect that information.

4. Research organizations must give respondents access to their personal information to correct or delete it.

5. Research organizations must protect data in onward transfer situations by ensuring that internal privacy officers protect data from unauthorized access and that subcontractors also comply with the regulations.

6. Research organizations must verify and certify their compliance and have adequate security systems and enforcement mechanisms in place.

Research practitioners have been on the forefront in protecting respondent confidentiality (Bowers 2002a). As shown in Exhibit B.1.1, the Council of American Survey Research Organizations (CASRO) spells out the requirements research firms need to meet in order to comply with federal and international data privacy rules (Bowers 2002c).

B.2 INTERNET PRIVACY

At the beginning of the twenty-first century, new technologies of communication have increased the danger that intimate personal information originally disclosed to our friends and colleagues may be exposed to—and misinterpreted by—a less understanding audience. For as thinking and writing increasingly take place in cyberspace, the part of our life that can be monitored and searched has vastly expanded. E-mail, even after it is ostensibly

> deleted, becomes a permanent record that can be resurrected by employers or prosecutors at any point in the future. On the Internet, every Web site we visit, every store we browse in, every magazine we skim, and the amount of time we spend skimming it, create electronic footprints that increasingly can be traced back to us, revealing detailed patterns about our tastes, preferences, and intimate thoughts. (Rosen 2000b, p. 7)

These words from Jeffery Rosen's (2000b) book *The Unwanted Gaze: The Destruction of Privacy in America* capture people's fears about today's world of computing and communications. While the Internet and the applications that serve it have been a boon to direct marketing, consumer research, and competitive intelligence, they pose a serious threat to personal privacy. "The battle for privacy," says Rosen (2000a, p. 53), "must be fought on many fronts—legal, political, and technological—and each new assault must be vigilantly resisted as it occurs."

The highest-profile data privacy issue today is the collection and use of personally identifiable information over the Internet. Consumer concern over how Web site operators collect and use visitors' personal information, combined with a slew of media stories about Web site operators' privacy violations, have kept Internet privacy in the forefront of public debate and a major focus for legislators.

Congress passed the first Internet privacy law in 1998, the Children's Online Privacy Protection Act (COPPA), which requires online services and Web site operators that knowingly collect information from children under thirteen years of age to inform parents of their information practices and obtain verifiable parental consent before collecting, using, or disclosing personal information from children. Congress has introduced numerous other bills that would prohibit online service providers and commercial Web sites from disclosing personally identifiable information without notice and consent from site visitors. As of early 2003, none of these bills has passed, with most sitting in a House or Senate committee or subcommittee. But legislation concerning the privacy practices of federal Web sites has been enacted (Smith 2002).

Another area of concern to consumer groups is online profiling, in which a company tracks the Web sites visited by a particular user and develops profiles of that user's preferences and interests for targeted advertising. In 2000, the FTC called on Congress to enact legislation to protect consumer privacy vis-à-vis online profiling, arguing that "bad actors" and others might not follow industry self-regulatory guidelines set out by online privacy seal programs (i.e. TRUSTe, WebTrust, and BBBOnLine). However, the current FTC Chairman's position is that broad legislation is not necessary at this time (Smith 2002).

Internet privacy and data privacy are interrelated, as are privacy and security. Privacy relates to policies of prior notice and research participant choice (opt-in and opt-out). Security relates to technology and prevention from unwarranted data access. Beth Mack puts it this way: "All too often, privacy and security are used in the same context, when, in actuality, the terms describe protection and prevention on the Internet, respectively. Privacy policies won't solve security problems, and without Internet security, there can be no online privacy" (Mack 2002, p. 21).

B.3 TELEPHONE PRIVACY

On the subject of telephone privacy, we can begin by discussing do-not-call legislation. In response to consumer concern over unsolicited sales-related telephone calls, lawmakers have passed do-not-call laws that require telemarketers to comply with individuals' do-not-call requests. The 1995 Telemarketing and Consumer Fraud and Abuse Prevention Act (Telemarketing Sales Rule) and the 1991 Telephone Consumer Protection Act are the primary federal laws restricting unsolicited telephone calls. And in March 2003, President Bush signed legislation creating a national do-not-call list. At the state level, twenty-seven states have imposed similar restrictions on the telemarketing industry. In addition, some states have established statewide databases of individuals who do not wish to be called.

Telephone calls made for survey research purposes currently are not bound by the laws. In the case of federal laws, for instance, research calls are implicitly exempt from the law's requirements because the activity is "outside the scope of the provisions." However, some state lawmakers have introduced do-not-call bills whose wording implicates marketing research activities, requiring companies to comply with do-not-call requests for calls that "seek marketing information for any purpose" (Bowers 2001). Thus far, lobbying efforts by the industry have ensured that marketing research is ultimately exempt from these laws. However, "with the increase in the number of do-not-call bills being introduced, the number of bills that pose a threat to the research industry has and will continue to increase" (Bowers 2001, p. 8). Furthermore, a perception problem exists for the industry because the public does not always draw a distinction between research calls and sales solicitations, with some respondents demanding they be placed on do-not-call lists when survey researchers call.

Telephone privacy also concerns electronic monitoring. Nearly all states require either one- or two-party consent for the electronic monitoring of telephone calls, while federal law requires one-party consent. Notifying research interviewers that calls will be monitored for quality-control purposes meets the one-party consent rule. However, two-party consent, required in more than a dozen states, can only be met by also notifying the respondent that the call may be monitored. The safest approach for compliance is to inform all potential respondents that the phone call may be monitored for quality control (though firms can also identify the area codes in two-party-consent and only advise respondents in those states). The statement can be as short as, "this call may be monitored for quality control." However, this statement not only lengthens the introduction but also runs the risk of sending up red flags with potential respondents (O'Rourke 1998).

Bibliography

Akaike, H. 1973. Information theory and an extension of the maximum likelihood principle. In B. N. Petrov and F. Csaki (eds.), *Second International Symposium on Information Theory*, pp. 267–281. Budapest: Akademiai Kiado.

Alexander, W. and S. Grimshaw 1996. Treed regression. *Journal of Computational and Graphical Statistics* 5(2):156–175.

Anand, S. S. and A. G. Büchner 2002. Database marketing and web mining. In W. Klösgen and J. M. Żytkow (eds.), *Handbook of Data Mining and Knowledge Discovery*, Chapter 46.1, pp. 843–849. Oxford: Oxford University Press.

Andersen, P. K., Ø. Borgan, R. D. Gill, and N. Keiding 1993. *Statistical Models Based on Counting Processes*. New York: Springer.

Atkinson, A. and M. Riani 2000. *Robust Diagnostic Regression Analysis*. New York: Springer-Verlag.

Bacon, L. D. 2002. Marketing. In W. Klösgen and J. M. Żytkow (eds.), *Handbook of Data Mining and Knowledge Discovery*, Chapter 34, pp. 715–725. Oxford: Oxford University Press.

Baeza-Yates, R. and B. Ribeiro-Neto 1999. *Modern Information Retrieval*. New York: ACM Press.

Bar-Ilan, J. 2004. The use of web search engines in information science research. In B. Cronin (ed.), *Annual Review of Information Science and Technology*, Volume 38, Chapter 5, pp. 231–288. Medford, N.J.: Information Today.

Belew, R. K. 2000. *Finding Out About: A Cognitive Perspective on Search Engine Technology and the WWW*. Cambridge: Cambridge University Press.

Belsley, D. A., E. Kuh, and R. E. Welsch 1980. *Regression Diagnostics: Identifying Influential Data and Sources of Collinearity*. New York: Wiley.

Benôit, G. 2002. Data mining. In B. Cronin (ed.), *Annual Review of Information Science and Technology*, Volume 36, Chapter 6, pp. 265–310. Medford, N.J.: Information Today.

Bergeron, P. and C. A. Hiller 2002. Competitive intelligence. In B. Cronin (ed.), *Annual Review of Information Science and Technology*, Volume 36, Chapter 8, pp. 353–390. Medford, N.J.: Information Today.

Berry, D. A. 1996. *Statistics: A Bayesian Perspective*. Belmont, Calif.: Duxbury.

Berry, M. W. and M. Browne 1999. *Understanding Search Engines: Mathematical Modeling and Text Retrieval*. Philadelphia: Society for Industrial and Applied Mathematics.

Berson, A., S. Smith, and K. Thearling 2000. *Building Data Mining Applications with CRM*. New York: McGraw-Hill.

Bessen, J. 1993, September–October. Riding the marketing information wave. *Harvard Business Review*:150–160.

Bishop, C. M. 1995. *Neural Networks for Pattern Recognition*. Oxford: Oxford University Press.

Bishop, Y. M. M., S. E. Fienberg, and P. W. Holland 1975. *Discrete Multivariate Analysis: Theory and Practice*. Cambridge: MIT Press.

Borg, I. and P. Groenen 1997. *Modern Multidimensional Scaling: Theory and Applications*. New York: Springer-Verlag.

Borrull, A. L. and C. Oppenheim 2004. Legal aspects of the Web. In B. Cronin (ed.), *Annual Review of Information Science and Technology*, Volume 38, Chapter 10, pp. 483–548. Medford, N.J.: Information Today.

Bowers, D. K. 2001, July–August. Privacy and the research industry in the US. *Research World* 9(7):8–9.

Bowers, D. K. 2002a, November 6. Telephone interview by Dana H. James. Reported in T. W. Miller and D. H. James, 2004. *Marketing Research and Information Services: An Integrated Approach*. Madison, Wis.: Research Publishers.

Bowers, D. K. 2002b, September 9. 2002 and beyond: A new research odyssey. American Marketing Association 23rd Annual Marketing Research Conference in Chicago.

Bowers, D. K. 2002c. New requirements for research: Privacy assurance and professional accountability. In J. H. Collins (ed.), *CASRO Journal 2002: Advancing the Business of Research*, pp. 115–116. Council of American Survey Research Organizations.

Bowman, A. W. and A. Azzalini 1997. *Applied Smoothing Techniques for Data Analysis*. Oxford: Oxford University Press.

Bozdogan, H. (ed.) 2004. *Statistical Data Mining and Knowledge Discovery*. Boca Raton, Fla.: CRC Press.

Breiman, L. 2001. Statistical modeling: The two cultures. *Statistical Science* 16(3): 199–215.

Breiman, L., J. H. Friedman, R. A. Olshen, and C. J. Stone 1984. *Classification and Regression Trees*. New York: Chapman & Hall.

Brian, D. 2003. Parsing natural language. In J. Orwant (ed.), *Games, Diversions & Perl Culture: Best of The Perl Journal*, Chapter 19, pp. 189–200. Sebastopol, Calif.: O'Reilly.

Burke, S. M. 2002. *Perl & LWP*. Sebastopol, Calif.: O'Reilly.

Burnham, K. P. and D. R. Anderson 2002. *Model Selection and Multimodel Inference: A Practical Information-Theoretic Approach* (second ed.). New York: Springer-Verlag.

Buvač, V. and P. J. Stone 2001, April 2. The general inquirer user's guide. Software developed with the support of Harvard University and The Gallup Organization.

Cameron, A. C. and P. K. Trivedi 1998. *Regression Analysis of Count Data*. Cambridge: Cambridge University Press.

Carlin, B. P. and T. A. Louis 1996. *Bayes and Empirical Bayes Methods for Data Analysis*. London: Chapman & Hall.

Carr, D. B. 1991. Looking at large data sets using binned data plots. In A. Buja and P. Tukey (eds.), *Computing and Graphics in Statistics*, pp. 7–39. New York: Springer-Verlag.

Carr, D. B., R. J. Littlefield, W. L. Nicholson, and J. S. Littlefield 1987. Scatterplot matrix techniques for large n. *Journal of the American Statistical Association* 83: 424–436.

Cate, F. H. 1997. *Privacy in the Information Age*. Washington, D.C.: Brookings Institution Press.

Caudill, M. and C. Butler 1990. *Naturally Intelligent Systems*. Cambridge: MIT Press.

Chakrapani, C. (ed.) 2000. *Marketing Research: State-of-the-Art Perspectives*. Chicago: American Marketing Association.

Chambers, J. M. 1998. *Programming with Data: A Guide to the S Language*. New York: Springer-Verlag.

Chambers, J. M., W. S. Cleveland, B. Kleiner, and P. A. Tukey 1983. *Graphical Methods for Data Analysis*. Belmont, Calif.: Wadsworth.

Chambers, J. M. and T. J. Hastie (eds.) 1992. *Statistical Models in S*. Pacific Grove, Calif.: Wadsworth & Brooks/Cole.

Chapman, P., J. Clinton, R. Kerber, T. Khabaza, T. Reinartz, C. Shearer, and R. Wirth 2000. CRISP-DM 1.0: Step-by-step data mining guide. 78 pp. Retrieved from the World Wide Web on March 19, 2003, at
http://www.crisp-dm.org.

Charniak, E. 1993. *Statistical Language Learning*. Cambridge: MIT Press.

Chaudhri, A. B., A. Rashid, and R. Zicari (eds.) 2003. *XML Data Management: Native XML and XML-Enabled Database Systems*. Boston: Addison-Wesley.

Chen, H. and M. Chau 2004. Web mining: Machine learning for web applications. In B. Cronin (ed.), *Annual Review of Information Science and Technology*, Volume 38, Chapter 6, pp. 289–329. Medford, N.J.: Information Today.

Chen, H., M. Chau, and D. Zeng 2002. CI Spider: A tool for competitive intelligence on the Web. *Decision Support Systems* 34:1–17.

Cherkassky, V. and F. Mulier 1998. *Learning from Data: Concepts, Theory, and Methods*. New York: Wiley.

Christensen, R. 1997. *Log-Linear Models and Logistic-Regression* (second ed.). New York: Springer.

Christiansen, T. and N. Torkington 2003. *Perl Cookbook* (second ed.). Sebastopol, Calif.: O'Reilly.

Churchill, Jr., G. A. and D. Iacobucci 2002. *Marketing Research: Methodological Foundations* (eighth ed.). Mason, Ohio: South-Western.

Clarkson, D. B., A. G. Gibbs, C. Gu, C. Kooperberg, S. Jin, C. J. Stone, and Y. Zhan 2002, January 10. S+Best user's guide. 158 pp. Retrieved from the World Wide Web on March 20, 2003, at
http://www.insightful.com/downloads/libraries/.

Cleveland, W. S. 1993. *Visualizing Data*. Murray Hill, N.J.: AT&T Bell Laboratories.

Cleveland, W. S. 1994. *The Elements of Graphing Data*. Murray Hill, N.J.: AT&T Bell Laboratories.

Congdon, P. 2001. *Bayesian Statistical Modeling*. New York: Wiley.

Congdon, P. 2003. *Applied Bayesian Modeling*. New York: Wiley.

Conway, D. 2000. *Object Oriented Perl*. Greenwich, Conn.: Manning Publications.

Cook, D., A. Buja, J. Cabrera, and C. Hurley 1995. Grand tour and projection pursuit. *Journal of Computational and Graphical Statistics* 4(3):155–172.

Cook, R. D. 1998. *Regression Graphics: Ideas for Studying Regressions through Graphics*. New York: Wiley.

Cook, R. D. and S. Weisberg 1999. *Applied Regression Including Computing and Graphics*. New York: Wiley.

Corter, J. E. 1996. *Tree Models of Similarity*. Thousand Oaks, Calif.: Sage.

Council of American Survey Research Organizations 2003. CASRO code of standards and ethics for survey research. Retrieved from the World Wide Web on February 24, 2003, at
http://www.casro.org/codeofstandards.cfm.

Cox, T. F. and M. A. A. Cox 1994. *Multidimensional Scaling*. London: Chapman & Hall.

Cranor, L. F. and B. A. LaMacchia 1998. Spam! *Communications of the ACM* 41(8): 74–83.

Crawley, M. J. 2002. *Statistical Computing: An Introduction to Data Analysis Using S-Plus*. New York: Wiley.

Cristianini, N. and J. Shawe-Taylor 2000. *An Introduction to Support Vector Machines and Other Kernel-Based Learning Methods*. Cambridge: Cambridge University Press.

Cross, D. 2001. *Data Munging with Perl*. New York: Manning.

Daconta, M. C., L. J. Obrst, and K. T. Smith 2003. *The Semantic Web: A Guide to the Future of XML, Web Services, and Knowledge Management*. New York: Wiley.

Dalgaard, P. 2002. *Introductory Statistics with R*. New York: Springer-Verlag.

Date, C. 2003. *An Introduction to Database Systems* (eighth ed.). Upper Saddle River, N.J.: Pearson Addison Wesley.

Davison, A. C. and D. V. Hinkley 1997. *Bootstrap Methods and their Application*. Cambridge: Cambridge University Press.

de Ville, B. 2001. *Microsoft Data Mining: Integrated Business Intelligence for e-Commerce and Knowledge Management*. Boston: Digital Press.

Denzin, N. K. and Y. S. Lincoln (eds.) 2000. *Handbook of Qualitative Research* (second ed.). Thousand Oaks, Calif.: Sage.

Dole, D. 1999. Cosmo: A constrained scatterplot smoother for estimating convex, monotonic transformations. *Journal of Business and Economic Statistics* 17(4): 444–455.

Draper, N. R. and H. Smith 1998. *Applied Regression Analysis* (third ed.). New York: Wiley.

Duda, R. O., P. E. Hart, and D. G. Stork 2001. *Pattern Classification* (second ed.). New York: Wiley.

Dumais, S. T. 2004. Latent semantic analysis. In B. Cronin (ed.), *Annual Review of Information Science and Technology*, Volume 38, Chapter 4, pp. 189–230. Medford, N.J.: Information Today.

Dyché, J. 2002. *The CRM Handbook: A Business Guide to Customer Relationship Management*. Boston: Addison-Wesley.

Efron, B. and R. J. Tibshirani 1993. *An Introduction to the Bootstrap*. London: Chapman and Hall.

Everitt, B. and S. Rabe-Hesketh 1997. *The Analysis of Proximity Data*. London: Arnold.

Everitt, B. S., S. Landau, and M. Leese 2001. *Cluster Analysis* (fourth ed.). London: Arnold.

Feldman, R. 2002. Text mining. In W. Klösgen and J. M. Żytkow (eds.), *Handbook of Data Mining and Knowledge Discovery*, Chapter 38, pp. 749–757. Oxford: Oxford University Press.

Fenzel, D., J. Hendler, H. Lieberman, and W. Wahlster (eds.) 2003. *Spinning the Semantic Web: Bringing the World Wide Web to Its Full Potential*. Cambridge: MIT Press.

Fielding, N. G. and R. M. Lee 1998. *Computer Analysis and Qualitative Research*. London: Sage.

Fienberg, S. E. 1980. *The Analysis of Cross-Classified Categorical Data* (second ed.). Cambridge: MIT Press.

Fogel, D. B. 2002. *Blondie24: Playing at the Edge of AI*. San Francisco: Morgan Kaufmann.

Fox, J. 2002. *An R and S-PLUS Companion to Applied Regression*. Thousand Oaks, Calif.: Sage.

Franses, P. H. and R. Paap 2001. *Quantitative Models in Marketing Research*. Cambridge: Cambridge University Press.

Frees, E. W. and T. W. Miller 2004. Sales forecasting with longitudinal data models. *International Journal of Forecasting* 20:99–114.

Friedman, J. H. 1991. Multivariate adaptive regression splines (with discussion). *The Annals of Statistics* 19(1):1–141.

Fuld, L. M. 1994. *The New Competitor Intelligence: The Complete Resource for Finding, Analyzing, and Using Information about Your Competitors*. New York: Wiley.

Gardyn, R. 2001, July. Swap meet: Consumers are willing to exchange personal information for personalized products. *American Demographics* 23(7):51–57.

Garfinkel, S. 2000. *Database Nation*. Sebastopol, Calif.: O'Reilly.

Geisler, C. 2004. *Analyzing Streams of Language: Twelve Steps to the Systematic Coding of Text, Talk, and Other Verbal Data*. New York: Pearson Education.

Gelman, A., J. B. Carlin, H. S. Stern, and D. B. Rubin 1995. *Bayesian Data Analysis*. London: Chapman & Hall.

Gentle, J. E. 2002. *Elements of Computational Statistics*. New York: Springer.

Gentle, J. E. 2003. *Random Number Generation and Monte Carlo Methods* (second ed.). New York: Springer.

Gilley, O. and R. Pace 1996. On the Harrison and Rubinfeld data. *Journal of Environmental Economics and Management* 31:403–405.

Gnanadesikan, R. 1997. *Methods for Statistical Data Analysis of Multivariate Observations* (second ed.). New York: Wiley.

Gower, J. C. and D. J. Hand 1996. *Biplots*. London: Chapman & Hall.

Greenacre, M. J. 1984. *Theory and Applications of Correspondence Analysis*. London: Academic Press.

Greenacre, M. J. 1993. *Correspondence Analysis in Practice*. San Diego: Academic Press.

Greenbert, P. 2002. *CRM at the Speed of Light: Capturing and Keeping Customers in Internet Real Time* (second ed.). New York: McGraw-Hill.

Gustafsson, A., A. Herrmann, and F. Huber (eds.) 2000. *Conjoint Measurement: Methods and Applications*. New York: Springer-Verlag.

Han, J. and M. Kamber 2001. *Data Mining: Concepts and Techniques*. San Francisco: Morgan Kaufmann.

Hand, D., H. Mannila, and P. Smyth 2001. *Principles of Data Mining*. Cambridge: MIT Press.

Hand, D. J. 1997. *Construction and Assessment of Classification Rules*. New York: Wiley.

Hanssens, D. M., L. J. Parsons, and R. L. Schultz 2001. *Market Response Models: Econometric and Time Series Analysis* (second ed.). Boston: Kluwer.

Harrell, Jr., F. E. 2002. *Regression Modeling Strategies*. New York: Springer-Verlag.

Harrison, D. and D. Rubinfeld 1978. Hedonic housing prices and the demand for clean air. *Journal of Environmental Economics and Management* 5:81–102.

Hart, R. P. 2000a. *Campaign Talk: Why Elections Are Good for Us*. Princeton, N.J.: Princeton University Press.

Hart, R. P. 2000b. *DICTION 5.0: The Text Analysis Program*. Thousand Oaks, Calif.: Sage.

Hart, R. P. 2001. Redeveloping Diction: Theoretical considerations. In M. D. West (ed.), *Theory, Method, and Practice in Computer Content Analysis*, Chapter 3, pp. 43–60. Westport, Conn.: Ablex.

Hastie, T. and R. Tibshirani 1990. *Generalized Additive Models*. London: Chapman and Hall.

Hastie, T., R. Tibshirani, and J. Friedman 2001. *The Elements of Statistical Learning: Data Mining, Inference, and Prediction*. New York: Springer-Verlag.

Haughton, D., J. Deichmann, A. Eshghi, S. Sayek, N. Teebagy, and H. Topi 2003. A review of software packages for data mining. *The American Statistician* 57(4): 290–309.

Hausser, R. 2001. *Foundations of Computational Linguistics: Human-Computer Communication in Natural Language* (second ed.). New York: Springer-Verlag.

Haykin, S. 1999. *Neural Networks: A Comprehensive Foundation* (second ed.). Upper Saddle River, N.J.: Prentice Hall.

Heiberger, R. M. and B. Holland (in press). *Statistical Analysis and Data Display: An Intermediate Course*. New York: Springer.

Helberg, C. 2002. *Data Mining with Confidence* (second ed.). Chicago: SPSS Inc.

Hemenway, K. and T. Calishain 2004. *Spidering Hacks: 100 Industrial-Strength Tips & Tools*. Sabastopol, Calif.: O'Reilly.

Herold, R. (ed.) 2002. *The Privacy Papers: Managing Technology, Consumer, Employee, and Legislative Actions*. Boca Raton, Fla.: CRC Press.

Hesterberg, T., S. Monaghan, D. S. Moore, A. Clipson, and R. Epstein 2003. *Bootstrap Methods and Permutation Tests*. New York: W. H. Freeman and Company. Companion Chapter 18 to *The Practice of Business Statistics*.

Hinkley, D. V., N. Reid, and E. J. Snell (eds.) 1991. *Statistical Theory and Modeling*. London: Chapman and Hall.

Huberman, B. A. 2001. *The Laws of the Web: Patterns in the Ecology of Information*. Cambridge: MIT Press.

Johnson, R. A. and D. W. Wichern 1998. *Applied Multivariate Statistical Analysis* (fourth ed.). Upper Saddle River, N.J.: Prentice Hall.

Kaufman, L. and P. J. Rousseeuw 1990. *Finding Groups in Data: An Introduction to Cluster Analysis*. New York: Wiley.

Kelle, U. (ed.) 1995. *Computer-Aided Qualitative Data Analysis: Theory, Methods and Practice*. Thousand Oaks, Calif.: Sage.

Kennedy, J. and R. C. Eberhart 2001. *Swarm Intelligence*. San Francisco: Morgan Kaufmann.

Klösgen, W. and J. M. Żytkow (eds.) 2002. *Handbook of Data Mining and Knowledge Discovery*. Oxford: Oxford University Press.

Kohonen, T. 2001. *Self-Organizing Maps* (third ed.). New York: Springer-Verlag.

Krause, A. and M. Olson 2002. *The Basics of S and S-PLUS* (third ed.). New York: Springer-Verlag.

Lam, L. 2001. *An Introduction to S-PLUS for Windows*. Amsterdam: CANdiensten.

Langley, P. 1996. *Elements of Machine Learning*. San Francisco: Morgan Kaufmann.

Lawrence, S. and C. L. Giles 1998. Searching the World Wide Web. *Science* 280(3): 98–100.

Le, C. T. 1997. *Applied Survival Analysis*. New York: Wiley.

Le, C. T. 1998. *Applied Categorical Data Analysis*. New York: Wiley.

Leamer, E. E. 1990. Specification problems in econometrics. In J. Eatwell, M. Milgate, and P. Newman (eds.), *The New Palgrave: A Dictionary of Economics–Econometrics*, pp. 238–245. New York: W. W. Norton.

Lebart, L. 1998. Visualizations of textual data. In J. Blasius and M. Greenacre (eds.), *Visualizing of Categorical Data*, Chapter 11, pp. 133–147. San Diego: Academic Press.

Leeflang, P. S. H., D. R. Wittink, M. Wedel, and P. A. Naert 2000. *Building Models for Marketing Decisions*. Boston: Kluwer.

Lilien, G. L., P. Kotler, and K. S. Moorthy 1992. *Marketing Models*. Englewood Cliffs, N.J.: Prentice-Hall.

Lilien, G. L. and A. Rangaswamy 2003. *Marketing Engineering: Computer-Assisted Marketing Analysis and Planning* (second ed.). Upper Saddle River, N.J.: Prentice Hall.

Little, J. D. C. 1970. Models and managers: The concept of a decision calculus. *Management Science* 16(8):B466–B485.

Little, R. J. A. and D. B. Rubin 1987. *Statistical Analysis with Missing Data*. New York: Wiley.

Louviere, J. J., D. A. Hensher, and J. D. Swait 2000. *Stated Choice Methods: Analysis and Application*. Cambridge: Cambridge University Press.

Luna, F. and A. Perrone (eds.) 2001. *Agent-Based Methods in Economics and Finance*. Norwell, Mass.: Kluwer.

Luna, F. and B. Stefansson (eds.) 2000. *Economic Simulations in Swarm: Agent-Based Modeling and Object-Oriented Programming*. Norwell, Mass.: Kluwer.

Lyman, P., H. R. Varian, J. Dunn, A. Strygin, and K. Swearingen 2000. How much information? Retrieved from the World Wide Web on December 12, 2003, at: http://www.sims.berkeley.edu/research/projects/how-much-info/internet.html.

Lyon, D. 1994. *The Electronic Eye: The Rise of Surveillance Society*. Minneapolis: University of Minnesota Press.

Mack, B. 2002, November 25. Online privacy critical to research success. *Marketing News*:21.

Maindonald, J. and J. Braun 2003. *Data Analysis and Graphics Using R: An Example-based Approach*. Cambridge: Cambridge University Press.

Malhotra, N. K. 2004. *Marketing Research: An Applied Orientation* (fourth ed.). Upper Saddle River, N.J.: Prentice Hall.

Mani, I. and M. T. Maybury (eds.) 1999. *Advances in Automatic Text Summarization*. Cambridge: MIT Press.

Manly, B. F. J. 1994. *Multivariate Statistical Methods: A Primer* (second ed.). London: Chapman & Hall.

Manning, C. D. and H. Schütze 1999. *Foundations of Statistical Natural Language Processing*. Cambridge: MIT Press.

Maybury, M. T. (ed.) 1997. *Intelligent Multimedia Information Retrieval*. Menlo Park, Calif./ Cambridge: AAAI Press / MIT Press.

McCullagh, P. and J. A. Nelder 1989. *Generalized Linear Models* (second ed.). New York: Chapman and Hall.

McHugh, J. 2000, February 7. The Web hall of mirrors. *Forbes*:120–122.

McLachlan, G. J. 1992. *Discriminant Analysis and Statistical Pattern Recognition*. New York: Wiley.

McManus, J. 2003, July/August. Street wiser. *American Demographics*:32–34.

Meadow, C. T., B. R. Boyce, and D. H. Kraft 2000. *Text Information Retrieval Systems* (second ed.). San Diego: Academic Press.

Merkl, D. 2002. Text mining with self-organizing maps. In W. Klösgen and J. M. Żytkow (eds.), *Handbook of Data Mining and Knowledge Discovery*, Chapter 46.9, pp. 903–910. Oxford: Oxford University Press.

Miller, G. A. 1956. The magic number seven, plus or minus two: Some limits on our capacity for processing information. *Psychological Review* 63:81–97.

Miller, T. W. 1994. Model selection in tree-structured regression. *1994 Proceedings of the Statistical Computing Section of the American Statistical Association*:158–163.

Miller, T. W. 1996. Putting the CART after the horse: Tree-structured regression diagnostics. *1996 Proceedings of the Statistical Computing Section of the American Statistical Association*:150–155.

Miller, T. W. 1998. Problems in data mining: Masking. *1998 Proceedings of the Statistical Computing Section of the American Statistical Association*:153–158.

Miller, T. W. 1999. The Boston splits: Sample size requirements for modern regression. *1999 Proceedings of the Statistical Computing Section of the American Statistical Association*:210–215.

Miller, T. W. 2000. Marketing research and the information industry. *CASRO Journal 2000*:21–26.

Miller, T. W. 2002. Propensity scoring for multimethod research. *Canadian Journal of Marketing Research* 20(2):46–61.

Miller, T. W. (ed.) 2004. *Cases in Business Research: Understanding Customers, Competitors, and Markets*. Madison, Wis.: Research Publishers.

Miller, T. W. and D. H. James 2003. *Marketing Research and Information Services: 2003 Industry Report*. Madison, Wis.: Research Publishers.

Miller, T. W. and D. H. James 2004. *Marketing Research and Information Services: An Integrated Approach*. Madison, Wis.: Research Publishers.

Miller, T. W. and J. Walkowski (eds.) 2004. *Qualitative Research Online*. Madison, Wis.: Research Publishers.

Mitchell, M. 1996. *An Introduction to Genetic Algorithms*. Cambridge: MIT Press.

Moore, D. S. 2001. *Statistics: Concepts and Controversies* (fifth ed.). New York: W. H. Freeman.

Mosteller, F. and J. W. Tukey 1977. *Data Analysis and Regression*. Reading, Mass.: Addison-Wesley.

Mosteller, F. and D. L. Wallace 1984. *Applied Bayesian and Classical Inference: The Case of the Federalist Papers*. New York: Springer. Earlier edition published in 1964 by Addison-Wesley, Reading, Mass. The previous title was *Inference and Disputed Authorship: The Federalist*.

Nelson, W. B. 2003. *Recurrent Events Data Analysis for Product Repairs, Disease Recurrences, and Other Applications*. Series on Statistics and Applied Probability. Philadelphia and Alexandria, Va.: ASA-SIAM.

Neter, J., M. H. Kutner, C. J. Nachtsheim, and W. Wasserman 1996. *Applied Linear Statistical Models* (fourth ed.). New York: McGraw-Hill.

Neuendorf, K. A. 2002. *The Content Analysis Guidebook*. Thousand Oaks, Calif.: Sage.

Oakman, R. L. 1980. *Computer Methods for Literary Research*. Columbia, S.C.: University of South Carolina Press.

O'Rourke, D. 1998. Electronic monitoring: Do you know the laws? *Survey Research* 29(1):1.

Orwant, J. (ed.) 2003a. *Computer Science & Perl Programming: Best of The Perl Journal*. Sebastopol, Calif.: O'Reilly.

Orwant, J. (ed.) 2003b. *Games, Diversions & Perl Culture: Best of The Perl Journal*. Sebastopol, Calif.: O'Reilly.

Osgood, C. 1962. Studies in the generality of affective meaning systems. *American Psychologist* 17:10–28.

Osgood, C., G. Suci, and P. Tannenbaum (eds.) 1957. *The Measurement of Meaning*. Urbana, Ill.: University of Illinois Press.

Paul, P. 2001. Mixed signals: When it comes to issues of privacy, consumers are fraught with contradictions. *American Demographics* 23(7):45–49.

Peppers, D. and M. Rogers 1993. *The One to One Future: Building Relationships One Customer at a Time*. New York: Doubleday.

Pfeifer, U. 2003. Information retrieval. In J. Orwant (ed.), *Computer Science & Perl Programming: Best of The Perl Journal*, Chapter 25, pp. 245–253. Sebastopol, Calif.: O'Reilly.

Piatetsky-Shapiro, G. and W. Frawley (eds.) 1991. *Knowledge Discovery in Databases*. Menlo Park, Calif.: AAAI Press.

Pinheiro, J. C. and D. M. Bates 2000. *Mixed-Effects Models in S and S-PLUS*. New York: Springer-Verlag.

Pinker, S. 1994. *The Language Instinct*. New York: W. Morrow and Co.

Pinker, S. 1997. *How the Mind Works*. New York: W.W. Norton & Company.

Pinker, S. 1999. *Words and Rules: The Ingredients of Language*. New York: Harper-Collins.

Popping, R. 2000. *Computer-Assisted Text Analysis*. Thousand Oaks, Calif.: Sage.

Press, S. J. 2004. The role of Bayesian and frequentist multivariate modeling in statistical data mining. In H. Bozdogan (ed.), *Statistical Data Mining and Knowledge Discovery*, Chapter 1, pp. 1–14. Boca Raton, Fla.: CRC Press.

Pyle, D. 1999. *Data Preparation for Data Mining*. San Francisco: Morgan Kaufmann.

Quigley, E. 2002. *Perl by Example* (third ed.). Upper Saddle River, N.J.: Prentice Hall.

Quinlan, J. R. 1993. *C4.5: Programs for Machine Learning*. San Mateo, Calif.: Morgan Kaufmann.

Quinn, J. B., P. Anderson, and S. Finkelstein 1998. Managing professional intellect: Making the most of the best. In H. B. School (ed.), *Harvard Business Review on Knowledge Management*, pp. 181–205. Harvard Business School Press. Original article appeared in the March 1, 1996, issue of *Harvard Business Review*.

Radcliff, C. 2002. *Perl for the Web*. Indianapolis: New Riders.

Rasmussen, E. M. 2003. Indexing and retrieval for the web. In B. Cronin (ed.), *Annual Review of Information Science and Technology*, Volume 37, Chapter 3, pp. 91–124. Medford, N.J.: Information Today.

Ray, E. T. 2001. *Learning XML*. Sebastopol, Calif.: O'Reilly.

Ray, E. T. and J. McIntosh 2002. *Perl & XML*. Sebastopol, Calif.: O'Reilly.

Ray, R. J. and P. Kulchenko 2003. *Programming Web Services with Perl*. Sebastopol, Calif.: O'Reilly.

Reed, R. D. and J. I. M. Robert 1999. *Neural Smithing: Supervised Learning in Feedforward Artificial Neural Networks*. Cambridge: MIT Press.

Ribic, C. A. and T. W. Miller 1998. Evaluation of alternative model selection criteria in the analysis of unimodal response curves using CART. *Journal of Applied Statistics* 25(5):685–698.

Ridgeway, G. and D. Madigan 2003. A sequential Monte Carlo method for Bayesian analysis of massive datasets. *Data Mining and Knowledge Discovery* 7(3):273–300.

Riehl, M. and I. Sterin 2003. *XML and Perl*. Indianapolis: New Riders.

Ripley, B. D. 1996. *Pattern Recognition and Neural Networks*. Cambridge: Cambridge University Press.

Roberts, C. W. (ed.) 1997. *Text Analysis for the Social Sciences: Methods for Drawing Statistical Inferences from Texts and Transcripts*. Mahwah, N.J.: Lawrence Erlbaum Associates.

Rosen, J. 2000a, April 30. The eroded self. *The New York Times Magazine*:46–53,66–68,129.

Rosen, J. 2000b. *The Unwanted Gaze: The Destruction of Privacy in America*. New York: Vintage.

Rossi, P. E. and G. M. Allenby 2003. Bayesian statistics and marketing. *Marketing Science* 22(3):304–328.

Rubin, D. B. 1987. *Multiple Imputation for Nonresponse in Surveys*. New York: Wiley.

Schafer, J. L. 2000. *Analysis of Incomplete Multivariate Data*. London: Chapman and Hall.

Schrott, P. R. and D. J. Lanoue 1994. Trends and perspectives in content analysis. In I. Borg and P. Mohler (eds.), *Trends and Perspectives in Empirical Social Research*, pp. 327–345. Berlin: Walter de Gruyter.

Schwartz, R. L. and T. Phoenix 2001. *Learning Perl* (third ed.). Sebastopol, Calif.: O'Reilly.

Schwartz, R. L. and T. Phoenix 2003. *Learning Perl Objects, References, & Modules*. Sebastopol, Calif.: O'Reilly.

Schwarz, G. 1978. Estimating the dimension of a model. *Annals of Statistics* 6:461–464.

Sebastiani, F. 2002. Machine learning in automated text categorization. *ACM Computing Surveys* 34(1):1–47.

Seber, G. A. F. 1984. *Multivariate Observations*. New York: Wiley.

Sharma, S. 1996. *Applied Multivariate Techniques*. New York: Wiley.

Silverman, D. 2000. *Doing Qualitative Research: A Practical Approach*. Thousand Oaks, Calif.: Sage.

Silverman, D. 2001. *Interpreting Qualitative Data: Methods for Analysing Talk, Text, and Interaction* (second ed.). Thousand Oaks, Calif.: Sage.

Simon, H. A. 2002. Foreward: Enhancing the intelligence of discovery systems. In W. Klösgen and J. M. Żytkow (eds.), *Handbook of Data Mining and Knowledge Discovery*, p. xvii. Oxford: Oxford University Press.

Simonoff, J. S. 1996. *Smoothing Methods in Statistics*. New York: Springer-Verlag.

Smith, M. S. 2002. Internet privacy: Overview and pending legislation. Retrieved from the World Wide Web on June 20, 2002, at: http://usinfo.state.gov/usa/infousa/tech/reports/rl31408.pdf.

Snedecor, G. W. and W. G. Cochran 1989. *Statistical Methods* (eighth ed.). Ames, Iowa: Iowa State University Press.

Society of Competitive Intelligence Professionals 2003. What is CI? Retrieved from the World Wide Web on December 11, 2003, at: http://www.scip.org/ci/.

Stone, P. J. 1997. Thematic text analysis: New agendas for analyzing text content. In C. W. Roberts (ed.), *Text Analysis for the Social Sciences: Methods for Drawing Statistical Inferences from Texts and Transcripts*, Chapter 2, pp. 35–54. Mahwah, N.J.: Lawrence Erlbaum Associates.

Stone, P. J., D. C. Dunphy, M. S. Smith, and D. M. Ogilvie 1966. *The General Inquirer: A Computer Approach to Content Analysis*. Cambridge: MIT Press.

Sullivan, D. 2000, September 8. Eye on the competition: Why text mining is the key enabler of automated competitive intelligence. *Intelligent Enterprise* 3(14). Retrieved from the World Wide Web on December 4, 2003, at: http://www.intelligententerprise.com/000908/feat1.shtml.

Sullivan, D. 2001. *Document Warehousing and Text Mining: Techniques for Improving Business Operations, Marketing, and Sales*. New York: Wiley.

Swayne, D. F., D. Cook, and A. Buja 1998. Xgobi: Interactive dynamic data visualization in the X Window system. *Journal of Computational and Graphical Statistics* 7(1):113–130.

Tanner, M. A. 1996. *Tools for Statistical Inference: Methods for the Exploration of Posterior Distributions and Likelihood Functions* (third ed.). New York: Springer.

Therneau, T. M. and P. M. Grambsch 2000. *Modeling Survival Data: Extending the Cox Model*. New York: Springer.

Trybula, W. J. 1999. Text mining. In M. E. Williams (ed.), *Annual Review of Information Science and Technology*, Volume 34, Chapter 7, pp. 385–420. Medford, N.J.: Information Today, Inc.

Tufte, E. R. 1990. *Envisioning Information*. Cheshire, Conn.: Graphic Press.

Tufte, E. R. 1997. *Visual Explanations: Images and Quantities, Evidence and Narrative*. Cheshire, Conn.: Graphic Press.

Tufte, E. R. 2001. *The Visual Display of Quantitative Information* (second ed.). Cheshire, Conn.: Graphic Press.

Tukey, J. W. 1977. *Exploratory Data Analysis*. Reading, Mass.: Addison-Wesley.

Venables, W. N. and B. D. Ripley 2000. *S Programming*. New York: Springer-Verlag.

Venables, W. N. and B. D. Ripley 2002. *Modern Applied Statistics with S* (fourth ed.). New York: Springer-Verlag.

Venables, W. N., D. M. Smith, and R Development Core Team 2001. *An Introduction to R*. Bristol, UK: Network Theory Limited.

Wainer, H. 1997. *Visual Revelations: Graphical Tales of Fate and Deception from Napoleon Bonaparte to Ross Perot*. New York: Springer-Verlag.

Wall, L., T. Christiansen, and J. Orwant (eds.) 2000. *Perl Programming* (third ed.). Sebastopol, Calif.: O'Reilly.

Wedel, M. and W. Kamakura 1999. *Market Segmentation: Conceptual and Methodological Foundations* (second ed.). Boston: Kluwer.

Weisberg, S. 1985. *Applied Linear Regression* (second ed.). New York: Wiley.

Weiss, M. J. 1994. *Latitudes & Attitudes: An Atlas of American Tastes, Trends, Politics, and Passions*. Boston: Little, Brown and Company.

Weiss, M. J. 2000. *The Clustered World: How We Live, What We Buy, and What It All Means about Who We Are*. Boston: Little, Brown and Company.

Weitzman, E. A. 2000. Software and qualitative research. In N. K. Denzin and Y. S. Lincoln (eds.), *Handbook of Qualitative Research: Context and Method* (second ed.)., Chapter 30, pp. 803–820. Thousand Oaks, Calif.: Sage.

Weitzman, E. A. and M. B. Miles 1995. *Computer Programs for Qualitative Data Analysis*. Thousand Oaks, Calif.: Sage.

Weller, S. C. and A. K. Romney 1990. *Metric Scaling: Correspondence Analysis*. Quantitative Applications in the Social Sciences. Newbury Park, Calif.: Sage.

West, M. D. (ed.) 2001. *Theory, Method, and Practice in Computer Content Analysis*. Westport, Conn.: Ablex.

Wilkinson, L. 1999. *The Grammar of Graphics*. New York: Springer.

Witten, I. H. and E. Frank 2000. *Data Mining: Practical Machine Learning Tools and Techniques with Java Implementations*. San Francisco: Morgan Kaufmann.

Witten, I. H., A. Moffat, and T. C. Bell 1999. *Managing Gigabytes: Compressing and Indexing Documents and Images* (second ed.). San Francisco: Morgan Kaufmann.

Wolfram, S. 2002. *A New Kind of Science*. Champaign, Ill.: Wolfram Media, Inc.

Ye, N. (ed.) 2003. *The Handbook of Data Mining*. Mahwah, N.J.: Lawrence Erlbaum.

Zhang, H. and B. Singer 1999. *Recursive Partitioning in the Health Sciences*. New York: Springer-Verlag.

Zhong, N., J. Liu, and Y. Yao (eds.) 2003. *Web Intelligence*. New York: Springer-Verlag.

Zipf, H. 1949. *Human Behavior and the Principle of Least Effort*. Cambridge, Mass.: Addison-Wesley.

Zivot, E. and J. Wang 2003. *Modeling Financial Time Series with S-PLUS*. Seattle: Insightful Corporation.

Index

O

P

Q

R

S

T